THE
MONEY
MESSENGER

Control Your Money.
Live the Life You Want.

ANGELA SANTALIA

Published by Wilkinson Publishing Pty Ltd
ACN 006 042 173
PO Box 24135, Melbourne, VIC 3001, Australia
Ph: +61 3 9654 5446
enquiries@wilkinsonpublishing.com.au
www.wilkinsonpublishing.com.au

Cover and book design by Tango Media.
Printed and bound in Australia by Griffin Press, a part of Ovato.

ISBN: 9781925927610
A catalogue record for this book is available from the National Library of Australia.

 WilkinsonPublishing

 wilkinsonpublishinghouse

 WPBooks

CONTENTS

Preface 6

Introduction 12

Chapter 1: Saving money (why bother?) 25

Chapter 2: Top reasons (excuses) for not saving 29

Chapter 3: Paying yourself first 36

Chapter 4: Track, budget, spend 44

Chapter 5: Separating bank accounts 64

Chapter 6: Buying what you want (without debt) 83

Chapter 7: Personal loans (the real cost) 95

Chapter 8: Credit cards (weapons of financial destruction) 105

Chapter 9: Erase credit card debt (in 3 easy steps) 130

Chapter 10: Are you wasting money? 136

Chapter 11: How to increase your income 147

Chapter 12: Why you must invest 154

Chapter 13: Buying your first property 181

Chapter 14: Home vs. investment property (which is best?) 209

Chapter 15: The secret to buying multiple properties 225

Chapter 16: Understanding superannuation 236

Chapter 17: Insurance (do you really need it?) 246

Chapter 18: Death and your money 274

Final word 282

DISCLAIMER

The information in this book is provided by the author and is general in nature. It's based on the author's experiences and the experiences of others.

It doesn't take into account the objectives, financial situation or needs of you or any other particular person. You need to consider your financial situation and needs before making any decisions based on the information. You may have to modify the information and do further research for it to suit your financial situation.

All information presented is given for illustration purposes only and mustn't be construed as a specific investment recommendation or considered as an offer to buy or sell a financial product, or as financial product advice.

The author doesn't provide financial, legal or tax advice. Statements made in this book on results achieved by the author or results achieved by others and are not indicative of future results or results that you may achieve by implementing the information.

The laws relating to investment, taxation, benefits, and the handling of money are constantly changing and are often subject to changes in Government policy. Whilst every care has been taken to ensure the accuracy of the material contained herein at the time of publication and presentation, neither the Publisher nor the author will bear any responsibility or liability for any action taken by any person, persons or organisations on the purported basis of information contained in this book.

Therefore, before acting on the information, we recommend you consider its appropriateness to your circumstances or consult a Financial Planner to assist you.

PREFACE

Why you and your friends need this book...

I am going to assume that because you picked up this book in the first place, you are looking for a way to bring more money into your life. You are not alone. A lot of people are in the same situation.

Life can be expensive, I know, I completely understand. Right from the start as a young child, we are introduced to the nicer things in life which we then want for ourselves... toys, clothes, pets, etc. So, we ask our parents, and if we are lucky enough, we receive. As we grow a little older and want more of those nicer things, clothes, computers, tech gadgets, bigger toys... again, we ask our parents. After all, they are our only avenue for getting anything in life at that stage.

As the years go on, we get used to putting out our hand, then all of a sudden, when we are old enough to move out from our parents' home and live a grown-up life, we get a huge shock that things actually cost money. Sometimes lots of money.

Not only are we not told that living out of home is costly and a serious game (that we so eagerly wanted to play when admiring adults as a child), but we slowly and surely realise that to have the nicer things in life, we actually have to pay for them too (somehow).

Maybe you are noticing that there always seems to be more 'month at the end of your money' rather than 'money at the end of the month'. Do you wonder how others afford to travel, shop, buy gadgets and upgrade their cars when they don't seem to earn much more than you? Do you have credit card debt which is growing by the minute?

How did you go wrong? Life wasn't meant to be this serious. Why can't you afford to buy a new outfit whenever you want to, whether it's an expensive one or just that special something that catches your eye as you walk past a shop? Why can't you afford a new computer, in full and upfront when your old computer suddenly quits? Why can't you enjoy dinner and drinks out on the town every Friday and Saturday night, perhaps even the occasional Sunday if you feel like it?

◆ Why can't you stop living payday to payday?

◆ Why do you always seem to struggle with money?

◆ How will you ever be able to afford to buy a home?

◆ Why do they not teach this stuff in school?

◆ Why did your parents not show you how to manage money successfully—did they also struggle with money?

◆ How are you meant to know, if you were not taught? What's the secret?

Now some people may think that the answer is to get a better job and make more money, maybe become a career person, a lawyer, a doctor or some other well-paying occupation. Yes, by all means, go for it, more power to them. No one will ever say that to get an education and secure a high paying job is not a good way to go about your life. In fact, it's an excellent start. But, perhaps, you don't want to be a lawyer or doctor, perhaps you didn't finish high school because of circumstances at the time, or maybe you are already working to support yourself, have moved out from your parents' home and can't possibly afford to stop working and become a student again.

Maybe, just maybe, you are already a lawyer or doctor or some other occupation that earns a good income and yet you still find that you have no money left at the end of the month, because you grew accustomed to earning more money and therefore spending more money (on those nicer things in life that you just had to have).

The more money you earn, the more money you spend. You can go broke earning even $100,000 per year—you just have to spend $100,001.

You don't actually need to earn more money to have a better lifestyle than you do now and to have more of the things you want in life when you want them, all whilst growing your wealth at the same time. Yes, it's true, there is another way. There are strategies which you can use straight away to organise your money and get ahead financially. You can create more in life using what you have now, even if all you have is your income. You simply need to use your income in a better way.

How do I know? Because I have done it, I do it; I live by it.

I am here to teach you the forgotten fundamentals of money management and to fill the knowledge gap of what's not taught at home or school. My aim is to reprogram your everyday spending habits and the structure of your cash flow so you take control of your own money to achieve a better financial outcome. I will also expose some common but unknown truths about money and reveal facts about money that you didn't know.

The financial secrets and strategies that I will share with you are simple to follow. They are tried, tested and proven to work. I have lived by them (ever since starting my working life) and they have served me well (and other people too). They are the essential foundations of successful money management. They are REAL. They WORK. I am proof of that.

After working in the Australian Financial Planning industry for nearly two decades and through my personal investment and life experience, I have definitely learnt a lot about money, people, and their spending habits. I have seen what works and what doesn't. I know how to get ahead financially and what to steer clear from.

For over ten years, I have been self-employed as a freelance Financial Paraplanner. I work for myself, in my own business, from home. My clients are Financial Planners. I help them to prepare financial plans for their clients, which detail recommendations about how to manage money, repay debt, increase wealth and protect assets; together we show clients how to solve their money troubles.

Throughout my career, I have written well over 10,000 Financial Plans for various types of clients—from young couples just starting out their lives together, everyday Mums and Dads planning for retirement, high-income earners with assets in the eight figures to corporate clients managing millions of dollars of staff retirement savings and trustees managing royalty payments for Mining Rights.

The good news is that your education level doesn't matter, the amount of income you earn doesn't matter. What matters is your desire to change what you are doing now, so you achieve different results. It's as simple as that.

To keep doing the same thing and expect different results is the definition of insanity.

If I can do it, anyone can. I didn't come from money, didn't have any handouts and even had my fair share of a tough childhood with every excuse available to me.

I am an ordinary Aussie girl who is extremely good with money.

In this book, you will learn step-by-step how to:

◆ Master the forgotten fundamentals of successful money management.

◆ Afford the 'nicer things' in life.

◆ Stop living payday to payday, increase savings and have money left over.

◆ Set up bank accounts correctly (and put bills on auto-pilot).

◆ Control your money and reduce financial stress.

◆ Know the hidden truths behind personal debt (the real cost to you).

◆ Master the art of credit cards (and get out of debt in 3 steps).

◆ Stop wasting money and increase income.

◆ Understand the basics of investing and why it's riskier not to invest.

◆ Buy your first property and calculate how much it will really cost.

◆ Decide whether it's better to buy a home or an investment property.

◆ Buy multiple properties over time—starting from zero.

◆ Understand superannuation and retirement savings.

◆ Know what insurances you need (and what you don't).

◆ Be in control of your money, even after death.

◆ Secure your financial situation to be comfortable.

These are my personal financial secrets, which I share with you.

A word of warning...

Don't get caught up on the figures used in this book or the so called 'lifestyle purchases' mentioned such as clothes, computers, tech gadgets, cars and holidays etc. They will change over time and therefore the specifics are irrelevant. For example, a new iPad today will not cost the same in a year and may not be worth as much in several years. Perhaps in time, iPads or the like will be a dime a dozen and everyone will own one, or no longer desire them. The salary you earn today will not be the same as you earn in the future. The expenses you have today will not be the same in the future. Maybe you are not interested in things, perhaps you prefer experiences such as travelling, skydiving, dining out etc, or perhaps you want to be able to give away more money to family or charity. The financial secrets and strategies that I will share with you (and the fact that they work), are the important parts of this book, no matter what the specific figures are, or your age, your income, where you come from or your reason for wanting more money.

They are TIMELESS.
They are PRACTICAL.
They are APPLICABLE to EVERYONE.

INTRODUCTION

E ver wondered why some people are rich and others are not? Why the poor get poorer, and the rich get richer? Money is a 'game' and how well you play the game determines your financial outcome. Rich people play the game better than poor people.

The banking system: A quick introduction

'It is well enough that people of the nation do not understand our banking and monetary system, for if they did, I believe there would be a revolution before tomorrow morning.'

HENRY FORD

Simply put, people deposit their money in banks. Banks then lend that money out and charge interest to consumers, or to entrepreneurs willing to borrow the money to invest it in some profitable enterprise.

Banks are allowed to lend out considerably more money than which they hold in reserve and if customer savings account balances are not enough, then private banks can seek to borrow more from the Central Banks.

Is the design of the banking system fair? Was it created by 'the rich' many, many years ago to further their own agendas and to create a monopoly over money on a global scale? Does the power of the Central Banks dictate how successful an individual can be? Maybe. Maybe not. It depends on who you listen to.

Actually, it's irrelevant to your personal financial success.

This book won't teach you how to get rich overnight, but it will teach how best to use the 'cards you are dealt' in the game of money—how to use what you have, in a better way, so you can be extraordinary with your money, even if you come from an ordinary start. You can design your own financial success, regardless of the banking system that surrounds you. There are many different aspects of the banking industry. I am not going to teach you the in-depth workings of it because quite frankly it's not important in the scheme of things. I am not going to change the banking industry overnight nor is that level of industry knowledge important for you to be able to manage your finances successfully. Remember, what is important, is that you learn how to play the game of money better than you are now. Excel in areas that you can control. Forget the rest. Our focus is not to bring on global change or get rich quick, but instead, learn how best use your income to grow your wealth, whilst also enjoying your lifestyle. At the same time, shedding some light on the 'hidden truths' when it comes to everyday money matters.

In today's world, you are over-stimulated with marketing (companies pushing you to buy) and the feeling of instant gratification (buying things you don't need or can't afford, in order to make yourself or others feel better), which then leads to financial strife. It's no wonder that many people get stuck in the 'rat race' and live payday to payday.

How to set up your bank accounts, how to borrow money correctly and when to borrow, how to manage money properly and invest to make more money—THAT is what you need to know and focus on.

Unfortunately, none of that is taught in school, and so there is a cycle that repeats itself from generation to generation. If your parents were not taught correctly about money, then how do they correctly teach you about money?

The system is set so that we go to school to get an education—an education that covers various subjects except how to run personal finances when you start your working life. You get a job, pay your taxes and work until retirement. Go to work, pay taxes, go to work and pay taxes. Repeat the cycle and figure out the rest in between by yourself. In the past, the government took care of you financially in retirement with a modest pension. These days, especially for younger generations, government pensions are all but disappearing quickly, and you are told to save for your own retirement. Whether you like it or not, the government is extending the retirement age, so you work longer, pay taxes longer and save for retirement for longer.

When do you learn about every day, practical money management? When do you learn about investing? When do you learn how to get ahead financially?

Some people will seek advice from a Financial Planner, but in my experience, that tends to happen around age 30-something to 50-something, as people enter a particular stage of life, such as starting a family, taking on more debt to upgrade their home or nearing retirement for example. What about before that?

For most people, secondary school in Australia ends around age 17. Some go on to tertiary education for a few years afterwards and then their working lives start, but for a lot of people, work starts even earlier for one reason or another. Potentially, that's a good 10 to 15 years before feeling the 'need' to seek the services of a Financial Planner, with years of trial and error when it comes to everyday money management (and more than enough time to make a mess of it).

Common reasons why people don't have a Financial Planner

◆ Feel they are too young to need financial advice, perhaps just starting their working life.

◆ Think they don't earn enough income, don't have enough savings or have too many personal debts to be able to put the advice into practice.

◆ Embarrassed by their current financial position—have the feeling of hopelessness.

- Afraid of the fees payable (cost) to seek financial advice.
- Unsure of what a Financial Planner actually does or can do for them.
- Concerned with unscrupulous Financial Planners (the media loves that)!

There is definitely a knowledge gap when it comes to successful money management—evident by people spending more than they earn and taking on more personal debt as a result.

Australia is one of the richest countries in the world. It's an expensive country to live in, however Australians also earn some of the highest incomes in the world. If you can 'make it' anywhere in the world, it's Australia. We have every opportunity available, yet there seems to be more people struggling to make ends meet and living payday to payday. Surely as times change and more and more households earn double incomes, the wealth of ordinary Australians should increase accordingly. But instead, it's proven time and time again by rising personal debt levels, that more people are forgetting the basics of money management and simply not playing the game right. There should be no excuses in a rich country such as Australia.

Australia's personal debt has been reported as the 'highest in the world' but what does this really mean?

'Australian household debt has steadily risen over the past three decades as more of us aim to own homes and continue to rely on products such as car loans and credit cards. In fact, the ratio of household debt to income has almost tripled between 1988 and 2015, going from 64% to 185%, according to the AMP.NATSEM Income and Wealth Report released in 2015.

While many other developed countries have seen a decline or 'levelling out' of personal debt since the 2008 global financial crisis, Australia's debt levels have continued to increase. As a result, Australia is now reported to have the highest personal debt levels in the world.

WWW.FINDER.COM.AU

17 FEBRUARY 2017

What if, instead, you learnt how to set your money up correctly from the beginning to avoid common pitfalls of cash flow mismanagement and personal debt traps? The difference between rich people and poor people is WHAT they spend their money on.

Let's clarify some important terminology right from the start:

Cash flow: Money you make
Expenses: Money you spend
Assets: Something that pays you (goes up in value)
Liabilities: Something that costs you (goes down in value)

- **Poor People** buy 'stuff'; things of fairly low value that lose more value over time. By 'poor' I don't mean people who are unemployed and homeless. I mean those that are living a regular working life, paying bills and with low amounts of personal wealth, often living payday to payday. Filling their home with knick-knacks and clutter, of which most are either considered 'junk' or for 'entertainment value' and doesn't help to increase their wealth. 'Little Aussie Battlers.'

- **Middle-Class People** buy 'liabilities'; more expensive stuff like tech gadgets, cars, boats, etc, which cost them more money and lose more value over time. They buy big homes, then buy more stuff to fill it, so whilst their home may increase in value, the extra stuff they buy detracts from it. They may seem richer or that they have 'made it' in life, but quite often have personal debt up to their eyeballs and may still live payday to payday, even if their household income is higher. A lot of good income earners still spend too much money on stuff and liabilities; they use debt to buy those things to impress the neighbours and don't invest enough. The more they earn, the more they spend. They should have much higher net wealth, given the level of income they earn.

- **Rich People buy 'assets'**; they invest a lot of their income to make more money so that they can enjoy more of the nicer things in life, but without using personal debt. The more they invest, the more they make. They have money available for a rainy day. They have good cash flow (relative to expenses). They look at the 'return on investment' that a purchase may make them (how much money it will return to them) BEFORE they spend. They have more assets than stuff. They don't necessarily earn a high income or come from money.

To change your financial situation, you must be more observant with your spending. You don't need to become a finance guru or let money management take over your entire life, however, you need to be conscious of all incomings and outgoings. When it comes to your money, become a Financial Pitbull.

The 10 BIGGEST mistakes made with money

1. Not Learning About Money Management (Feeling Powerless)

You don't know what to do or where to start. You were not taught in school how to manage money, so you trial and error over time but can't see what you are doing 'wrong'. Ignoring the issue will only make it worse. The definition of insanity is to keep doing what you are currently doing and expect a different outcome. The good news is that anyone's financial position can be improved. Learn from others' mistakes, then learn from those with results.

2. Inconsistent Income

The level of income you earn is not as important as the consistency in which you earn it. If your income varies very significantly from payday to payday, or you work on a contract basis or chop and change your jobs with large periods of unemployment or irregular income, then it's hard to make a plan on how to use it most effectively. You need a regular income year after year to be able to stick to a plan. If you are currently unemployed or jumping between jobs often, then get a stable job ASAP. Without an income, you can't do much in life.

3. Not Paying Yourself First (Always)

If you are paying your taxes, housing, bills, and other expenses all before you pay yourself, then you are 'living to work' instead of 'working to live'. It will always be harder to save at the end of the month (after paying everyone else) than if you save first (before anything else). Often there is rarely any money left over at the end of the month, so you need to switch it around and give you the priority which you deserve.

4. Not Having Emergency Money

Things change in life. Unexpected expenses pop up in life. They always do. You always need access to some cash. Having a cash buffer will give you peace of mind that you have funds to draw on if an emergency or an extraordinary, unexpected bill arises, or worse yet if you lose your job or get hurt and can't work.

5. Not Knowing Where Money Is Going (Wasting Money)

Ever tracked your expenses for a month or two? Written down every single dollar spent? If not, then how can you possibly know where your money is being spent? You may have a rough idea, but you need concrete figures. It's hard to redirect money to what you really want in life if you don't know where you are really spending it. Without analysing your actual spending, it's hard to accurately budget, and if you don't have a budget, then it's hard to determine what surplus income you have, if any, or whether you are overspending. Knowing where you spend money helps you to cut back.

Budgeting is important. It's boring, but important, especially until you get the hang of money management. Afterwards, when your finances are in order, sticking to a budget can be more relaxed, but initially, it's critical to analyse your incomings and outgoings and have a budget to work from. If you are not conscious of where you spend your money, it can leave your pocket in ways in which you don't even realise and which adds further insult to injury. Whether you are paying for things you don't need or use, paying unnecessary fees, paying costly bank interest or just not thinking of ways to save money each time you spend it, then you are wasting money. A dollar saved, is a dollar in your pocket (rather than someone else's).

6. Spending More Than You Earn

Recipe for disaster—simple. Living within your means is crucial. You will go bankrupt unless you make changes. It's blunt but true. The good news is that you can change your spending habits. You were not born a 'spender'. You learnt that habit over time, so you can also change that habit, i.e. track your expenses for at least two months, review each area of spending and cut back. Spend less and give your-self some breathing room. Later, you can also look at increasing your income, initially though, your budget will show you areas where you can make some immediate savings. There are always solutions.

If you live with a partner, and have separate finances and different spending habits, then it's hard to be on the same financial page. You need to talk about money to understand each other's income, spending, and financial goals. If one per-son is a great saver, but the other is constantly spending, then you will go around in circles and get nowhere. If you are both 'spenders' then you need to know that, to keep each other accountable. You don't necessarily need every single bill or bank account to be in joint names, however at least a couple of bank accounts need to be e.g. one account for short/medium-term savings (emergencies and larger cost items, holidays etc) and another account for long-term savings (the 'don't touch' account, to buy a property together or other investments to grow your joint wealth). It's important you both save money together, so both people in the relationship are less tempted to dip into joint savings.

7. Spending Too Much On Housing

Spending too much on housing (rent or mortgage) is a major reason why people struggle financially, which is easy to do, especially when property prices and rents keep increasing. Prices will continue to rise; you can't control that. What you can control is the amount that you choose to spend on housing, especially if you are living a lifestyle that you can't afford (right now).

Whilst there is no definite rule, aim to spend no more than 25%–35% of your gross income on housing and that amount includes all property related expenses such as utility bills (electricity, water, gas) and property insurance or other fees, etc. If you need to, consider living in a smaller place, change suburbs or share the cost with someone else. Live within your means. You can always upgrade later down the track when you can afford to do so. Even if you earn a good income and can afford to spend more on housing, consider spending a little less rather than always the maximum—leave yourself some breathing room because life circumstances change. What if you lose your job tomorrow? Or get sick or injured and can't work for a period of time? What if interest rates rise to those seen in the 1980s (ask your parents about it). What if you start a family (planned or unplanned) and your combined household income significantly reduces? For couples, consider housing costs that you can afford on just one income, rather than two—that's a great buffer. Imagine what you can then achieve with more of the second income at your disposal, rather than being over-committed to high housing costs and other bills which need 100% of both incomes to make ends meet.

Always have a backup plan for the backup plan and don't over-extend yourself, just in case. The money you don't spend on housing can be used for so many other things—to increase your savings/ investments and improve other areas of lifestyle. It's okay to make some short-term sacrifices to invest in your long-term success. First homeowners, don't spend big and buy your dream home the first time you buy.

8. Racking Up Personal Debt

When your day-to-day finances are not in order, it's easy to fall into the cycle of using debt to help you along the way, so you can buy whatever you want, or make ends meet as a short-term fix when you have no other cash funds available to you (for emergencies or unexpected expenses). Whether it's a credit card used incorrectly or a 'Payday Loan' type of scheme, the cost of holding personal debt can increase quickly and see you in a position whereby you have several credit cards, a car loan and maybe some store debt (Interest-free Payment Plans)—none of which will help you to get ahead financially and will send you broke.

Spending money you don't have, on things you don't need and racking up personal debt is a vicious cycle which will not end well—stop that immediately. Personal loans and credit cards will be discussed more throughout this book to increase your knowledge of the do's and don'ts when it comes to those mischievous little tempters. I will teach you the truth about personal debt and what it really costs you.

Most people don't use credit cards correctly. Most people shouldn't use them at all. If you have existing credit card debt right now then don't use credit cards anymore. Simple as that. I will show you how to get rid of that debt; then you must steer clear in the future. Cash is king.

9. Buying Stuff, Instead of Investing

If you keep buying stuff which goes down in value over time such as clothes, tech gadgets, household items, bikes, cars or holidays, dining out (any life experience) etc, then your wealth also goes down. Remember, those are not assets; they are liabilities, regardless if you use debt to buy them or not. Regardless of whether you spend money on things or experiences, spending is spending! If you are using credit cards and/or personal loans to fund those items, you will cripple your financial life. Knowing the difference between an asset and a liability will help you make better choices about where you spend your money. Knowing the difference between 'good debt' and 'bad debt' can be a game changer for making money and will be discussed later.

10. Not Saving Regularly

Are you putting today's happiness before tomorrow's needs? Instant gratification is the desire to have everything now. Spending everything you earn. Living payday to payday, whether it's intentional or somehow just how you 'end up' each week, because of circumstance. If your budget doesn't match your lifestyle (extravagant or not), then you need to reassess. Sometimes you need to sacrifice a little now, to get more in the future, especially if you are jeopardising your financial security by not having money left over. What does it cost you in the long-term to be spending everything now and never saving?

Without regular savings, you will not progress, and you will be tempted to use personal debt. If ants can put a little away for tomorrow, then so must we. Surely ants can't be smarter and more disciplined than us humans? Don't be stingy with money, be selective. Live deliberately. Spend in a balanced way.

It's okay to consume, but not okay to 'compulsively consume'. You will not get happier by consuming more. Keep your ego in check. Really think about what you need vs. want. If you are a consumption machine and constantly spending money on stuff (liabilities) to the detriment of your finances, stop—rethink—take a breath—refocus your spending.

If you are in a position where you do in fact have money left over each payday, and you do regularly save, but are still not getting anywhere with your finances, then reassess what you do with those savings (does it eventually get spent)? Essentially, you are in the same predicament as those who don't save.

Introduction Summary

- The 10 biggest mistakes made with money are:
  1. Not Learning About Money Management (Feeling Powerless)
  2. Inconsistent Income
  3. Not Paying Yourself First
  4. Not Having Emergency Money
  5. Not Knowing Where Money Is Going (Wasting Money)
  6. Spending More Than You Make
  7. Spending Too Much On Housing
  8. Racking Up Personal Debt
  9. Buying Stuff, Instead of Investing
  10. Not Saving Regularly
- An asset is something that pays you. A liability costs you.
- The difference between poor people and rich people is what they spend their money on.
  - Poor People buy 'stuff' (go down in value).
  - Rich People buy assets (go up in value).
- Spend money on experiences (memories) to grow as a person and assets to grow your wealth, rather than more stuff which goes down in value.
- Buying more stuff will not make you happy. It will make you poorer.
- Become conscious of money. Be observant with spending.
- Take responsibility for your own money management.

CHAPTER 1

Saving money (why bother?)

Dictionary.com defines 'save' as:
'to avoid the spending, consumption, or waste of i.e. to save money.'

One of the best things my mum ever taught me was how to save money and to 'put some away for tomorrow'. Actually, mum forced me to save some of my income as soon as I started working in my first job and I am forever grateful she did, as it was one of the best lessons I learnt (and thankfully learnt from a young age).

Think about it, how can a person ever possibly pay for everything they need or want with one week's wage? I am not talking about buying a private jet or your own island in the tropics, simply affording the things which you need or want in 'normal' day-to-day life.

Treat your personal finances as a business and you are the Chief Financial Officer (CFO). It's your responsibility to ensure that the business runs smoothly. Without successful money management, even at a basic level, the business (you) will struggle and may even go bankrupt.

Just like a business, you too must save money regularly to:
◆ Regulate Cash Flow
◆ Afford Larger Purchases
◆ Survive Emergencies & Unexpected Expenses
◆ Make More Money (Investing)

Regulate Cash Flow

There are things in life you need for survival and things you want for enjoyment. Regardless of what category your expenses fall into, they will never all be paid at the same frequency as you receive your income (salary). Your payday may be weekly, but your phone bill may be due monthly, etc. If you don't save some of your weekly income (you spend it all from week to week) and instead pay the entire bill using the income you earned in the week that the bill arrives, you will leave yourself short that week, meaning other bills or your lifestyle will be affected. Perhaps you will not be able to go out that weekend, because you had to pay a few 'monthly bills' during the week, or worse yet, you may be short for rent or a mortgage repayment, because you also had to pay other necessities like food and fuel, which couldn't wait for another week. That cycle can drain your money confidence and take too much energy to juggle. There is a better way.

Afford Larger Purchases

If you want to fund larger expenses such as holidays, clothes and tech gadgets, how will you pay for it all at once? If your weekly income is less than the cost of a holiday, for example, then you need to save a small amount on a regular basis to be able to accumulate the necessary funds. The earlier you start saving, and the more consistent you are, the better, but it's never too late to start. Later I'll show you how to afford larger expenses, regardless of the amount.

Survive Emergencies & Unexpected Expenses

Life throws all sorts of scenarios at us. Whether it's a cash emergency, such as your car breaking down and needing a substantial number of repairs, or an 'emergency to you' type of unexpected expense, such as your favourite band is in town for one show only and you need the cost of a ticket. Or, perhaps friends invite you on an overseas trip which needs to be paid in full in two weeks, otherwise you miss out on a special airfare deal. Or, you drop your phone and it breaks (we've all been there). How will you cope with no savings to access because you live from payday to payday? Are you going to borrow money from loved ones (if they have it to lend in the first place) and be someone who can't look after themselves financially? Are you going to borrow money from a bank or credit card and be someone who always pays too much (for things) because of the interest costs you pay on top of the borrowings? Then stress about how to repay the debt, especially as you weren't able to afford it in the first place? Or, are you going to miss out?

Make More Money (Investing)

Saving money is the first step to creating wealth and means more money in your back pocket. It's the fundamental basis of all successful money management. However, simply saving money does not get your money working for you. You are working for the money. To create real wealth, you also need to invest. Save first. Invest second. Without investing, you will never have any more money than what you can save. The first step is in understanding the importance of saving. Unless you can master that, you won't be able to do much else financially.

Saving is not an option; it is a necessity. Just as a business must afford its expenses and pay staff in order to continue operating, you too must be able to meet certain expenses in life. The optional extras you choose to enjoy thereafter is up to you. By putting money aside on a regular basis, even if just a small amount, you can regulate your cash flow, afford larger expenses and have cash available for emergencies as they arise… and believe me, they always do.

By being the best 'CFO' of your money life, you can have what you want, when you want and without putting yourself in financial strife.

You can proudly rely on yourself and make those scenarios an affordable part of day-to-day life, rather than a stressful drama. The earlier you start to save, the better and the easier it becomes. That's because the older you get, the more expenses you have such as children, bigger homes, more debt plus retirement savings. It's never too late. Start today, then practice being GOOD at it. You can HAVE your cake and EAT it too.

Chapter 1 summary

- Having savings available provides a level of financial security.
- You must save some money on a regular basis to regulate your cash flow, survive emergencies, afford the nicer things in life and to make more money.
- Without regular savings, your wealth (and buying ability) is limited to the income you earn each week and no more.
- Once you have consistent savings in place, later you can invest in assets—things that make you money—such as property and shares to create real wealth over time and financial security.
- Without regular savings, don't even consider other investments.
- Life is about balance—spend some, save some. Some for today, some for tomorrow. There has to be some give and take. Life is not about missing out but having it all—in time.
- Be the best 'CFO' of your money life.

CHAPTER 2

Top reasons (excuses) for not saving

There are a lot of people who will say that they understand the importance of regularly saving, after all, you can't pay for everything using one week's wage, yet a lot of people don't actually save money on a regular basis. Some do manage to save a certain amount, then spend it and repeat the cycle. Honestly, I think I have heard just about every excuse under the sun when it comes to saving (or lack thereof). Four of the most common excuses are:

Don't earn enough (can't afford to).
You can afford it, everyone can, you just don't know how.
Will start next week.
Yeah, yeah heard that before, why not this week?
Do save, but then spend it.
Then you need to change what you are doing.
Don't need to save; I live for now.
You are limiting your lifestyle and how much you 'live'.

Each excuse has a payoff which is something you want to be doing for instant gratification and happiness (such as spending the rest of this week's pay on a big weekend out or a new tech gadget), rather than doing what needs to be done in order to keep up some regular savings (perhaps going out one night a week instead of two, or cutting back on some other area of spending, if that's what it takes).

Saving regularly doesn't need to feel like a sacrifice if you start now and are consistent. A regular amount put away on a consistent basis is the key. A small amount saved for a long time can be more powerful (and easier) than saving a large amount for less time.

> *My mum was a classic example of this after needing to find a job to support us children. Not earning much at all, we lived payday to payday. Not because of any fault or intention of Mum, it really did feel as though we needed every single dollar that she earned, just to cover our basic expenses, let alone many luxuries. Any savings that Mum did manage to put away then went on larger necessities, such as school fees or car repairs, etc.*
>
> *Later on, as I got older and started my financial journey, I shared with Mum about the most amazing strategy I know 'Paying Yourself First'—the 10% Savings Rule.*
>
> *Mum chose to give it a go, implemented the strategy and it completely changed her savings results. I will explain in detail later on, but for now, the important part is that Mum chose to try it, to do something different and to change her thinking—and it worked.*

Let's investigate further and understand that reasons for not saving regularly are just excuses, not the truth; they are stories that we tell ourselves and which sabotage our success.

DON'T EARN ENOUGH (CAN'T AFFORD TO SAVE)

I don't buy into that one, sorry. 'Saving' is not a new phenomenon, it's been around since the dawn of time. It actually doesn't matter how much you earn or how much you save, what's important is that you save something, anything, regularly and consistently.

When I started working full-time at age 17, I was earning the grand sum of $230 per week (net after tax). It wasn't a lot of money then and it's definitely not a lot today, but it was what I had to work with. After a couple of weeks of working and happily spending, my mum asked me how much I was saving. I looked at her blankly. Mum suggested that I put $50 every week into a second bank account for a 'rainy day'. Ok, it wasn't so much a suggestion but more of an ultimatum—either I save $50 per week into a separate savings account or I pay it to her as 'rent/board'. I took advantage of Mum's generous offer and I chose the savings. I knew a good deal when I saw one. At 17, I was still living at home and basically my only expenses were a mobile phone ($30 per month) and fuel for my car ($25 per week), plus going out on the weekends and clothes of course, but they were not necessities, only the phone and fuel were necessities, the rest was optional.

TABLE 1: My Actual Figures

Income	Amount (weekly)
Wages (net after tax)	$230
Expenses	
Less Fuel	-$25
Less Phone*	-$7
Surplus Income **(Income less Expenses)**	**$198 per week** **($10,296 yearly)**

*Monthly phone expense pro-rata over 52 weeks then divided by 12 months to calculate the average monthly cost.

Now, I realise that the price of things today may be higher than they were in the past, but so are most salaries. I am not 17 anymore, my current fuel costs are more than $25 per week, but my income is also much more than $230 per week. However, the basic principles of saving are the same. I know of young 'tradies' today who are 17–18 and earn much more than $1,000 per week (net after tax), with not much to financially show for it. It's all relative.

After paying for my necessities, I still had $198 per week leftover to spend on 'stuff'. That is $10,296 per year—which was enough to buy a small car in cash or a trip to Europe (even at today's prices).

When you convert a weekly amount to a yearly amount, it's much more grounding. All of a sudden, the stuff that can be bought each week no longer seems as appealing, not when compared to what can be bought over a longer period of time if the weekly amount is saved up. Saving $50 per week as suggested by Mum really didn't seem like such a problem and still left me with $148 per week for other stuff. So, I started saving that $50.

Whether you pay rent/board or not, or what your expenses are, is irrelevant. Remember, the amounts used throughout this book are examples only and will differ to your situation—it's the lesson of saving regularly which is important. Naturally, if you no longer live at home then your expenses will be much higher and probably take up most of your income (a likely reason why you are reading this book), however, your salary will also likely be higher than mine was. Whilst living at home with your parents, make the most of your savings during that time. If already living out of home, just do what you can.

Whether you save $5 per week, $50 per week or $500 per week is not important, it's the act of saving an amount on a consistent basis which is important (and not dipping into it too often in the early stages).

The Government ('Tax Man') automatically takes a percentage of your salary each payday, usually before you even have a chance to hold the money in your own hands. If the Government was to all of a sudden increase tax rates by 1%, 5% or even 10%, you wouldn't have a choice and would have to find a way to give up that extra chunk of your income. You would force yourself to afford it. Pretend that tax rates increased today and instead save that extra amount for yourself. The key to financial success is to save first before you spend. Pay yourself first and then pay your bills (more in Chapter 3).

YOU WILL START SAVING NEXT WEEK

Unfortunately, most likely you won't. We humans are creatures of habit. What you don't do today, you probably won't do tomorrow, unless you choose to make a change. If you don't save this week, how or why will you all of a sudden save next week? If you can't afford to save this week, how will you magically be able to afford to save next week? Saving money is a consistent effort.

A little each week goes a long way over time and makes it less of a burden. It's not about the amount, it's about creating a good habit, automatically each payday, rather than a chore, done ad-hoc when you feel like it.

Remember, the government is consistent when deducting your income tax. You don't have a choice and the amount fluctuates depending on how much you earn. You know that you can't use that portion of your earnings for your lifestyle. Often, you don't even see that portion of the money. Treat your savings the same—think of it as a mandatory deduction that starts today.

YOU DO SAVE… BUT THEN SPEND IT

Perhaps you are saving on a regular basis. Perhaps your bank account balance grows to $1,000 and then you spend it. You manage to save up $1,000 again, and then you spend it. A vicious cycle. Are your savings bundled together in one bank account? This is a common problem if you have just one main bank account in which you hold all money—money for spending and money for savings, all lumped in together—it rarely works. You need to separate your savings from your spending money, so you know exactly what you have saved and what you have left to spend.

For some, seeing a separate savings account grow in value also creates motivation to keep going and save more money. If you know you will be tempted to spend that growing savings account balance, you must use a different banking institution to hold your savings. If you can't see your savings account balance on a regular basis, you are less likely to spend it. Remove the temptation by moving your funds away from you. Use separate bank accounts for Everyday Spending and your Savings. The key is to move the money you need for your bills and necessities into an account out of sight. Use technology to your advantage and set up automated transfers through your bank (direct or online) to automate the process and make it one less thing to worry about or to actively have to manage (more in Chapter 5).

YOU DON'T NEED TO SAVE; YOU LIVE FOR NOW

A friend literally said this to me one day when we were talking about savings. Well, living payday to payday is not living life to its fullest potential if you ask me. Your spending is limited by what you earn in a particular week, which can bring unnecessary stresses and limits the type of lifestyle you can enjoy. You never know what's around the corner, so you need extra funds at your disposal if you don't want to miss out when opportunity knocks.

Life is about balance, save some and spend some. You only get one life, and it needs to be enjoyed to the fullest. I don't believe in saving everything for 'one day' and never enjoying the nicer things in life. Life is not about being frugal to the extreme. Whilst your health is good, and you can experience all that life has to offer, you need to organise your finances to be able to do so. If your car breaks down next week and you need $1,000 to fix it (which you don't have), then I can guarantee your attitude of 'don't worry about it' and 'she'll be right mate' will quickly change and you will suddenly be living (and working) to repay your car repair costs, rather than living for now. Or even worse, you may still be living for now with ever-increasing credit card debt to cover those car repairs, etc. That is unnecessary stress.

SAVING REGULARLY IS A HABIT (BORING, BUT NECESSARY) ...

Having your finances in order creates the feeling of abundance and reduces stress. Plus, you can experience the joy of being able to help yourself and others in life, mentally, emotionally, physically and monetarily. Remember, all excuses are created equal. Just because one person earns more than another, it doesn't mean they necessarily save more or that their savings ability comes any easier to them. Usually, when a person earns more, they spend more—a common occurrence.

Through my work, I regularly see people earning over $100,000 per year, in their mid-40s, with minimal financial assets and always some credit card debt. And no, the cars that they own (usually with loans attached) are not considered to be assets as the value goes down over time. When it comes to money, the only assets of importance are those that go up in value over time.

A high-income earner must choose to save, just as a low-income earner must choose to save. Only the amounts saved may change. Start to think in percentages: if one person earns $100,000 and saves $10,000 each year that equates to 10% of income saved, likewise another person who earns $50,000 and saves $5,000 each year saved 10% too. Whatever your income level, start saving using a percentage rather than a dollar amount.

Chapter 2 summary

- Create a healthy cash flow so you have choices in life.
- Regular savings means you won't need expensive and unnecessary personal debt and you will stress less about money.
- When it comes to not saving regularly, all excuses are equal.
- Each excuse has a payoff—something you want to be doing now for instant gratification and happiness instead of also thinking about tomorrow.
- Earning more money is not always the answer.
- Don't worry about what you are saving for as a reason, purpose, item or expense will come along—trust me they always do—just start your savings today.

CHAPTER 3

Paying yourself first

Have you ever felt as though there is more 'month at the end of your money' rather than 'money at the end of the month'?

To try and save a portion of your income after paying tax, rent, bills, etc, can take a lot of discipline. If any area of your spending blows out, quite often the 'elective savings' that you intended to do will be the part that gets missed or postponed until next week. The problem is, if that blow out keeps happening each week for any reason at all then saving a portion of your income regularly will never occur and you will find yourself in the cycle of living payday to payday and wondering why there is never anything leftover to save.

Ask yourself… why do you work?

Usually, the answer is to earn income for living expenses. Yet most employees will have income tax deducted from their salary before they even see a dollar 'in the hand'. Then, usually, most people pay the larger mandatory expenses next, like rent or mortgage repayments, other personal loan repayments, followed by food, utilities, petrol, etc. So, in essence, you are really working to pay:

1. The Tax Man (Government)
2. The Landlord or Bank
3. The Grocers
4. The Utility companies
5. The Oil Companies… and so on.

When do you start to work for you as a priority and not as the last person in a long list? An easy and simple way to change this all-too-common predicament is to:

Pay Yourself
FIRST

This is one of the best strategies that I ever learnt. It changed my world. It's the fundamental basis for saving regularly and getting ahead financially. It's been around since ancient Babylonian times. It's tried, tested and works every time it's implemented.

I came across it in a book called *The Richest Man in Babylon* by George S. Clason, first published in 1926. I highly recommend that book to everyone. Read it next. The strategy is to pay yourself first because a part of all you earn is yours to keep.

Step One Save a minimum 10% of your gross income, before taxes, rent, bills, food etc.

Step Two Use only the remaining 90% for expenses (and other savings). No less, no more.

I have been using this strategy for some years now and have shared the results with many friends and family who have also achieved great results. However, I do it a little differently to George S. Clason as I pay myself 10% of net income (take home after tax). This keeps it more practical in real life as most people have income tax deducted before receiving any income, so it's generally easier to calculate 10% of the amount that is actually received into your bank account. It doesn't matter if you receive the same net income each payday or if it varies. 10% is always 10%, the percentage doesn't change.

To implement this strategy, come next payday, follow these steps:

1. Calculate 10% of the net income you receive.
2. Transfer the 10% to a separate bank account (your '10% Savings Account'). Do this first before anything else.
3. The remaining funds are yours to pay other living expenses like rent or mortgage, food, utilities, clothes, entertainment, etc and for other savings goals.

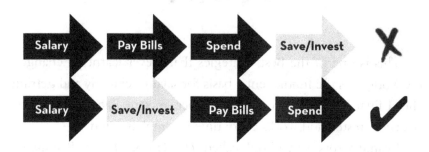

For example, if your net income is $850 per week then 10% = $85. Transfer $85 to your 10% Savings Account FIRST. Use the remaining $765 for other savings and expenses.

Make sure you pay yourself FIRST before you pay anything else—that removes the psychological barrier of feeling as though you can't afford to save. Subconsciously, if you can't see it (the 10%) then you won't spend it. Your budget will automatically adjust to allow for it. It works every time.

It's essential that the 10% Savings be transferred into a separate bank account held with a different banking institution (to your everyday account). You must keep it separated otherwise how will you know what are savings and what's for spending? Using a different institution will remove the temptation to spend it. If you can't see it, you won't spend it.

Just like you currently spend whatever money is in your everyday bank account, when you move 10% away first, you still end up spending only what's left in your everyday bank account. Your brain doesn't automatically register the money that you no longer see.

Ten per cent is the minimum—choose a higher amount as your budget allows. Start with 5% if you must (after all, anything is better than nothing), however 10% is practical for everyone and is tried and tested time and again. If 10% works for everyone else, it will work for you too. You will not even notice that it's 'gone' and you will also see results faster.

So, forget the excuse 'I can't afford 10%'—remember, if the government all of a sudden put up income tax by that amount, you would have to go without that money and find a way to afford it. By paying yourself first, the 10% is still for you, for your future benefit.

DON'T TOUCH THE 10% SAVINGS ACCOUNT (FOR NOW).

The 10% Savings is not for lifestyle expenses such as clothes, tech gadgets, concert tickets, holidays, cars, etc, it's to grow your wealth and get ahead financially:
- A home loan deposit (or investment property)
- Extra loan repayments (to clear debts faster)
- Investments/Assets/Businesses (to make more money).

Keep adding to the account each payday—it's a never-ending strategy. Remember, the whole point of the 10% Savings Rule is not to analyse whether you can afford to save that amount or not. By moving that money into a separate account first, before anything else, you remove the opportunity to over-analyse it.

Later, when you are ready, you can consider investments such as a term deposit, shares and/or property etc, those are assets which will increase in value over time and make you more money. For now, you need to create a habit of saving, before worrying about how to invest.

Mum's Real-Life Results

A few years after Mum went back to work she found herself with not much to financially show for it. She felt as though things were getting more and more expensive and that her wage was just not keeping up (sound familiar?).

Mum never seemed to be able to save, as there was never any money left over at the end of her fortnightly pay. Being a single lady, she had to pay all rent and expenses (for two children and herself) on her own. Mum felt hopeless. After a while, she started to go to work unhappy and unable to see her future as anything different. How was she to get off the mouse wheel of work, pay bills, work, pay bills, work, pay bills? I suggested she start the 10% Savings Rule. Mum was willing but hesitant because her budget was tight. How was she possibly able to put aside 10%? Mum also knew that the temptation of having savings building up in an account that she was able to access would likely mean it might be spent on larger expenses like car repairs. No doubt something always pops up in life to spend the savings. I needed to separate Mum from the account.

Mum and I are very close and have a relationship of trust and love. So, I suggested I open a bank account in my name, into which she deposited the money each fortnight using internet banking. Each fortnight Mum looked at her net pay, calculated 10% and transferred that amount into the new bank account—even before paying her rent. Every now and again I told Mum the balance of the account, and she was happily blown away by her progress. Over time, Mum's account grew to $1,000, then $3,000, then $5,000-plus.

Here was someone who was 'not able to save' and felt that she needed at least 100% of her income to cover expenses (if not more), to someone who was now saving 10% of her income each fortnight into an account, which she didn't touch and now had over $5,000 cash and yet she was still able to pay her other expenses with the remaining 90%.

Mum's expenses had not changed. Mum's income had not changed. Only Mum's mindset and actions had changed. After a while, I asked Mum if she missed the 10% income or even noticed it gone from her everyday bank account. She said to me:

'No, I really don't miss it (the money), I don't even notice it's gone and hearing about how the account balance is growing gives me more motivation to keep going.'

It's funny, the more we earn, the more we spend. If you can't see the 10% Savings in your everyday bank account then it's as though you don't have it and therefore you don't spend it. You make do with what you have left, and the beauty is, you will not even miss that 10%. That's why it's essential that you pay yourself FIRST before you pay anything else. It will not work if you pay yourself LAST. Believe it or not—paying yourself first works. Every time. (You don't have to ask someone else to open an account on your behalf. Being stuck in a rut took some more extreme measures for Mum and we worked together on that.)

Want another example of this working?

Christine's Real-Life Results

I have a friend, let's call her Christine. Christine was struggling with credit card debt, wasn't able to save and so asked for my help. I asked Christine to track her expenses for two months, which she did. Christine's income vs. spending showed that in theory it was possible for her to have $700 per month left over, even without changing any existing spending.

That was a surprise to Christine because, in reality, she didn't have $700 building up in her bank account each month. If Christine had access to the money, it was being spent. This is a pretty common scenario, it's human nature. So, it was a case of needing to get money into a savings account at the start of the month, rather than at the end of the month. Move it out of sight.

We ignored the full $700 per month that Christine should have had in theory. We started off slow and simply applied the 10% Savings first, which for Christine equated to $145 per fortnight ($314 per month). Christine set up an automatic funds transfer (direct debit) from her everyday bank account to a separate account (with a different institution), which we nicknamed the '10% Savings Account'. The automatic payment was set to lodge the day after Christine's fortnightly pay day so that the money was redirected to the new account immediately and before Christine even noticed it.

We didn't change any of Christine's existing spending. We took baby steps and only redirected $145 per fortnight as Christine's 10% Savings for now. Christine's income hadn't changed. Christine's expenses hadn't changed. The only change made was to pay Christine first, rather than last.

I then left Christine to it for a few fortnights and was happy to confirm that Christine had successfully been saving, and actually laughed when she too realised that she wasn't even noticing the money leaving her bank account because the automatic fund transfer occurred so close to her payday.

Chapter 3 summary

- You must pay yourself first. Always. That is the secret to saving.
- Your 10% Savings Account must be held at a different institution to move the funds out of sight.
- Choose a high-interest account with no ATM access or fees. If you have an existing home loan, use an offset account.
- The 10% Savings is not for lifestyle expenses. It's only for:
  1. A home loan deposit (or investment property).
  2. Extra loan repayments (to clear debts faster).
  3. Other Investments/Assets/Business Ideas (to make more money).

CHAPTER 4

Track, budget, spend

D o you know what you spend your money on? I mean actually know? Before you can ascertain if there is a problem with your spending, you first need to analyse where your money is being spent... actually being spent that is. True numbers, not estimations. Only then can you make changes to create more money. Two people can earn the same amount of income yet have vastly different lifestyles (where and how they live, etc), simply because of how they choose to spend money.

Tracking Expenses

Take a notepad with you everywhere you go for at least one month (preferably two) and write down every single dollar that you spend each day. In today's world, there are also Apps such as Monefy, Daily Expenses 3 or Travel Expenses (the latter can be used for holiday budgeting). A notepad and pen work just as well. Whether you spend $1 on gum, $4 on a coffee, $50 at the fuel pump or $200 on an electricity bill, write it all down and at the end of the month you will be able to total your expenses and see where you actually spent your money. If, for example, you don't receive an electricity bill in the month that you are tracking (that bill may come every two months), then average out what will be your approximate monthly equivalent spend so you don't exclude those larger bills.

Even if you think you know what your expenses are, this can be an extremely valuable exercise to do as it will give you an insight into the little extras that you spend, which may not necessarily register in your mind each time, in comparison to larger, more noticeable expenses like rent, phone, fuel, electricity, etc.

Creating A Budget

A budget is a plan on how to spend your money and shows you whether you have enough money to do everything you need and want to do. A budget can be as complex and analytical as one wants, with spreadsheets and graphs. A piece of paper with your income listed on one side and your expenses listed on the other side works just as well. By listing all income and all expenses, you will easily be able to see if you are spending more or less than you can afford. A budget also acts as a measuring tool to check if your future spending is in line with the amount you had budgeted for in each area i.e. housing, food, transport, entertainment etc. Your budget can be over any timeframe that you like. I suggest monthly to give you a broad overview of your expenses, especially because not all expenses are paid as frequently as weekly or fortnightly. To know your expenses, you first need to track them. Then you can create a budget using your actual figures, rather than guessing.

Everyone needs a budget of some kind. Some people don't think they need a budget, because they perhaps don't earn enough money or because they feel that they already know what they spend. Some people resist making a budget because they think it will force them to restrict spending. Not true. Everyone can benefit from having a budget.

The purpose of a budget is to give you an understanding of your spending, not to force you to save as much as possible or make you go without. Rather than telling you how to spend your money, a budget gives you the choice to continue spending as you are, or to redirect your money elsewhere (to where it matters most), so you stay on top of bills and can put money aside for other goals.

Without some idea of whether you earn enough to pay for the lifestyle you have (or want), how can you possibly know? When it's too late? After you are already behind your bills? Later when your finances are in order, sticking to a budget can be more relaxed, however to start with, it's a critical part of being able to analyse your incomings and outgoings.

To create a successful budget which you can stick to, it has to be reasonable. You must always allow yourself a proper amount for essentials like groceries, plus some 'treats'. If you are struggling right now with your cash flow then minimise the treats (for a time).

> If your income is **more** than your expenses
> you have **surplus income.**
> If your income is **less** than your expenses
> you have an **income shortfall.**

Below is real life example of a friend's budget, let's call her Sarah. Sarah is having trouble managing her expenses, has rising credit card debt as a result and feels that she doesn't know where her money is going. Sarah first tracked her expenses for two months to know exactly what she was spending and put together the following budget:

TABLE 1: Sarah's Monthly Budget (Average Expenses Each Month)

Income (Monthly)	Amount	Expenses (Monthly)	Amount
Net Salary (after tax)	$3,349	Rent ($340 per week)	$1,473
		Home Contents Insurance	$20
		Car Insurance/ Servicing/ Registration	$100
		Petrol ($50 per week)	$217
		Mobile Phone	$49
		Groceries ($75 per week)	$325
		Health Insurance	$50
		Utilities (Electricity/ Water/ Gas)	$85
		Lunches/ Coffees at Work ($15 per week)	$65
		Gym Membership	$50
		Hairdresser ($150 every 6 weeks)	$108
		Clothes	$200
		Entertainment ($100 per week)	$433

Income (Monthly)	Amount	Expenses (Monthly)	Amount
		Dining out ($50 per week)	$217
		Alcohol ($20 per week)	$87
		Magazines	$9
		Gifts	$50
		Donations	$10
Total IN	**$3,349**	**Total OUT**	**$3,548**

Sarah earns $45,000 per year, which is $3,349 per month (net after tax, estimation using 2020/21 Australian Tax Resident Rates & Medicare Levy). Sarah is spending $3,548, which means -$199 per month shortfall (overspending!). Sarah's budget easily shows that she is overspending by a whopping $2,388 per year! No wonder Sarah has rising credit card debt.

As a rule of thumb, a healthy budget allows you to save around 20% of income, meaning 80% is spent on living expenses. This gives a buffer so you can save more than just the mandatory 10% Savings Rule.

Sarah is spending much more than 80% of income on expenses, she is spending 106% and paying high rent for someone with her level of income. Ideally, she should only spend around $2,680 per month on expenses (and save the rest).

Currently, Sarah isn't able to save any income on a regular basis because she is spending more than she earns. Without savings, Sarah won't get ahead financially. She can't implement the 10% Savings Rule until she rejigs her spending and reduces her expenses.

This is a recipe for disaster = bankruptcy!

Bankruptcy may sound extreme, but no matter who you are or what you earn, if you spend more than you earn, you will lose in the end. Simple.

This example shows the importance of tracking expenses and having a budget. Until Sarah tracked her expenses and created a budget, she wasn't even aware of her overspending. The budget clearly shows that to her in black and white. Without clarifying the problem, it's easy to fall behind in your bills and rack up credit card debt to fund the shortfall or to borrow money from friends/family here and there (without being able to repay). Nothing good can come from not being able to afford your bills or repay debts and if you don't have surplus income then you can't put money aside for emergencies or to afford big-ticket items such as holidays or a home loan deposit.

For Sarah, it's no wonder that she feels as though she is stuck in a rut and not progressing with her finances (not able to buy a new car or her first home). Sarah is living payday to payday and in a vicious spending cycle.

Sarah has two options:
1. EARN MORE or
2. SPEND LESS

Earning more income may or may not be an option right now but spending less is something that everyone can do to create immediate surplus income. It's the easiest, most guaranteed way to get fast results. Remember, it's not about going without and giving up all enjoyment in life, but rather identifying where your money is being spent, so you can make an informed decision to continue as you are or to redirect some spending, so you have what is important to you (rather than overdue bills and stressful credit card debt).

Sarah's next step will be to categorise her expenses as either 'essential' or 'non-essential'. Then Sarah can see what expenses must be paid and what expenses can be changed.

Essential vs Non-Essential Expenses

◆ Essential Expenses: those which you must pay, life necessities such as shelter (rent/mortgage), food, utilities, and some insurances.

◆ Non-Essential Expenses: those which give you enjoyment and are spent by choice, such as dining out, alcohol, takeaway coffee/food, beauty services (hairdresser/beautician), regularly buying new clothes and shoes etc.

Getting our hair done professionally or buying a new outfit for Saturday night can definitely seem like essential expenses, but they are not. Be truthful to yourself when assessing your expenses. Take budgeting seriously, give it the attention it deserves.

Having trouble differentiating between essential and non-essential expenses? Start by stripping back your expenses to zero. Then add back your expenses one by one, in order of importance starting with the most important expenses that you can't live without (those that mean you would starve or go to jail if you didn't pay); those are your essential expenses. Keep adding back in terms of importance. Then add back your 'essential but not life-threatening' expenses such as mobile phone, home internet and so on. The purpose of this is to know your absolute base level of spending—your essential expenses which are non-negotiable in terms of need, which differ to your non-essential expenses which, if you had to, you will manage to live without.

TABLE 2: Categorising Sarah's Budget into Essential vs. Non-Essential Expenses

Income (Monthly)	Amount	Expenses (Monthly)	Amount
Net Salary (after tax)	$3,349	**Essential**	
		Rent ($340 per week)	$1,473
		Home Contents Insurance	$20
		Car Insurance/ Servicing/ Registration	$100
		Petrol ($50 per week)	$217
		Mobile Phone	$49
		Groceries ($75 per week)	$325
		Health Insurance	$50
		Utilities (Electricity/ Water/ Gas)	$85
		Sub-Total	**$2,319**
		Non-Essential	
		Lunches/ Coffees at Work ($15 per week)	$65
		Gym Membership	$50
		Hairdresser ($150 every 6 weeks)	$108
		Clothes	$200
		Entertainment ($100 per week)	$433
		Dining out ($50 per week)	$217
		Alcohol ($20 per week)	$87
		Magazines	$9
		Gifts	$50
		Donations	$10
		Sub-Total	**$1,229**
Total IN	**$3,349**	**Total OUT**	**$3,548**

For Sarah, her total expenses which are 'essential' equate to $2,319 per month and must be paid, they are non-negotiable. All other expenses Sarah can choose to live without if she had to and therefore expenses of $1,229 are considered 'non-essential'.

In one month, if Sarah only spent money on essential expenses ($2,319) her new outcome would be $1,030 per month surplus (money left over). Sarah then immediately changes her cash flow position from -$199 shortfall to +$1,030 in surplus. Sarah can potentially save up to $12,360 per year and do so much more with it.

Wow! What can you do with $12,360? A new car, overseas travel, school fees, put towards a home loan deposit, an emergency fund, other debt repayment—that extra money provides flexibility, security and choices.

Now in reality, Sarah may not want to live on the complete basics for a whole year and scrimp and save to the maximum, unless of course she is focused on saving for a particular goal or clearing unwanted debt. The key is to find a balance between two extremes of over-spending vs. underspending. To live and spend deliberately, so you also have extra funds available when needed. Life isn't much fun if you over-spend and send yourself bankrupt, nor is it fun to be overly stingy with money and never spend anything on yourself. You get one chance at life—you need to enjoy it too.

Sarah needs to decide which of the non-essential expenses are most important to her and which can be cut, or at least reduced. Wherever a reduction can be made, that money can go towards essential expenses and create surplus income. Once Sarah has surplus income, she can start saving towards things that she may truly desire.

Changing Your Spending Choices

Let's look at each non-essential expense with suggestions to cut the spending completely, plus alternative solutions to reduce the spending:

Expense	Ideal Solutions (cut)	Alternative Solutions (reduce)
Lunches/ Coffees at Work ($15 per week)	• Make homemade lunches using groceries bought each week (which cost less). *If short on time, cook a big batch of soup or casserole once or twice a week to supply a week's worth of lunches or cook extra for dinner for lunch the next day.* • Make coffees at work or take supplies from home (thermos) if not provided at work. *Ask your employer to supply a 'pod coffee machine.' Staff can then choose to pay 50c-$1 per pod for a 'cappuccino experience' on a smaller low-cost scale.*	• Nominate one day a week or month to buy a café made lunch/ coffee and take homemade lunches on other days. In the past, I worked in a large office and my colleagues and I went out for lunch on Fridays. It was something to look forward to. The rest of the week I took homemade lunches and drank the office tea.
Gym Membership ($50 per month)	• Use free methods to exercise like walking or running in a park. Have a friend join you. • Make an aerobics routine at home with body strength exercises e.g. lunges, squats, triceps dips, etc. For ideas simply Google it or visit your local library for fitness magazines. *YouTube has an endless supply of programs for FREE. www.youtube.com*	• Exercise DVDs from eBay. The average cost is under $20 and can be used numerous times. Consider buying one DVD this month and one next month for some variety. *I have a collection of five or six exercise DVDs I bought over the years, which I use at home in my lounge room when having a break from the gym, needing a change or wanting to reduce expenses. I still love them.*
Hairdressers ($150 every 6 weeks)	• Colour your hair at home. • Visit a salon only for haircuts. *No...? Fair enough - we all have limits, move on to the Alternative Solutions.*	• Stretch salon visits from 6 weeks to 9 weeks to reduce the cost from to $108 to $73 per month (saving $420 per year) • Use a lower cost salon. • Hairdressing Uni Student Salons offer cheap cuts and colours as practice work for their qualifications. Personally, I prefer local, small salons rather than a large chain or high-end salons. Not only do the prices tend to be better than the 'pay for the name' salons but the experience is personable and you support small business.

New Clothes ($200 per month)

• Buy clothes that are classic cut, rather than always on trend, so they don't go out of style so soon.

• Revamp the clothes you already have by having a 'clothes swapping' party with friends.

• See a Colour Stylist so you know what colours actually suit you. It helps to stop buying clothes that don't suit you and don't make you feel good (and therefore are not worn). You will save money and time in the long run and definitely cover the cost of the stylist consultation.

I had my 'colours done' a few years ago. It changed my clothing/ shopping life. No longer do I buy clothes that don't suit me or go together, but now all my clothes mix and match easily. I buy less but better quality.
www.houseofcolour.co.uk

• Dig through the goodies at Vintage and Op-Shops especially when travelling overseas, you never know what name brand items you can find and it can be fun to pick up something unique.

I have a friend who shops for new clothes a lot. She regularly changes her mind soon after she buys an item and ends up 'donating' brand new clothes to op-shops, some never worn and with tags.

• Buy new clothes less frequently. Instead of a new outfit each week, try one new outfit every month or two.

• Buy from lower cost shops and look for savings online.

Buying clothes online can often be cheaper (even with postage) compared to retail stores as their overheads are less. Plus you can pick up unique items/ international items that not everyone in your town is wearing. Whilst this doesn't support local business, there are plenty of other people who perhaps can better afford the retail department stores, which tend to be owned by large corporates anyway. Instead, I choose to support local business through local hairdressers and small boutiques, for example. Support in 'swings & roundabouts' I say. Remember, buy less, buy better quality.
www.ebay.com
www.asos.com
www.boohoo.com

Entertainment, Dining Out & Alcohol ($170 per week)

• Review your lifestyle. Spending $170 per week on yourself is fun (plus hairdresser, plus clothes, etc), but is pretty luxurious if you are having budgeting problems. Prioritise what's really important and what you could go without. (or at least reduce).

• Reduce overall 'going out' and be more selective about the invites you accept.

• If you have a big event coming up in a few weeks, limit going out before then to save your dollars and make you appreciate the big event when it finally rolls around.

Think of FREE or low-cost activities like a picnic, going to the beach, walking in a beautiful park, coffee at a café with a friend (now and again rather than every day at work), outdoor cinemas, etc.

• Reduce dining out to once or twice per month. If also drinking alcohol whilst out, refrain from buying additional alcohol (or buy less) throughout the month.

Eat and drink at home with friends. Have friends 'bring a plate' for dinner parties. Alternate dinner parties with friends at their homes (take turns in hosting).

Magazines ($9 per month)

• Read articles online or borrow books/ magazines from friends.

• Recycle magazines between friends rather than each of you buying the same copy.

Prefer books? Become a member of your local library. It's FREE.

• Look for 'Bookshop Cafes' where you can buy a coffee and enjoy a book or magazine supplied by the café.

• If you are spending money on books/ magazines, look for community Book Swap Shops whereby you swap a book that you own for another.

• Nothing beats the smell of old books and turning paper pages but eBooks tend to be cheaper than hardcopy (as they cost less to manufacture) and are also easier to travel with.

www.amazon.com
www.apple.com/itunes

Gifts ($50 per month)

• Make cards or gifts yourself for a lot less, such as homemade chocolate wrapped in beautiful paper and ribbon.
• Send online e-cards for birthdays www.123greetings.com
• Make an agreement with your close friends and family not to exchange gifts or to limit gifts to young children only.
• Have a Christmas 'Secret Santa' rather than buying gifts for all.

Be selective with who you share your generosity with. *You can't always buy for everyone.*

• Giving to people in need is always a fantastic idea. However, you will not be helping anyone if you send yourself broke. Stop this expense whilst you take control of your finances then restart when your budget allows.
• If you are worried that you may not restart if you stop or it's very important to you to make donations then consider reducing other expenses and donate that money instead, i.e. the savings made from not buying magazines.

Having to give up something of yours (magazines) to maintain your donations only makes the donations more special.

• Donate to a charity on behalf of someone as their 'gift'. You select the donation amount. Helps to create more 'value', for example a $50 individual donation goes much further when pooled with other peoples' donations, compared to what $50 can buy these days as a gift.

Rather than buying a material item for a friend (who probably doesn't need it anyway and has enough 'stuff'), redirect the funds to charity.

• Reduce the amount that you donate.
• Reduce the number of charities that you support to one or two.

I donate to the RSPCA and sponsor a child in Africa through a local-run non-profit organisation. Those are the charities that I have chosen for myself. I donate once a year and only to those charities.

I've had a 'revolving donation' in place through an charity called KIVA for a long while, whereby the original donation I made was loaned to business owners in poorer countries that are in need. The loan has been repaid into my account and reloaned several times over now, without me having to donate more cash. Amazing concept.

www.rspca.org.au
www.worldfamilies.org.au

The possibilities are endless if you focus on making a change.

If you buy a lot of new clothes because you go out so much, then reducing the amount of times you go out each month will also reduce your need to buy new outfits—if the thought of not going out on the town at least once per week drives you crazy with boredom then be more creative with what you do for entertainment and add some variety. For example, rather than drinking at a pub or dining out at a restaurant, have a Mexican night at a friend's house with everyone pitching in (Bring-A-Plate Parties). Be conscious of your spending. Every time you spend. Don't be stingy with money—be selective.

If Sarah changes nothing then she will get more of the same results. Sarah must take action. She needs to reduce some essential expenses, especially those that vary in cost such as groceries, however non-essential expenses must be reduced first. Sarah very much enjoys going to the gym and out with friends, so let's keep some of that and instead start with:

TABLE 3: Sarah's Proposed Budget Changes (To Create Surplus Income)

Action	Expense	New budget/ Limit	Reduction
Reduce	Lunches at work	$10 per week limit (from $15)	$20 per month
Reduce	Hairdresser	Extend to every 9 weeks ($150 limit)	$35 per month
Reduce	Entertainment/ Going Out	$100 per week limit (from $170)	$304 per month
Reduce	Gifts	$25 per month limit (from $50)	$25 per month
Reduce	New clothes	$100 per month limit (from $200)	$100 per month
Stop	Magazines	Borrow from a friend or visit a library	$9 per month
Stop	Donations	Stop until finances are under control	$10 per month
Potential Budget Reduction			**$503 per month**

TABLE 4: Sarah's New Budget after Those Changes

Income (Monthly)	Amount	Expenses (Monthly)	Amount
Net Salary (after tax)	$3,349	**Essential**	
		Rent ($340 per week)	$1,473
		Home Contents insurance	$20
		Car Insurance/ Servicing/ Registration	$100
		Petrol ($50 per week)	$217
No Changes		Mobile Phone	$49
		Groceries ($75 per week)	$325
		Health Insurance	$50
		Utilities (Electricity/ Water/ Gas)	$85
		Sub-Total	**$2,319**
		Non-Essential	
		Lunches/ Coffees at Work ($10 per week)	$45
		Gym Membership	$50
		Hairdresser ($150 every 9 weeks)	$73
		Clothes	$100
Changes Made		Entertainment/Dining out/Alcohol ($100 per week)	$433
		Magazines	Nil
		Gifts	$25
		Donations	Nil
		Sub-Total	**$726**
Total IN	**$3,349**	**Total OUT**	**$3,045**

After reducing Sarah's non-essential expenses from $1,229 to $726, her total spending will reduce from $3,548 to $3,045 per month, which means $304 per month in surplus (money left over). Sarah has immediately improved her cash flow position from a -$199 per month shortfall to a $304 per month surplus and kept many of her luxuries such as gym membership, new clothes, going out each week, buying lunch each week and getting her hair professionally done. By simply scaling back the more costly activities or extending the frequency, Sarah can now save $304 per month which equals $3,648 per year. That is enough for an overseas holiday!

Sarah's new budget is a far better outcome than having a negative cash flow of -$2,388 per year. Imagine Sarah's results if she also stopped her gym membership (at least for a while), exercised for free and reduced more of her non-essential shopping. These changes won't be forever. For now, they are a must. Now that Sarah has some surplus income, she can do more with her money.

Applying the 10% Savings Rule

Currently, Sarah is not saving any money for a rainy day or towards larger expenses. She is not growing her wealth or saving to buy a home one day. To get ahead financially, although her budget is still tight, Sarah must at least start her 10% Savings. Even if Sarah changes her budget and creates a $304 per month surplus, if she doesn't start paying herself first that extra surplus money will likely be spent elsewhere and barely even noticed. It will be absorbed into day-to-day life.

By implementing the 10% Savings Rule, Sarah will be able to save on a regular basis first—rather than leaving it to will. It will also help her to only spend what's left in her everyday bank account. Money that's out of sight is money that's out of mind. It's one thing to afford just to pay your bills, it's another to afford to put funds aside and create wealth, get ahead in life and be able to spend as you like in the future.

TABLE 5: Sarah's New Budget (With 10% Savings Rule)

Income (Monthly)	Amount	Expenses (Monthly)	Amount
Net Salary (after tax)	$3,349	**10% Savings**	
		$3,349 x 10%	$335
		Essential	
		Rent ($340 per week)	$1,473
		Home Contents Insurance	$20
		Car Insurance/ Servicing/ Registration	$100
		Petrol ($50 per week)	$217
		Mobile Phone	$49
		Groceries ($75 per week)	$325
		Health Insurance	$50
		Utilities (Electricity/ Water/ Gas)	$85
		Sub-Total	**$2,319**
		Non-Essential	
		Lunches/ Coffees at Work ($10 per week)	$45
		Gym Membership	$50
		Hairdresser ($150 every 9 weeks)	$73
		Clothes	$100
		Entertainment/Dining out/Alcohol ($100 per week)	$433
		Magazines	Nil
		Gifts	$25
		Donations	$0
		Sub-Total	**$726**
Total IN	**$3,349**	**Total OUT ($3,045 spent and $335 saved)**	**$3,380**

If we apply the 10% Savings Rule, Sarah's new outcome is -$31 per month shortfall.

Sarah is now saving, but because Sarah was overspending by so much in the first place and living beyond her means, she also needs to reduce her non-essential expenses a little further if she wants to make this work. Regular savings is a must otherwise her financial situation won't change. To help Sarah spend within her means, she needs to implement the 10% Savings Rule first, pay essential expenses and then spend only the remaining money on non-essential expenses (and no more):

Net Income	$3,349 per month
Less 10% Savings	-$335 per month
Less Essential Expenses	-$2,319 per month
Remaining funds for Non-Essential Expenses	$695 per month

That will give Sarah more of an idea as to what she can afford for non-essential expenses with her level of income. Remember, a healthy budget allows you to save more than the mandatory 10% Savings. Maybe aim to save around 20% (or more).

It's up to Sarah what else she cuts from her spending, but something has to give. She can either choose to reduce more non-essential expenses so she can save at least 10% of her income, or she can instead choose to have luxuries which she can't afford. Will Sarah value going to the hairdresser or gym as more important than her financial future? The fact is, someone with Sarah's financial situation simply can't afford to have a gym membership and spend $150 at the hairdressers (even if done every nine weeks instead of six). Sarah can't afford to go out weekly and needs to reduce it to, say, fortnightly. Those expenses are luxuries in life (even if social media and advertising have us believe that they are essentials, unfortunately, they are not).

If Sarah wasn't already overspending the 10% Savings Rule could be applied and not even be noticed.

TABLE 6: A New 'Successful' Budget for Sarah

Income (Monthly)	Amount	Expenses (Monthly)	Amount
Net Salary (after tax)	$3,349	**10% Savings**	
		$3,349 x 10%	$335
		Essential	
		Rent ($340 per week)	$1,473
		Home Contents Insurance	$20
		Car Insurance/ Servicing/ Registration	$100
		Petrol ($50 per week)	$217
		Mobile Phone	$49
		Groceries ($75 per week)	$325
		Health Insurance	$50
		Utilities (Electricity/ Water/ Gas)	$85
		Sub-Total	**$2,319**
		Non-Essential	
		Lunches/ Coffees at Work ($10 per week)	$45
		~~Gym Membership~~	~~$50~~
		~~Hairdresser ($150 every 9 weeks)~~	~~$73~~
		Clothes	$100
		Entertainment/Dining out/Alcohol ($100 p/f)	$217
		Magazines	Nil
		Gifts	$25
		Donations	$0
		Sub-Total	**$387**
Total IN	**$3,349**	**Total OUT ($2,706 spent and $335 saved)**	**$3,041**

New cash flow position: $308 per month surplus.

In this example I cut the gym membership (instead try exercising for free), removed the hairdresser visits (instead try colouring hair at home), and reduced going out to once per fortnight.

Sarah is now spending around 80% of income on expenses and saving $335 per month (10% Savings). After that, Sarah is also $308 per month in surplus (money left over).

Sarah can achieve these results and get ahead financially if she wants to, but Sarah has to want to change her situation. Only Sarah can take those steps for herself.

Non-essential expenses (luxuries) that are cut from a budget initially can still be enjoyed now and again when extra funds are available or reintroduced as Sarah's income increases over time. They must not be paid using the 10% Savings.

The aim of budgeting is to move money around to get the best result for you.

Remember, the 10% Savings Rule works every time someone chooses to implement it. In this scenario Sarah had to cut some non-essential expenses, because Sarah was overspending, with a large cash flow shortfall. This was a real-life example of a friend.

Sarah's example is to show the power of tracking expenses and creating a budget.

For people that don't have a cash flow shortfall and are affording their bills but just not sure why there isn't any money left over each payday, the 10% Savings Rule is easy to apply and won't need any intentional reduction to expenses like with Sarah's budget.

Something happens to our mentality with money—when we can't see it, we don't spend it, and we don't even miss it. We then make it work (affording bills) only with the remaining money, including some luxuries and without even realising it our non-essential spending reduces. Things just fall into place.

Remember Mum's great results (page 40)?

Remember Christine's great results (page 41)?

Track and analyse your expenses to understand where your money is really being spent. The changes you make to your spending and the alternatives that you create for yourself are limited only by your imagination and your desire to succeed. How strict you are with your budget is up to you. Obviously the more savings you can make, the quicker your financial results will be and the more choices you will have in life.

Do you need to budget forever? Some people do. Some people don't. Depends on how much you need to keep yourself in check. If things aren't going right in your financial life and you have been living without a budget for a while then it's time to get into the habit (again). Time to tighten the reins for a while until you get back on track. Track your expenses for a couple of months.

Where is your money going?

Chapter 4 summary

- Everyone needs a budget.
- Track your expenses for one to three months to really know what you spend.
- Categorise your essential vs non-essential spending.
- Review and reduce non-essential spending to create an immediate surplus.
- Be conscious of your money every time you spend.
- Don't be stingy with money, be selective.
- The 10% Savings Rule is non-negotiable. Do that before any other expenses.
- Aim to spend no more than 80% of your income on expenses. Give yourself a buffer so you can save more than just the mandatory 10% of income.
- Reassess your budget and spending over time. Make changes as needed.
- Repeat the process until you perfect your personal system. Congratulate yourself.

If you do what a lot of other people do not,
you will achieve what a lot of other people will not.

CHAPTER 5

Separating bank accounts

How many bank accounts do you have? One, two, three... more? I am a big believer in holding different accounts for different purposes as a way to separate savings from spending money, and to separate savings further into short-term and long-term. This may sound like an 'obvious' strategy but I have met a lot of people who don't do it. If you don't separate savings from spending money, how can you tell which is what?

Disadvantages of having just one bank account:

◆ Mixed Up: if money is mixed up and held in just one account you are unable to easily see what's available for spending and what's meant to be your savings.

◆ Hard to Track: it's hard to determine exactly what you have saved or if you are overspending. How do you tell if you are getting ahead with your savings, staying the same or going backward?

◆ Too Accessible: if savings are too accessible, it will be easily spent.

My money management philosophy revolves around moving money out of sight (and easy access), into a few different accounts which are earmarked for various purposes, whether it be to pay regular bills or for holidays—so that money is available when needed, instead of accidentally being absorbed (spent) from week to week... just because it's in your everyday bank account. After putting money aside to cover commitments, whatever is left over can then be spent without worry or confusion.

Having A Second Bank Account

The minimum number of bank accounts you need to have is two (one for saving and one for spending):

Account 1: Everyday Account
Step 1: Your salary is deposited into this account
Account 2: 10% Savings Account
*Step 2: Transfer 10% to this account (before anything else)
and hold with a different institution*

Remember Mum's ultimatum, mentioned in Chapter 2? Either I pay $50 per week (to Mum) for board or I put it in a separate savings accoount (for my future).

At the time, I didn't understand the importance of using a separate account for savings but regardless, the very next payday I opened a second account and deposited $50 of my $230 weekly wage. The remaining $180 stayed in my original Everyday Account. That meant I was saving more than 10% (almost 22%) because I lived at home and my expenses were low; I took advantage of that whilst I could. Mum's generosity not only taught me about the importance of saving but also the need for separate bank accounts. I was grateful that mum had instilled in me one of the most important lessons I was ever taught—how to save, correctly. I then chose to continue it.

You may or may not have a choice in paying board, and your income/expenses may be higher than the figures mentioned above, but the basic principle is the same—separate your savings from your spending money.

Advantages of having separate accounts:

◆ Savings are separated from spending money.
◆ Easier to tell exactly how much you have accumulated in savings.
◆ Easier to identify how much you have left to spend on living expenses and lifestyle.
◆ Motivation increases as your savings balance grows.

◆ It's impossible to accidentally 'dip into' your savings unless you consciously withdraw funds from the savings account.

In today's world, with fee-free bank accounts available, it's a crazy idea for anyone to hold just one account into which all income is deposited and all expenses are debited. Why mix it all up? Why make budgeting harder than it has to be?

TABLE 1: Two Accounts (Example)

Account	Purpose
Everyday Account	Everyday Expenses (*your salary is paid into this account*) **Why?** Easier to see how much money is left for expenses and other savings once your 10% Savings has been done.
10% Savings Account (*use a different institution*)	10% Savings (*to save for a home or other investments & make more money*) **Why?** Easier to tell how much has been saved and motivates to keep going the higher the balance grows. **Don't touch this money** unless you plan on buying a property or investing it to make more money.

The basic structure that everyone needs to have is at least two accounts (Everyday Account & 10% Savings Account). Those accounts will never change throughout the following examples and instead additional accounts are added on as needed.

In addition to an Everyday Account and a 10% Savings Account, I regularly use at least another three additional accounts to help me save for emergencies and other goals—those things that are also important but not reason enough to dip into a 10% Savings Account.

Multiple Accounts—One for This, One for That

Separating savings in different accounts helps to:
◆ Manage and afford regular expenses
◆ Survive emergencies
◆ Save for different purposes (goals)
◆ Know what money can be spent & what needs to be left untouched (for long-term investing)

Saving for a tech gadget such as an iPad, for example, will take a different amount of time to saving for an overseas holiday, and both of those goals will take less time than saving for a home loan deposit or just for a 'rainy day' (unexpected emergencies). For example, your 10% Savings Account is for longer-term wealth creation goals (funds are left untouched for a longer period of time), whereas saving for a holiday is a shorter-term goal (funds will definitely be spent in the near future for the holiday). Ideally, have around five accounts in total, as follows:

1. Everyday Account
2. 10% Savings Account (use a different institution)
3. Bills Account
4. Emergency Account
5. Just In Case Account

This may seem like a lot of accounts, but when four of the five are held with the same banking institution you can easily view them all together and move money between them online. Don't go crazy and overcomplicate your life but be sure to have a few different accounts to make your money management easier. The number of accounts you hold is up to you and will depend on what savings goals you have or how much help you need to separate your money. Some accounts will be permanent and some can come and go as needed.

TABLE 2: Account Set Up (Example)

Account	Purpose
Everyday Account	Everyday Expenses
10% Savings Account (use a different institution)	Home loan deposit savings, investing (or extra debt repayments)
Add-On	
Bills Account	Regular, fixed bills and debts (the 'necessary')
Emergency Account	Emergencies & unexpected expenses (the 'unknown')
Just In Case Account	To save for things you want in the future, whether you have something specific in mind right now or not (the 'what if')

Notice that the Everyday Account and 10% Savings Account have not changed? Additional accounts have been added on as needed.

THE 'EVERYDAY' ACCOUNT

All income is paid into this account. It's your main 'cash hub'.

THE '10% SAVINGS' ACCOUNT

This is money for your 'future', to make more money and to get ahead in life. Use these funds for a future home loan deposit (or investment property), or to invest in other assets that will make more money (shares or businesses etc). Use the 10% Savings to make extra credit card or car loan debt repayments (so long as you also stop accruing new personal debt).

If/When you have a home loan, definitely use the ongoing 10% Savings to make extra loan repayments to repay the debt faster and save thousands of dollars in interest (more on that in later chapters).

THE 'BILLS' ACCOUNT

A sure way to not spend money which is earmarked for a specific purpose (such as bills), is to move it out of sight, to avoid accidentally dipping into it for anything else. It's so much easier to manage regular, reoccurring bills (such as rent, utilities, phone, car registration/maintenance, insurances, gym membership etc), by putting money in a 'Bills Account' to pay each bill as they fall due.

Simply calculate what those bills roughly equate to over a year and divide by 12 for the monthly amount. Every payday, after your 10% Savings is done, transfer that amount to a 'Bill's Account' to have on-call for when the bill arrives. Match the frequency of your payday—if you are paid fortnightly then divide the annual amount by 26. If paid weekly, divide the annual amount by 52.

This strategy also enables you to take advantage of available discounts by paying bills less frequently (half yearly or yearly), knowing that money is building up in a separate account for when your bill arrives. Whatever is left over in your Everyday Account after moving funds out to pay yourself first and cover regular bills is for fun/ entertainment and other ad-hoc living expenses. Stress-free spending knowing that your commitments are taken care of. If you find that there's not much money left over (for fun), review and cut back your bills.

Take care of your 'have to' first. Then splurge.

You can use a Bills Account for multiple expenses and minimum debt repayments, just make a note of what those funds are earmarked for so you don't forget. Bills are bills regardless of what they are for; you know that money in the Bills Account is not to be spent elsewhere.

Did you know...?

Car Registration Fees were payable on a yearly basis in Melbourne (until recently), compared to quarterly or half-yearly payments available in Perth, for example. Without a Bills Account, finding that yearly payment puts strain on many budgets.

In Dubai, rent is paid yearly. Yes, you heard correctly, paid yearly to the landlord. That system is no surprise to the residents of Dubai, everyone living there knows how it works and that payment is required every 12 months, yet I met many other residents who stressed about it each year, worried because they hadn't saved the funds throughout the past year. Having a Bills Account into which the rent money was saved each month, was crucial.

THE 'EMERGENCY' ACCOUNT

Everyone needs some emergency money, that is, the money you only use in a real emergency, not to buy stuff or go out at the weekend, or because you are short of cash one week and dip into the account, but real emergencies which leave you in financial strife if you didn't pay. Without an emergency stash of cash, you will be tempted to dip into your other accounts for the wrong reasons.

Preferably, a minimum of a thousand dollars needs to be stashed away in a separate account for emergencies. Start by saving up a thousand dollars for emergencies, then increase the balance over time to at least one month worth of living expenses. Ideally, keep building the account to three months' worth of expenses (or more). This is something you do over time and it's very important, so if you need to scale back other non-essential expenses (e.g. entertainment) for a while until you create an initial emergency fund, then that is what you need to do. Kickstart your emergency fund by decluttering your home and having a garage sale. You don't need much stuff in life, but you definitely need an emergency stash.

THE 'JUST IN CASE' ACCOUNT

After setting up your 10% Savings Account, Bills Account and an initial Emergency Account, congratulate yourself because you have made sure that your 'have tos' are taken care of. Then, what about your 'want tos'? To be able to buy what you want, when you want, you need to be able to fund larger expenses which may cost a couple of hundred or a couple of thousand dollars (or more) as a lump sum. This is done with a 'Just in case' Account.

Larger expenses are those that you can't or shouldn't spend all at once using your regular weekly budget. For example, if you buy an iPad for $650 all at once when you get paid this week, how will you afford to pay your rent or mortgage and other living expenses? It may be impossible, and you will severely disadvantage yourself financially. Without any savings, you simply can't afford to buy the nicer things in life. Forget credit cards; they are not there to help you afford that iPad—I will discuss credit cards and the cost of instant gratification using borrowed funds in Chapter 8.

You can go without the iPad... or, what if you had an account into which you had been regularly saving a small amount and is easily accessed at short notice to buy luxury items, without hurting your budget (or even noticing it) and without feeling guilty that you dipped into your 10% Savings for non-essential luxury stuff?

Dividing your savings into different accounts will help you buy what you want when you want it without affecting your usual budget and avoiding the 'I can't afford that' feeling. Being able to buy what you want when you want without guilt or worry will do amazing things for your psyche and confidence. No longer will you have to go without the things you like, because you thought you weren't able to afford it. Anyone can save towards something they want— the only difference is that some people will be able to save more than others each payday, either because their expenses are lower or because they earn more and choose to save more (rather than spend those extra earnings). Remember, a person can earn more and yet have less to show for it than a person who may earn less.

It's important to limit how often you dip into your Just In Case account, especially at the beginning whilst you establish a savings habit (and a decent account balance).

Over time, as you spend some here and there, it becomes less noticeable (as the balance is continually topped up).

Add additional accounts as you like... I am a very visual person and need to separate money in order to save regularly and, more importantly, not dip into money which is for some other purpose. If I have a particular goal that I am saving for (holidays etc.), I may even use another separate account for that. My travel is ongoing (remember I love to travel and explore the world) and therefore my 'Holiday Account' is completely separate from my 'Just In Case' account and actually never closes (and is continually topped up). It's easy to reduce travel costs and pay less by taking advantage of specials/flight deals when there are savings to access. For me, six accounts work perfectly. Five I see regularly via Internet Banking and one is tucked away at a different institution (10% Savings Account), so I don't see it as often.

These days, bank accounts can easily be opened and closed over the phone or internet. When not in use, leave the account dormant for future use.

TABLE 3: Adding Another Account (for specific goals)

Account	Purpose
Everyday Account	Everyday Expenses
10% Savings Account (*use a different institution*)	Home loan deposit savings, investing (*or extra debt repayments*)
Add-On	
Bills Account	Regular, fixed bills and debts (*the 'necessary'*)
Emergency Account	Emergencies & unexpected expenses (*the 'unknown'*)
Just In Case Account	To save for things you want in the future, whether you have something specific in mind right now or not (*the 'what if'*)
Extra Savings Account (*i.e.: Holiday Account*)	To save a regular amount for a specific goal you may have e.g. holidays or extra savings towards a home loan deposit. **Why?** Helps to know what money has been saved for that goal and how much more is needed to reach it. The earlier you start saving for a goal with a fixed timeframe, the less you need to save each time. Even if you have no particular upcoming holiday plans, it never hurts to have a 'Holiday' account or replace 'Holiday' with whatever pleases you more.

The aim is to move as much money from your Everyday Account into other accounts so you don't just spend it by default, simply because it's there.
Save a small amount of money into each account for a long period of time (regular savings is ongoing and never stops).

Set up the number of savings accounts to suit you. You don't need a separate account for every single expense in your life, but it does help to separate short-term and long-term savings away from your regular bills.

TABLE 4: Account Set Up Summary

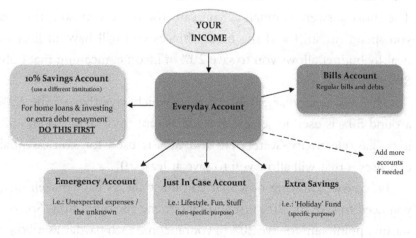

Transfer a set amount to each account every payday.

I have a friend who has an account specifically for Car Maintenance. She transfers $50 per week into that account for car registration, insurance, servicing, etc. If she has funds left over in the account at the end of the year (if her actual car maintenance costs didn't exceed the $50 per week allocated), then she has bonus savings to use elsewhere.

Another friend uses a separate account for Child Education Fees. She transfers a specific amount into that account each fortnight for school fees, uniforms, books, etc.

If you struggle with spending too much on the weekends and not leaving enough in your Everyday Account for other expenses, then consider adding a Fun Account. Put a budgeted amount aside in an account for fun/entertainment/dining out, to control what you spend. Relax and have fun with this money, but when it's gone, it's gone until next payday. If you find yourself dipping into your other accounts for more money—then you are overspending.

Saving regularly is not an option it's a must.

How Much Do You Need to Save?

The short answer: as much as you can (the more you save, the less you spend on stuff and the more choices you will have in life). A healthy budget allows you to save 20% of income, meaning that only 80% is spent.

There is a popular 50-30-20 rule, which says that of the 80% around 50% is used for essentials such as rent/mortgage, food, utilities (gas/electricity/water) etc and 30% is used for non-essential expenses = that will allow you to save at least 20%.

Of course, knowing now that you must always pay yourself first, you need to save the 20% first and then spend the other 80%. So, as a starting point, aim to save 20% of your income each payday as follows:

10%	10% Savings Account (non-negotiable)
10%	Emergency Account/Just in Case Account

Which leaves 80% for living expenses and minimum debt repayment. This is an example, as everyone is different. It isn't a finite rule and it will be broken from time to time. For example:

◆ What are you saving for? Do you need to save more or less to reach that goal in the timeframe you have available?

◆ If you earn a high income then take advantage of that whilst you can and keep your expenses low so that you save more than 20%.

◆ Are you struggling with your expenses right now and need to work on a more affordable budget? Saving 20% of your income may seem astronomical right now. In that case, just save what you can; the 10% Savings is non-negotiable, but the rest can be reduced a little to something more affordable.

Some savings, any savings are better than nothing. Start with the maximum, scale back if needed, but remember, moving money out of your Everyday Account and out of spending sight will help to adjust your budget. You will end up spending only what's left in your Everyday Account and your non-essential spending will reduce.

It's much more important to have some emergency savings than to treat yourself to non-essential luxury items (iPads, holidays etc) in the short-term. So, you want to concentrate on establishing an initial emergency fund of at least $1,000 before you start your Just In Case savings. You can do both at the same time, but it will just take you longer to establish a decent emergency stash.

Automated Payments: Set and Forget

In today's modern world there are additional electronic tools to help you stay on top of your regular bills. No longer do you need to visit a Post Office to pay your bills or stick them to the fridge door to constantly remind you. Automated payments will simplify your financial life. Regular electronic funds transfers (EFT) can be set up to occur each payday, so you don't even have to think about what money will be going into which account. Automated payments make the 10% Savings Rule a breeze to implement (and stick to), especially if you earn the same amount each payday (as the 10% amount won't change). Use automated payments to transfer regular amounts into the Bills Account, Emergency Account and Just In Case Account.

Most people have access to Internet Banking these days which can be used to set up your automated payments quickly and easily, but if for some reason you don't have access to Internet Banking then visit your bank to set up automated payments—for free.

Advantages of automated payments:

◆ Money is moved out of sight quickly and effortlessly.

◆ Funds are transferred to different accounts for different purposes.

◆ Creates good saving habits, with little effort needed from you to maintain it.

◆ Payments can continue for a set period of time, or with no end date.

◆ Transfer amounts are easily altered as your income changes over time.

♦ This part of your 'financial life' is automated (one less thing to think about).

Even if you are not in front of your computer or are away on holiday your transfers will be done for you. You just need to make sure there is money available in the Everyday Account for the transfers to lodge. Set your automated payments to occur the day after your payday (before you have a chance to spend it and to allow for different banks' processing times). If your income varies each payday then manually transfer funds to your 10% Savings Account (before anything else) and use automated payments for everything else.

DIRECT DEBIT

Most companies offer direct debit payments whereby you authorise bill payment to be directly debited from your nominated bank account on the due date (for free). To set up a direct debit payment agreement, contact each company you deal with to complete a form or login to their online system to add your bank account details to your account. This works best for regular, fixed bills such as rent, utilities, memberships, insurances etc (paid from your Bills Account). You will still receive a bill in advance (paper or online) so that you are aware of your upcoming charges and the debit date. The date is usually around the same time each month or quarter, depending on the frequency.

Benefits of direct debits:

♦ Bills paid on time: no more late fees or unfriendly 'overdue' notices.
♦ Payments not missed: unless your Bills Account has insufficient funds.
♦ Saves time: no need to leave your computer screen or smartphone.
♦ Reduces administration work: no need to remember when to pay the bill.
♦ Improves cash flow: payments made around the same time each month.
♦ Usually no payment fees: but always confirm with the company or your bank.

Things to remember:

◆ You still need to check each bill that you receive to ensure the charges and amount owing is correct. Don't ignore the amounts being debited from your Bills Account just because they are automatic.

◆ If your nominated Bills Account has insufficient funds when the direct debit lodges, the payment will be missed, and you will need to manually make the payment yourself. Usually, you will receive an email/letter/SMS text message informing you of a missed payment.

◆ You need to contact the company to set up/stop the direct debit authorisation.

◆ If you change bank accounts, you need to inform each company.

BPAY

Rather than having a company directly debit from your bank account, you instead pay the bill yourself, either via telephone or online banking. Money is transferred to the company using a Biller Code and your Customer Number (shown on the statement). Automated BPAY payments can be set up for bills if the amount due doesn't fluctuate.

Benefits of BPAY:

◆ Control: you control when the bill is paid.

◆ Security: payments are made using your bank's secure telephone or online banking system, with access from a computer, tablet or smartphone.

◆ Saves time: no need to leave your computer screen or smartphone.

◆ Usually no payment fees: but always confirm with the company or your bank.

Things to remember:

◆ You have to remember to pay the bill, so diarise it.

◆ Use automated payments wherever possible.

- You will still receive a bill in advance (paper or online), don't forget to check that the billed charges are correct.
- You are responsible for entering the BPAY details correctly—if a payment lodges incorrectly, the funds will generally bounce back to your account for you to retry. This can occur some days later, so you might have missed the due date of the bill, therefore you need to regularly monitor your bank accounts.

A credit card can be used for all direct debit and BPAY payments. In fact, it can be very convenient to charge most living expenses to a credit card and then repay the balance (in full) from the Bills Account. Doing so can help to avoid fees if your bank account or ATM card have limits on how many fee-free transactions you can make each month for example. However, this only works well if you use a credit card properly and repay the full balance every month. So, you still need to accumulate sufficient money in your Bills Account.

This strategy takes more discipline. You need to have the money available to repay the card in full and not spend it elsewhere before the final credit card payment is due. Smaller, more frequent card repayments can be made weekly or fortnightly to help with staying on top of budgeting and to keep the card balance low. Never use a credit card like this unless you are confident with your budgeting and overall money management (as you need to monitor your expenses and be able to repay the balance).

If you are tempted to overspend (or currently overspending) then avoid credit cards completely. If you already have any outstanding credit card debt, any at all, then don't use a credit card for your daily expenses. Stick to a regular debit card which offers online payment capabilities (just like a credit card, but without a credit facility attached) and make direct debit and BPAY payments from a regular bank account (Bills Account). With the introduction of Visa Debit Cards, you actually don't need a credit card to successfully manage your cash flow.

Types of Bank Accounts

With all of the different accounts from banks and other institutions, which one do you use? Here is a summary of the main accounts available:

EVERYDAY 'TRANSACTION' ACCOUNTS

The basic account sometimes called a cheque account. Suitable for everyday transactions such as shopping, paying bills and depositing salary. Some banks will charge monthly Account Keeping Fees, especially if they have other services attached to them like a Cheque Book, whilst others don't. The number of transactions allowed per month will vary according to the institution. Electronic banking facilities are usually available such as ATM Access and Internet Banking. Negligible interest is earned if anything at all.

Avoid accounts with Account Keeping Fees and Transaction Fees—they are unnecessary for regular day-to-day banking, especially when there are so many institutions to pick from which don't charge fees (and a lot of transactions can be done online for free). Services such as Cheque Books are fast becoming irrelevant in today's world, and so there is no point paying for features that you don't need or use.

SAVINGS ACCOUNTS

Can also be used for everyday banking, although some accounts pay higher interest if no withdrawals are made over a certain period. Some accounts have minimum balance requirements. A higher amount of interest is earned compared to a Transaction Account, but usually still negligible and nothing to get particularly excited about unless you have a substantial account balance and leave the funds untouched for some time. I use these types of accounts for my savings accounts. Quite often they can be set up online as 'Online Access' accounts, meaning you use them only through your Internet Banking and with a higher Interest Rate attached—although still negligible in many cases.

HIGH-INTEREST ACCOUNTS

This is another version of a savings account but offering higher Interest Rates (e.g. 1%-3% p.a.). Often opened online. High-Interest accounts are great to use for Long-term Savings (10% Savings Account) in order to maximise interest earned on your money from the bank, whilst you are not using the funds. Open an account with an institution that differs from your other bank accounts, to remove the temptation to spend your savings. Make sure it is fee-free and no ATM access.

OFFSET ACCOUNTS

An account which is attached to a home loan or investment property loan. The funds held in the offset account reduces the loan balance so that interest for the loan is calculated on a lower amount. This helps to reduce interest costs, instead of earning a negligible amount of interest income. The less interest you pay, the faster you repay the loan. The amount saved is equal to the loan interest rate and without any risk. If you have a home loan, use an offset account for your Long-term Savings (10% Savings Account) to reduce your interest costs (Chapter 13). Ask your loan provider to open the account for you.

Speak to your bank for assistance in setting up the right accounts for you or go online. Use your common sense. Don't pay Account Keeping Fees or Transaction Fees. Don't pay for features or services you don't need.

Don't worry too much about the interest rate attached to an everyday bank account, it won't be much. Just select a high-interest rate account for your 10% Savings (or offset account), then stick to regular run-of-the-mill accounts for everything else.

If you are self-employed, it's a good idea to use a different bank account, debit card or credit card for your work-related expenses, to easily keep track of tax-deductible expenses for tax time. This keeps business expenses separated from personal expenses and minimises your Accountant's fees.

CASE STUDY

Kate's Real-Life Story

I have a friend; let's call her Kate. A few years ago, Kate's way of budgeting and separating her money was to withdraw most of her salary in cash each week, except for:

1. 10% Savings, which she transferred to a separate account.
2. Additional savings for holidays, which she transferred to another account.
3. A little extra which she left in her Everyday Account.

Kate withdrew the rest, which was the exact amount needed to cover her fixed, regular bills such as rent, groceries, fuel etc. She then divided the cash into little plastic money bags, labelled each one with its intended purpose and kept it in her purse. Throughout the week, Kate visited the real estate office to hand over the money in the 'rent' bag, then visited the grocery shop and spent up to the amount in the 'groceries' bag, filled up her car with fuel and paid using the money in the 'fuel' bag etc.

To some people, Kate's method may seem very time consuming or perhaps old-fashioned (a manual Bills Account if you will), but like I said, it was a few years ago and it worked for Kate—that was the important part. Kate's story is an example of the steps that some people will take to manage their money in a way that works for them—no excuses. This method was Kate's way of being able to separate her money and stay on budget.

Chapter 5 summary

- Saving regularly is not an option, it's a necessity.
- Use multiple bank accounts—one for this, one for that.
- Separate your savings into short-term and long-term goals.
- Saving regularly is easy if you use automated transfers (move money out of 'spending sight').
- Keep your 10% Savings separated from other savings—or use for extra debt repayments.
- Allow nothing to jeopardise your 10% Savings (non-negotiable).
- Set up an Emergency Account + Bills Account + Just In Case Account.
- Aim to save around 20% of your income + spend 80%.

CHAPTER 6

Buying what you want (without debt)

Savings are not just for a rainy day. You have to have some fun too. You only live once. Being able to buy things and experiences for greater enjoyment and a better lifestyle when you want and without financial worry or strain will bring joy into your life.

Say a friend asks you to go on an overseas holiday in 12 months from now and tells you that you will need around $5,000 for your airfare, accommodation and spending money. (Swap 'holiday' for anything else which motivates you more, if not travel.) You want to go on that holiday. How are you going to pay for it?

Your choices are:

◆ Miss out
◆ Borrow from someone you know
◆ Borrow from a bank
◆ Pay with savings (truly enjoy the experience, stress-free)

This is not a multiple-choice question. There is only one answer.

MISS OUT (YOU CAN'T AFFORD IT)

Well, that's just plain boring and quite frankly not an option in my view and definitely not the point of this book. What's the point of working if you are not really living? Let's forget this option and see how you can afford it.

BORROW FROM SOMEONE YOU KNOW (FAMILY/FRIENDS)

You have a choice, to be a person who relies on a loved one to borrow money from (if they have it to lend in the first place) or be someone who is financially responsible and able to stand on your own two feet. Will you rely on family and friends for money? At what age will you stop that and rely on yourself... 20, 30, 40, 50? Why would you want to burden someone else with your financial worries? We are all born equal and all have the ability to succeed if we put our minds to it, so it's not fair to lean on someone else for money all the time. Besides, it's a pretty risky strategy to let your happiness and financial success depend on someone else's bank balance.

Sure, if your parents can help you out financially from time to time then lucky you. If your first port of call is to ask for money whenever a larger expense pops up then that's lazy and takes advantage of another person's generosity. In most countries around the world, if you are over 18, you are legally an adult and therefore can't blame anyone else for what you do or don't have. It's up to you and not anyone else's responsibility to finance the lifestyle you want. If you are under 18 then your parents have the responsibility to financially look after you and provide shelter, food, education and other necessities of life. Necessities don't generally include overseas holidays, for example.

If you want more from life, then change what you are doing. No one will do it for you.

Often I see people who receive regular, significant financial assistance from parents who do not fully appreciate what they are given and end up wasting the money and the extra opportunity. If everything is given to you, there is no 'fear of loss' and therefore no need to assess 'risk vs. reward', take action or achieve financial success of your own. Why do you need to bother? That is a lazy way of thinking, whether it be conscious or unconscious. Parents, if your adult child refuses to grow up and get on with life—reassess your generosity. Cut the apron strings sooner rather than later, otherwise, you are not helping the situation.

If you borrow money, you are obliged to repay it. If you don't repay money to friends/family, you will put strain on and possibly ruin the relationship. It shows that you are unreliable and don't keep your word. It's highly unlikely that friendship will last after an experience like that and if it's family whom you owe money to, then future family Christmas and Birthday celebrations are likely to be a little tense, to say the least.

Have you ever heard these sayings?

'Don't mix business with pleasure.'
'Money and friends don't go together.'

However, if you are a person of your word and you do in fact want to repay the money, then first you have to find the money to be able to repay it with. It's the same as if you had borrowed money from a bank, repayments are due and must be made. The only advantage of borrowing from family/friends is that usually no interest will be charged and you will only need to repay the amount you originally borrowed.

If you feel that you can't 'afford' to put a portion of your income aside and save up for a holiday now, then how will you 'afford' to make the repayments back to family/friends?

And who wants the burden of being on a fabulous overseas holiday knowing that you will be returning home to debt? Isn't it preferable to save the money yourself first, pay for the holiday in full and travel without the financial worry? (This also assumes that your family/friends have the money to lend to you in the first place—if they don't then unfortunately you will simply miss out.)

BORROW FROM A BANK (PERSONAL LOAN OR CREDIT CARD)
Credit from banks and other financial institutions is more readily available than ever. Unfortunately, many people are using short-term debt such as personal loans and credit cards to fund lifestyle purchases which they really can't afford. It's the classic mistake of

taking on debt to afford a better lifestyle. A recipe for disaster, but commonly marketed to us by banks as a painless way of having what you want, when you want it. You are living in a 'want it now' society and banks know that many people will, in fact, give in to the temptation of instant gratification if the funds are made readily available.

The problem with borrowing money is that you are charged interest for the privilege, meaning you pay back the original amount borrowed plus extra (the interest), which pays the lender for their time, money and risk (the risk of lending you the money and whether you will repay it on time or not). It's how the banks make their money. Banks are not in the business of losing money.

Personal loans and credit cards are legally binding contracts— you have to meet your commitments. Even though most people know there is a cost attached to borrowing money, they will not make the conscious decision to calculate the extra cost beforehand and instead, as long as the loan repayment plan seems affordable— the issue of borrowing for lifestyle is ignored.

A question that continues to baffle me is: if you can afford loan repayments (when legally bound to do so) then why can't you save that same amount beforehand, starting now? The latter will get you so much more bang for your buck.

Debt does have advantages when used correctly, but it depends on what you use the borrowings for as to whether you get ahead financially or move backwards. If the debt is used to buy assets such as property and shares, which go up in value over time (make you money) then you can create real wealth—YOU WIN.

However, if the debt is used to buy stuff that goes down in value (costs you money)—which unfortunately is the case with lifestyle purchases such as tech gadgets, holidays, cars, boats etc—then you end up paying more than you should and YOU LOSE.

Say you end up borrowing $5,000 for an overseas holiday from ABC Bank as a personal loan (unsecured). The loan is considered 'unsecured' because the borrowed money will be spent on a holiday in this case and not a tangible item such as a car or boat (there will be no item for the bank to take as security for the loan which they will repossess and sell to recover the money if you don't repay the loan on time). Generally, a higher interest rate is payable for unsecured loans as the bank takes on more 'risk'. Credit cards are considered another type of short-term loan and come with very high-interest rates attached, as they are always unsecured.

How much extra money you end up repaying is dependent on the loan term and interest rate that you agree to with the lender. The lower the rate the less interest you pay. However, the longer the loan term, the more interest you pay. Your repayments will be less each time, although you will have the loan for longer meaning the lender has to wait longer for the money to be returned and therefore will charge you more.

TABLE 1: Borrowing For A $5,000 Holiday (Interest Rate @ 14.00% pa)*

Loan Term	Repayments	Total Interest (over the term)	Real Cost To You (loan + interest)	How Much Extra You Paid (compared to saving)
1 year	$449 per month	$387	$5,387	$387
2 years	$240 per month	$762	$5,762	$762
3 years	$171 per month	$1,152	$6,152	$1,152

*Figures calculated using Personal Loan calculator (www.moneysmart.gov.au) with an example Interest Rate, current at the time of writing and provided as estimations only and do not necessarily correspond to actual operations of banks.

Say you choose the three-year loan term. Your repayments will be $171 per month for three years and you would end up paying total interest of $1,152 to the bank. You would repay a total of $6,152 even though you originally only borrowed $5,000.

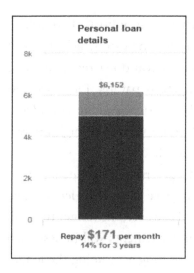

This graph shows the three-year loan. The darker portion (lower) is the amount you borrowed and the lighter portion (top) area is the interest = the 'cost to you' for borrowing the money. An amount of $5,000 borrowed will cost you $6,152 to repay = $1,152 interest, which means your $5,000 holiday actually cost you $6,152.

You paid over 23% more for the holiday.

Are you prepared to pay $6,152 for a $5,000 holiday?

That's $1,152 (23%) more than someone who saved up for it.

That extra $1,152 is better put towards more spending money or your next holiday.

If you choose a loan term of one or two years instead of three, you pay a lower amount of interest ($387 for a one-year loan or $762 for a two-year loan), however you need to be able to afford higher repayments. In the above example, repayments increase to $240 per month for a one-year loan or $449 per month for a two-year loan. Higher repayments may not be affordable, depending on your real-life budget. Either way, you will still pay more for the holiday compared to someone who chooses to save for it. Often, personal loans have terms of three, five or seven years. That's a long time to pay interest.

These figures also assume that you borrow $5,000 once only, however what if you want an annual overseas holiday and spend $5,000 per year per trip?

- Imagine the repayments for multiple loans (one for each holiday).
- Think of the interest cost for multiple loans.
- How will you afford your other living expenses?
- Will you enjoy those holidays as intended if you have a debt to return to?
- How will you feel with a growing amount of personal 'bad' debt?
- What's the likelihood of a bank continuing to lend you $5,000 per year, whilst you have money outstanding from previous loans?

How many times will you repeat that costly mistake over your lifetime and wonder why you slip further and further backwards financially? Don't be someone who borrows money for the wrong reasons, always ends up paying too much for everything and then wonders how on Earth you will repay the debt.

Loans cost money (interest) and in the time that it takes to repay a loan, you could have saved the same amount quicker and cheaper.
Save first. Spend second. Not the other way around.

You need to make the decision and start your savings first, knowing that there are lots of fabulous things and experiences in life that are there to be enjoyed. Perhaps you don't have any holiday plans now, but they will appear at some point in the future (especially if you know you have the savings to enjoy it).

PAY WITH SAVINGS (THE CHEAPEST AND THE BEST OPTION)
Although this may feel like a slower approach, it's not. It's about being prepared. It's not financially smart to be unprepared and borrow for lifestyle purchases as they pop up. Why pay more for things than you must, simply because you have no savings? Instead, save consistently. Your Just In Case Account must never be empty.

Remember, it's not about saving a big amount over a short time, but instead saving a smaller amount over a longer time.

If you start saving today (for a $5,000 holiday in 12 months' time), you only need to save $417 per month, compared to the $449 per month that it will take to repay a loan in the same timeframe (refer table 1). The timeframe is the same. The outcome is different. It costs less to be prepared.

In both situations, you are shelling out the money—the difference is whether you do it beforehand (into your savings account) or afterward (to a bank).

Being in control of your money so you can buy what you want when you want and without debt is not difficult but is intentional.

You must always save for lifestyle purchases such as tech gadgets, clothes, household items, holidays etc. Never use borrowings for those. Even cars can be paid for with savings. Saving for a car can take longer compared to a holiday, it is, however, definitely possible. The car I currently own cost me $22,000 second-hand a few years ago and was paid for in cash.

With brand new cars available today at affordable prices, there is no reason why an average salary earner can't save enough to be able to afford a $10,000, $15,000 or $20,000 car. As at December 2018, a brand-new Mazda 2 Hatch costs from $15,990 drive away—now it may not be your dream car, but it's a brand, spanking new car. If you save $100 per week, you can have enough cash in around three years. That's a lot less than the term of most car loans! Often, car loans have five or seven-year terms. Yes, circumstances change and the price of cars change, but it's a quick example of how achievable buying a car with cash really is—if you start saving before you want the car.

If you save on a regular basis and limit how often you dip into those savings initially, then the account balance will start to grow exponentially and make it less and less noticeable when you do choose to spend some here and there. Paying for a car in cash can be as unnoticeable as paying for a holiday. Of course, it also depends on your taste in cars and how much you are prepared to spend but saving even 25% or 50% towards the cost of the car is better than 0% and will reduce interest costs.

Have you ever heard this saying?

'Spend as little on a car as your ego will allow.'

If you have to borrow for a car now, for whatever reason, then at least limit the loan size and repay it as fast as you can by making extra repayments. Having a single personal loan in place for a car is very different from having multiple loans and credit cards in place. If borrowing to fund a big-ticket item such as a car, then all other lifestyle purchases need to be made with savings. People become unstuck when they have a number of personal loans and credit cards at one time and often use personal debt for lifestyle purchases.

The 'real cost' of Personal Loans and Credit Cards are detailed in Chapters 7 and 8.

Good Debt vs. Bad Debt

Borrowing to fund non-essential lifestyle expenses will increase your 'bad debt', waste your hard-earned money with unnecessary interest costs and slow your overall financial progress. However, not all debts are created equal, and some debt can be very beneficial when used correctly. Do you know the difference?

'Good Debt' is used to buy assets that make you more money such as property, shares, and businesses (investments)—they go up in value over time and outweigh the interest costs. When the asset produces income, the Government also allows the interest costs to be claimed as a tax deduction, meaning the investor (you) pays less income tax and in turn has a higher amount of take-home income to pay the interest or invest more.

'Bad Debt' diminishes your wealth over time. It's debt that's used to buy stuff—things that go down in value (cost you money) such as lifestyle purchases (clothes, tech gadgets, household appliances, holidays, cars etc). They are not investments, will not grow your wealth or earn extra income—therefore there are no tax benefits either. Bad debt will send you financially backwards.

Breaking it down and having it all (without debt)

Whether or not you have a specific lifestyle item or financial goal in mind, it makes sense to start saving now and get ahead in the game, just in case something catches your eye and you want to travel or want to buy something nice for yourself.

When I promise you that you can have what you want, when you want, I am not referring to a private jet or a penthouse apartment in Paris; most people will not be able to simply save for those types of luxury items with those price tags attached in one lifetime—that kind of wealth is outside the scope of this book. What I am talking about are the everyday needs and wants. Things you want in your day-to-day regular person's life, to enhance your lifestyle—such as nice clothes, tech gadgets, household items, holidays and cars etc.

You can save for larger expenses and big-ticket items as well as smaller ones.

To have it all you need to break it down, like this:

1. Determine the amount you need to save. (The cost of the item.)
2. Divide by the number of weeks you have to save for it. (The longer the timeframe, the less you will need to save each week.)
3. Set up an automatic payment to transfer that amount into a savings account the day after your payday. (Use your Just In Case Account or a separate account if needed.)
4. Watch your savings account balance grow. Get motivated by your progress. (If tempted to dip into the account prematurely, remind yourself of what you are actually saving towards and move the money to another institution if needed.)

5. When you reach your goal, happily spend that money and enjoy it!

Repeat this formula for every larger expense or lifestyle goal that you have. Sounds simple? It is simple—so why don't more people do it?

TABLE 2: Saving for $1,000 surfboard in 2 months (8 weeks)

Account	Purpose
Everyday Account	Everyday Expenses
10% Savings Account	10% Savings (*different institution*)
Add-On	
Just In Case Account	Save $125/week for the Surfboard ($1,000 / 8 weeks = $125) This can include the regular money you will already be saving into this account, but if you want to speed things up, make it in addition to.

If your budget doesn't allow you to save $125 per week for the surfboard, then you need to extend the timeframe in which you will aim to buy the item. Let's try four months.

TABLE 3: Saving for $1,000 surfboard in 4 months (16 weeks)

Extra Savings Account	Save $62.50/week for the Surfboard ($1,000 / 16 weeks = $62.50)

If you don't want to wait to have the money then I suggest you start saving a regular amount each payday starting now, to get ahead of the game. Save whatever you can comfortably afford in your budget (in addition to your 10% Savings of course). Have the money available before you see an item you want or opportunity knocks. As your Savings balance grows, you can access the funds as needed, so you can pay for your lifestyle purchases immediately, without borrowing the money.

Even if there's nothing in particular that you want right now, no particular item/experience or financial goal, you must still start saving regularly anyway. Something will pop up in the future—it always does. The more you save each time, the quicker your account balance will grow and the less you 'dip into' the account for smaller items along the way, the more you will have for big-ticket items. What expenses can you 'trim' in your budget to create extra savings?

Chapter 6 summary

- Never borrow money for 'stuff' (liabilities, things that cost you money).
- Only borrow money to buy assets (things that make you money).
- Know the difference between 'good debt' and 'bad debt'.
- Break down larger expenses to afford them over time (without debt).
- Don't buy lots of 'cheap stuff' (low-value items) regularly—instead buy good quality, but less frequently.
- Start your Just In Case savings sooner rather than later, you never know what you may want in the future.

CHAPTER 7

Personal Loans
(The Real Cost)

Too often people sign up for personal loans without fully understanding the real cost of doing so. Do you know how a personal loan actually works?

Repayments

The original amount borrowed from a bank or other lending institution is known as the 'principal'. The repayments you make consist of an amount that goes towards repaying the principal and an additional amount to cover the interest costs (the lender's profit)—those repayments are known as 'principal and interest' repayments. As the principal is reduced over time, so are your interest costs. The quicker you repay the principal, the less interest you pay and the quicker your loan is repaid in full.

Some loans are 'interest only' meaning the principal is not repaid. However, those loans are generally for investment purposes only and not personal loans. Interest only loans are usually repaid in full when the attached investment (property for example) is sold.

Loan term

This is the period of time by which you agree to repay the loan. The longer the term, the less the repayments will be each time, however, the more interest you will pay as you extend the amount of time that the lender has to wait for the money to be repaid. Generally, personal loans have terms of 1–7 years to select from (commonly five or seven years). Home loans (mortgages) generally have terms of 25–30 years.

You choose the term when you apply for the loan and generally can't change it throughout the life of a loan unless you want to extend it—some lenders will allow that type of change to the contract as you will pay more interest to them in the long-run.

Interest rate

Interest rates around the world can vary considerably anywhere from 0.00–24.00% per year or more and will have a huge impact on the total cost of a loan. It is wise to shop around for different lenders to determine what interest rate is on offer. However, the interest rate is not all you have to consider when borrowing money. Quite often, a low rate may mean that there are other higher fees and charges to pay to compensate for the low rate or an introductory interest rate which is lower at the start (to entice you to borrow) and then reverts to a higher rate after an agreed term.

Interest is usually calculated on a daily basis and charged to you at each repayment.

Always ask for a discount when it comes to interest rates. If you don't ask, you don't receive. If you have an existing loan(s), then phone your lender today to ask for a discount. This works because if your lender wants to keep your business, they will offer some discount (albeit small)—better those extra bucks stay in your pocket than the lender's pocket. Simply phone and say that you are considering changing lenders and ask if they can offer you a better rate.

Interest rates are either 'fixed' or 'variable'. A fixed rate doesn't change for the agreed term. It gives you certainty about interest costs and the repayment amount. For the benefit of fixed repayments and certainty in what your commitments will be each month, a fixed rate is usually higher than a variable rate. Extra repayments may or may not be possible with a fixed rate loan.

A variable rate is just that; it varies over time. This means that if your interest rate changes throughout your loan term, your repayments will also change. The payoff is that a variable rate is generally cheaper than a fixed rate however you are at the whim of the economy, so if lenders increase rates, your repayments will also increase as you will pay more interest to the lender. However, if rates reduce, your repayments will also reduce, and you will benefit from the interest savings compared to someone with a fixed rate.

In theory, fixed rates can be good if you think rates are likely to increase during the term of your loan. However, considering that no one has a crystal ball to see what rates will do in the future, most times you will be better off and save more money by choosing a lower variable rate and then doing everything you can to make extra repayments to repay the loan early, instead of paying a higher fixed rate from the start, on the off-chance that rates may increase one day in the future.

Also, fixed rate loans can also be tricky to refinance (which is when you move to another lender to reduce interest rates, for example), as you may be liable to pay break costs; an extra cost calculated to cover the interest that your current lender will miss out on by you breaking the agreed fixed term. So fixed rate loans have some extra considerations.

Fees and charges

Lenders also make money by charging fees, such as Application fees and Account Keeping fees. For example, a bank may charge you $150 to apply for a loan plus $10 per month whilst you hold the loan. The fees are generally added to the loan amount, so in the case of borrowing $5,000 for a holiday (Chapter 6), you may end up borrowing $5,150 plus $10 per month. Sometimes you will have the option of paying the $10 per month fee from a nominated bank account, instead of adding it to the loan. Some lenders will offer special deals whereby they waive the Application fee or Account Keeping fee for a limited time (to entice you to borrow). So, it pays to shop around to look for a lender with a low interest rate and no other fees and charges wherever possible.

Don't pay bank fees whenever it can be avoided. If the lender is charging interest on a loan then don't pay additional fees. Use your negotiating skills and ask the lender to waive the Application fee and Account Keeping fee if possible. It doesn't hurt to ask, and yes it does work. Or take your business elsewhere.

Repayment frequency

Repayments are usually set to monthly by default, but often you can also select weekly or fortnightly repayments, just ask your lender. Interest is generally calculated on a daily basis, and therefore it makes sense to make repayments on a more frequent basis, in order to reduce your interest costs.

Making monthly repayments is not generally as effective as fortnightly because you have to wait until the end of a whole month to make the repayment, meaning your principal was higher for the entire month and interest was charged on that higher balance, compared to if you had made fortnightly repayments. Fortnightly repayments mean you pay the equivalent of half of your monthly repayment every two weeks. This allows you in effect to make one extra monthly repayment per year.

For example, say your monthly repayments are $1,000, after one year you would have repaid $12,000 ($1,000 x 12). If you repay fortnightly, you split the monthly payment in half, making fortnightly payments of $500 ($1,000/2). There are 26 fortnights in a year meaning you will repay $13,000 ($500 x 26), rather than $12,000 (an extra $1,000, which is equivalent to 1 x monthly payment). The extra amount directly reduces the principal amount on which interest is calculated. As the interest costs are less, more of your regular repayments then go towards repaying the principal and paying off your loan sooner.

Making weekly repayments of $250 ($1,000/4) will not result in any extra repayments being made as you still repay $13,000 over a year ($250 x 52). However, you will still repay the loan faster as the principal will reduce more frequently resulting in less interest costs.

Early repayment

Most lenders will allow you to make extra repayments to repay your loan faster and return the money quicker. In turn, it also helps to reduce your interest costs. Repaying personal loans as soon as possible (well before the end of the loan term) will minimise your extra costs. Make sure no additional fees are payable to make extra repayments. If there are fees, you will still generally be in front by making the extra repayments (if the interest savings outweigh the fees), consider finding a different lender.

If you repay a fixed rate loan earlier than the agreed term, break fees may be payable and can be substantial, so read the fine print of your loan contract or ask your lender.

Redraw facility

Having a redraw facility attached to a variable rate loan allows you to redraw any extra repayments that you have made (if you are ahead of your payments). Having such as facility in place can provide extra flexibility in case something changes in your personal situation and you need to redraw some of your extra repayments; however, it can also be tempting to redraw funds for non-emergencies, especially if you don't have any other savings at your disposal, so know your temptation limits. You can't generally redraw from a fixed rate loan.

If you are struggling with personal debt and your overall spending, then it's not a wise choice to have a redraw facility. The more you redraw, the less progress you make in repaying the loan faster.

LOAN REPAYMENT EXAMPLE

Let's look at the real cost of borrowing $5,000 for an overseas holiday using a personal loan with a variable interest rate of 14.00% p.a. as an example. The following table shows various loan terms and repayment frequencies.

TABLE 1: Example $5,000 Personal Loan*

Loan Term	Repayment Frequency	Repayment Amount	Total Interest Payable	Total Cost Of Holiday	How Much Extra You Paid
1 year	Monthly	$449	$387	$5,387	$387
	Fortnightly	$207	$372	$5,372	$372
	Weekly	$103	$365	$5,365	$365
2 years	Monthly	$240	$762	$5,762	$762
	Fortnightly	$110	$746	$5,746	$746
	Weekly	$55	$739	$5,739	$739
3 years	Monthly	$171	$1,152	$6,152	$1,152
	Fortnightly	$79	$1,137	$6,137	$1,137
	Weekly	$39	$1,130	$6,130	$1,130

*Figures calculated using Personal Loan calculator (www.moneysmart.gov.au) and sample Interest Rate, current at the time of writing, provided as estimations only and do not necessarily correspond to actual operations of Banks.

The longer the loan term, the less the repayments are each time, but more interest is payable (so the real cost is much higher). The three-year loan was the example used in Chapter 6. Let's keep following that and assume you select weekly repayments.

1-Year Term (52 weeks) Repayments $103 per week
Total interest payable $365
Total holiday cost $5,365
(you pay $365 extra for the holiday)

Do you realise that to save $5,000 over one year you only need to save $96 per week, compared to $103 per week it will take to repay the loan? If you can't discipline yourself to save $103 per week right now (to save up for the holiday), how will you be able to repay it to the bank? Magic? Or will you find the motivation suddenly because you are now legally bound to do so?

If you decide to save $103 per week first, you can have $5,000 in only 48 weeks, instead of having to repay a loan for 52 weeks. You then have money for your holiday one month faster and save yourself $365. Isn't that motivation enough to start saving now?

What if $103 per week is unaffordable to your budget and so you select a two-year loan term to reduce your repayments? In that case, your interest costs increase because you borrow the bank's money for longer:

2-Year Term (104 weeks)   Repayments $55 per week
Interest payable $739
Total holiday cost $5,739
(you pay $739 extra for the holiday)

To save up $5,000 over two years takes only $48 per week, compared to $55 per week to repay the loan.

If you save $55 per week (instead of paying it to the bank) it would take 91 weeks to save up, instead of making loan repayments for 104 weeks. You then have the money about three months faster and save yourself $739. Crazy!

If you can choose to make loan repayments of $55 per week, why don't you instead choose to save that same amount beforehand?

What if you select a three-year loan term to further reduce your repayments?

3-Year Term (156 weeks)   Repayments $39 per week
Interest payable $1,130
Total holiday cost $6,130
(you pay $1,130 extra for the holiday)

To save $5,000 over three years, you only need to save $32 per week, compared to $39 per week it will take to repay the loan.

Or, if you instead save $39 per week, it will take around 128 weeks to save $5,000, instead of making loan repayments for 156 weeks. You now have the money seven months faster and save a whopping $1,130!

These examples show the real cost of the loan and the fact that it is less of a strain on a budget to save a regular amount over time than to borrow it.

You need to be clear about what you can or can't afford. Note that you can't simply try out a loan to see how you go. Once you are committed, you are committed—legally and if you don't repay the loan in the agreed time, you 'default' on the loan and the bank will repossess whatever item you used to secure the loan (car, boat, etc). The default will be recorded against your credit rating, which will definitely not look good to future lenders. Any item which is repossessed by the bank will be sold at auction for whatever amount they can get for it (not necessarily what it's worth), and the sale proceeds will be used to repay your debt. If the sale proceeds don't cover the entire outstanding loan balance, then it's also likely the bank will take legal proceedings and sue you to recover the rest of the money. This is not a good position to be in. If the loan is unsecured, meaning there was no item attached to the loan as security for the bank to be able to sell, the bank will most definitely sue you to recover the money.

Unfortunately, people often borrow for lifestyle expenses because:

1. Ill-Prepared: they have no savings available or have not started saving yet.
2. Insufficient Savings: they keep 'dipping into' savings accounts.
3. Overspending: they want everything now and are not selective enough with spending.

Consistently saving a regular amount will prepare you for when you need money. Holding back from spending your savings too often, especially if saving for a big-ticket item, will take some self-control. So, if needed, move your Just In Case savings to another institution (out of sight like your 10% Savings) and remove the temptation.

If you have an existing personal loan costing you interest then it's a good idea to reduce the amount you save into your Just In Case Account and instead also use that money to make extra loan repayments and repay the balance faster. Scale back your other expenses too (especially non-essential) whilst you have the loan to free up more money for extra repayments. You must get rid of the debt as quickly as possible. Generally, most savings accounts will not pay you much interest, if anything at all, and therefore every dollar of interest that you don't pay to your lender you keep in your own pocket—that means you effectively earn a rate of return on your money equal to the loan interest rate, which will always be much higher than any savings account. Even high-interest accounts can't compete with an average personal loan rate.

The more money you need to repay a loan, the less you have to save to improve your lifestyle and get ahead financially, so can you see why personal debt is no good for your financial health? Your savings ability reduces because you end up paying the money to someone else (the bank) instead of keeping it for yourself.

If you are considering taking on a personal loan for a car, for example, because you need a car and you didn't leave enough time to save up for it (or at least half of it), then you need to make sure your budget can afford the repayments without affecting your other savings. It's no good having a nice shiny new car if you can't really afford it (or afford anything else once you have the car). If a car loan will affect your savings ability then scale back the cost of the car and your other expenses to afford the repayments and maintain some other savings.

Allow nothing to jeopardise your 10% Savings. If you have existing personal debt, use your 10% Savings to make extra repayments to clear the debt faster. This strategy only works, however, if you stop accruing more debts in the meantime.

Chapter 7 summary

- Saving for a future expense will cost less than borrowing it (and takes less time).
- Personal debt (loans and credit cards) will make you poorer.
- Make loan repayments more frequently (fortnightly or weekly, not monthly).
- Make extra repayments to clear existing personal debt faster. Throw an extra $100 per week, $50 per week or even $20 per week against the loan, or your 10% Savings (for now). Some extra repayments are better than no extra repayments.
- Start saving sooner, rather than later. Avoid using personal debt.

CHAPTER 8

Credit Cards (Weapons of Financial Destruction)

B anks and other lending institutions are making it easier and easier to access short-term loans through credit cards and store cards. Some supermarkets are even offering their own branded credit cards. Around the world, there is an epidemic of people spending more than they earn because of easy to access credit cards and the pleasure of instant gratification; wanting more than they can afford, living outside of their means and paying the price for it. Credit cards can be tricky to understand and financially destructive if not used correctly—they can either make your life easier, or they can hinder your financial progress. Unfortunately for most people it's the latter.

Credit card debt is considered 'bad' debt, as the interest payable is not tax deductible and usually the items purchased with credit cards go down in value over time, not up. Having this type of debt will not increase your wealth. It's also looked upon unfavourably by lenders when you apply for other forms of credit, such as car and home loans, and this can hold you back from a successful application.

Credit card debt is one of the worst kinds to owe.

This book is unlikely to stop the world from using credit cards incorrectly, it will at least teach you how credit cards actually work in reality and how easy it can be to fall into the trap of credit card debt, so that you have a better understanding and steer clear.

Basically, the rule of thumb is that when you receive your monthly credit card statement, you must pay 100% of the closing balance by the due date. Don't just make the minimum repayment shown on the statement. If you don't repay 100% of the closing balance, then you will pay a very high rate of interest on the full amount owed (before 1 January 2019 that interest was also backdated to the beginning of your statement cycle). The interest rate can be as high as 24.99% p.a. or more. Ouch!

In the past I remember talking to a family member about credit cards and I asked her if she repays 100% of her bill each month. She answered 'No, but I always make sure I pay the minimum required plus usually some extra on the balance'. I then asked that family member if she was aware that she was being charged interest on the full amount owing and that the interest was backdated to the start of her statement cycle (i.e. the earliest date shown on the statement). She replied 'No' with a shocked looked on her face. Unfortunately, she thought that as long as at least the minimum repayment was made, as shown on the statement, then no interest would be charged. This conversation reminded me that many people are not actually aware of how credit cards really work, yet a lot of people are using them each day, unaware of the traps.

> *Paying interest for lifestyle items (stuff that goes down in value) is a waste of hard-earned money. It will set you back financially and keep you in a vicious cycle. Don't buy things on credit that you can't afford with cash in the first place.*

Since 1 January 2019, Australian credit card providers are no longer allowed to backdate interest costs, however, that doesn't change how financially devastating credit card debt can be.

International card providers still backdate interest so I have kept that in for the calculations shown on the following pages as an example.

Applying for a card

When applying for a credit card, from either a bank or other institution (the 'card issuer'), you are essentially applying for a loan—a form of 'credit'. The card issuer will ask you about your job, income and expenses, assets and liabilities and then use that information to assess your suitability for credit (i.e. whether you can afford the debt and be able to repay it), then decide on whether to approve or decline your application.

Every time you apply for credit, whether it be a credit card, personal loan, car loan, mobile phone contract or store credit (including Interest-Free Shopping Plans), it's listed on your 'Credit History' for five to seven years. Your Credit History is basically that—a history of each time you applied for credit. You can request a copy of your Credit History Report from Equifax Australia (previously Veda). Your Credit Score is what lenders can use when assessing your credit application.

Whether you are approved or declined for credit is not recorded on your Credit History, only the date, the lending institution and the amount of credit applied for. Your Credit History report will also contain personal details, loan inquiries, credit providers, serious debts and credit infringements, commercial credit and public record information including bankruptcy data and default judgments. Not paying a mobile phone bill on time could leave a mark on your Credit History and stop you getting a credit card or home loan. The more times you apply for credit, the more entries on your Credit History.

The catch-22 is that if you are declined for a credit card, for example, and you apply for another card with another institution (once or multiple times), the number of credit applications recorded on your Credit History increases and with each new application, your likelihood of obtaining new credit decreases—the more applications for credit (especially within a small period of time), the less likely you will obtain credit. Future lenders will wonder why you have so many recent applications and will assume that you either (1) were approved for several credit cards/loans or (2) you were declined for each application for some reason and therefore have to keep applying with other institutions—both scenarios don't look good to a potential lender. So, if you are declined for any type of credit, even just once, sit back and look at why and don't just reapply. Ask the lender for details if needed. Your income may be deemed to be insufficient for your existing level of living expenses and debt repayments, or you may have an unfavourable 'bad' Credit History.

If you are approved for credit, the card issuer will send you the card with an approved Credit Limit which is the amount you can spend up to. Usually, the minimum is $500 or $1,000. Often, a lot of people then apply for several credit cards over time (especially after one card is 'maxed out') and can easily end up with credit card debt of $5,000, $7,500, $10,000+. You can't simply apply for a Credit Limit of $10,000 or $20,000 straight away unless you earn sufficient (higher) income and have low expenses. Generally, you prove your 'good repayment behaviour' by repaying your credit card in full each month, and the card issuer then increases your Credit Limit over the years.

Some card issuers charge an Annual fee for the card—unnecessary in my view as many other card issuers don't. Often, it's possible to negotiate the removal of the fee simply by asking. Cards without fees may have less 'bells and whistles' like no Rewards Program and possibly a higher interest rate. However, the interest rate factor need not be a concern as you should never pay interest in the first place—read on.

Using the card

Once you receive your credit card, you sign the back of it and start spending. The card starts with a balance of $0, and when you use it to make purchases, you draw down on the Credit Limit. When you reach the Credit Limit, you can't make further purchases using the card until you reduce the balance.

Some card issuers will allow you to exceed the Credit Limit but then charge you an Overlimit Fee—some will require you to 'opt-in' for that service, but others will provide it automatically (so they can happily charge you extra fees). It's important to monitor your card to make sure all purchases are correct and were authorised by you, to avoid exceeding the Credit Limit and paying unnecessary fees.

If your Everyday Account is held at the same institution as your credit card, you can generally link the accounts and use the card as an ATM card (press either the credit button or the savings button when using Eftpos/an ATM, to select the account you wish to access) and enter your PIN. Many credit cards will have a PayPass Logo, meaning you can use them 'contactless' (without entering a PIN or signing a receipt) for purchases of under $100.

Credit cards, when used properly, are especially useful for:

◆ Paying bills over the internet, phone or at the Post Office.
◆ Shopping online.
◆ Booking tickets, airfares, and hotels online or by phone.
◆ Providing a security deposit for a booking (e.g. at a popular restaurant or hotel)—the venue may ask for your credit card details as security for a booking but not charge the card unless you are a no-show. Or a hotel may 'block' a certain amount from a card at check-in as security for the room (and mini-bar), then release (unblock) the funds after check-out.

Credit cards can, in fact, provide a lot of flexibility if used correctly—if used incorrectly, they can be financially devastating. Daily living expenses such as food, fuel etc can be charged to a credit card as a way of managing cash flow, particularly if you don't like to carry around much cash or as larger bills are received, i.e. you are paid fortnightly but a monthly bill is due. You pay the bill using the credit card knowing full well that you have the funds accruing in your bank account over that month to repay it in full. This is an alternative to using a 'Bills Account' but requires a lot more discipline as it's very easy to overspend on a credit card PLUS spend the cash that you had earmarked for the credit card repayment.

Until recently, many banks charged fees for cash withdrawals from ATMs and therefore credit cards became a good way to charge multiple expenses without having to frequently withdraw cash or worrying about incurring bank transaction fees, but with the introduction of debit cards, the need for credit cards are becoming less and less.

Being able to charge a larger expense/big-ticket item and repay it over time is possible with a credit card, i.e. say you need to buy a new computer suddenly because your old one stops working and needs replacing. You didn't expect this type of purchase and perhaps had not yet started your regular 'Just In Case' savings, but really need a new computer for school/work urgently. A credit card enables you to buy the computer straight away and repay the debt later. However, you need to repay 100% of the debt by the due date otherwise you will also pay interest costs (which makes the computer more expensive). If you spend money on a credit card and know you won't be able to repay it in full by the due date, then you are using the card incorrectly.

Repaying the card

All credit cards have a billing cycle (statement cycle), which represents the date your credit starts to the date that repayment is due. Card issuers often offer interest-free periods of 45 or 55 days, which is the time you can use the credit without interest costs. Shop around to get the best interest-free period. Your statement will detail your billing cycle dates and the due date for repayment:

◆ Billing Cycle Starts: First day of the month (e.g. 1 January)
◆ Billing Cycle Ends: Last day of the month (e.g. 31 January)
◆ Due Date: 45 days from the first of the month (e.g. 14 February)

In this example, if you make a purchase on the first of the month, you have up to 45 days before repayment is due. If you make a purchase on the 28th day of the month, you have only up to 17 days before repayment is due. To maximise the time before having to make a repayment, the best strategy is to make the purchase at the beginning of the billing cycle, so that you have the full 45 days to repay it (if needed) before being charged interest.

When I first applied for a credit card many years ago, it took me a while to understand the billing cycle, and it was quite confusing to keep track of initially, especially because my billing cycle started on an odd date and not the first of the month, which is simpler.

If using a credit card for your living expenses then the date of a purchase is not so relevant as smaller purchases are made frequently throughout the billing cycle (expenses don't all occur at the same time).

You must always make sure that you can repay the balance owing by the due date to avoid interest costs. If you don't have to pay interest costs then you don't have to worry about maximising interest-free periods—it becomes irrelevant.

Make repayments more frequently (each payday), to keep the balance low and more manageable, i.e. if paid weekly and not using a Bills Account for whatever reason then transfer a fixed amount weekly to your card to cover the expenses being charged (as budgeted). If your card balance increases higher than the amount being transferred, reassess your spending and cut back. What are you buying that's not budgeted? Adjust your weekly transfer, or your spending, or your budget. It's simpler to use a Bills Account and ditch the credit card.

Interest Costs & Repayments

At the end of the billing cycle, you will be sent a statement from the card issuer which shows the due date and the end of the interest-free period. You will also see a 'minimum repayment' amount shown on the statement. This is the amount you are required to repay as a minimum. With credit cards, you don't have to repay 100% of the debt straight away.

Now, that may seem like a generous alternative to repaying the full amount. However, banks are in the business of making money. If you don't repay the full amount owing by the due date, the bank will charge you interest each day that you don't make the full repayment. Interest is calculated daily and adds up quickly. The interest you end up paying will blow out the cost of your purchases. Interest rates can be 24.99% per year or more—much higher than a car loan.

For example:

♦ You purchase a computer on credit for $1,500 on 17 April.
♦ Your billing cycle ends on 30 April.
♦ You receive a statement which shows $1,500 is due on 15 May.
♦ The statement also says that the minimum repayment due is $10.

If you repay the full $1,500 on or before 15 May, no interest will be payable. If you don't make the full repayment, interest will be payable from 15 May and calculated daily. Beware, interest costs can add up fast and some (international) card providers will still backdate the charges!

Different card issuers use different systems to calculate the interest payable. Most will use an Average Daily Balance method, whereby interest accrues daily. The annual amount is then divided by 365 days to find the daily rate. That rate is applied to the balance (Average Daily Balance) for as long as it's unpaid in full. Card issuers often rely on the fact that you don't fully understand that interest is constantly compounding. The term 'compound interest' means that interest charges are added to the loan balance, so your debt grows exponentially. When investing, compound interest (that is paid to you) is a good thing and makes you richer, but when it comes to personal debt, compound interest (that you pay to someone else) will make you poor.

TABLE 1: How Interest Is Calculated (with backdated interest example)

$1,500 Amount Owing x 24.99% Interest Rate	= $374.85 per year interest
Daily interest	= $374.85 / 365 days = $1.03 per day
Backdated interest	= $1.03 x 45 days (from 1st April)
Interest Payable	= $46.21 on top of the $1,500 owing
Total Payable	**= $1,546.21**

The longer you don't repay the balance in full, the higher your debt will grow. In this example, you have paid $46.21. An extra $46.21 (3.08%) may not seem like much of a concern initially, but the bigger concern is that for each day you don't repay the full $1,500 owing plus the interest, that interest will continue to grow daily and be added to the balance until the total debt is repaid... and it can add up quickly. Say you don't repay the full balance for a further 30 days (75 days in total), your interest costs increase to $77.02—you now paid $77.02 (5.13%) more for the computer. This is a simplified calculation of interest charges.

TABLE 2: Interest Costs – Owing $1,500 Over Different Time Periods

Unpaid for	45 days	75 days	90 days	100 days
Total Cost	$46.21	$77.02	$92.43	$102.70

The higher the amount owing, the higher the interest costs. If left unpaid, interest costs compound. You will pay interest on top of interest!

What if the computer, together with other expenses made throughout that month totalled $3,000? You can't make the full repayment so your interest costs will be around $92.43 if left unpaid after the 45-day interest-free period (backdated). Perhaps you leave it until next month. After 75 days of not repaying the debt, your interest costs increase to approximately $154.05. Remember, 75 days is only about 2.5 months—time passes quickly and will catch up with you.

TABLE 3: Interest Costs Owing $3,000 Over Different Time Periods

Unpaid for	45 days	75 days	90 days	100 days
Total Cost	$92.43	$154.05	$184.86	$205.40

Say you instead went on an overseas holiday and spent $4,500 (who needs a new computer anyway), only to come back to a statement requesting full payment. If you can't make the full repayment and leave it for a while longer, your interest would be around $138.64 if left unpaid for 45 days, as an example. That interest cost would increase to $231.07 if left unpaid for 75 days and so on and so forth.

TABLE 4: Interest Costs – Owing $4,500 Over Different Time Periods

Unpaid for	45 days	75 days	90 days	100 days
Total Cost	$138.64	$231.07	$277.29	$308.10

See how the interest really starts to add up? You start paying interest on top of interest. The longer you leave it, and the more you spend, the quicker the debt can spiral out of control. These figures are provided for you as approximate examples to show you how interest is calculated in a simple way. Your card issuer will confirm the exact amounts on your statement; you will not need to calculate anything. Your statement will tell you how much you owe. The problem is, however, if you don't repay the card balance in full, you will not see the interest costs, until your next paper statement (unless you check in real-time via online banking). So, it can be quite surprising how fast the debt increases.

It's essential to repay 100% of the closing card balance shown on the statement to avoid paying interest. Small amounts of interest add up. Why pay more in life than you have to?

If you are considering buying a big-ticket item using a credit card and you know you will not be able to repay 100% of the amount by the due day, stop, do some simple calculations to determine what your approximate interest costs may be (or ask your lender)—you can then make an informed decision as to whether it's worth the extra cost to have the item now (instant gratification) or whether it is best to wait and save the money first. The latter is the only correct answer.

A simple rule of thumb: don't buy things on credit!
Never pay interest to buy an item that goes down in value.
Instead, save first. That will cost you less and
makes financial sense.

Computers break, holiday opportunities pop up, emergencies happen which can remove the luxury of time and why it's important to have an ongoing 'Just in Case' Account. Having access to savings gives you more options in having what you want (or need) now, rather than accruing debt and paying more than you need to because of interest costs.

If you can't afford to save a specific amount each week now, how will you suddenly be able to repay a debt in 45 or 55 days? Saving an amount over time instead of immediately spending and racking up debt is a good way to see if you can afford to manage a credit card.

Start your 'Just in Case' Account sooner rather than later to get ahead of the game and be ready for when money is needed. It's cheaper to be prepared.

Why Minimum Repayments Are Not Enough

Not paying your credit card bill at all is not an option—you are required to make at least a minimum repayment which is generally around 2% or $10 (whichever is greater).

The higher the amount owed,
the higher the minimum repayment.

If you have any past amounts overdue then the minimum amount you must repay will increase to include those amounts. Your statement will tell you the minimum amount due. The minimum repayment will be part principal and part interest. The principal repayment will be used to reduce your debt and the interest portion will go to the bank (as their profit) and will not reduce your debt at all. Therefore, assuming you make only the minimum repayments on a $1,500 credit card debt, it will take you approximately 18-and-a-half years to repay, and interest costs will total $4,036! You end up paying $5,536 for a $1,500 computer and have debt hanging over your head for 18.5 years!

Obviously that's not a correct approach to handling debt. You must repay the debt quicker to get ahead. You will not get anywhere by paying only the minimum.

FIGURE 1: Minimum Repayments Are Not Enough*

*https://www.moneysmart.gov.au/tools-and-resources/calculators-and-apps/credit-card-calculator

Look at the larger (lighter) portion. That's the interest payable! Much more than the principal amount borrowed. Nearly three times as much over the term of the loan.

If you find yourself in the position whereby you have more than one credit card, money owing on all of them and you are using one card to repay another—stop. You are probably paying exorbitant interest and cash advance fees on top. This is a recipe for disaster.

Have you ever heard this saying?

'Robbing Peter to pay Paul.'

You can continue like that for only so long. Stop your spending immediately to stop the debt from increasing. (Chapter 9 will show how to get out of credit card debt fast.)

If you do use a credit card to purchase a big-ticket item for whatever reason, then calculate what your weekly repayments need to be to repay the full amount in time.

As an example, if you buy the computer at the start of your billing cycle, with the full 45 days to repay, then your repayments will be around $34 per day ($1,500/45) or around $240 per week to repay in full. The further into the billing cycle that you buy the computer, the less time you will have to repay it and the higher your repayments must be to clear the debt in full. For example, if you buy the computer on the 17th of April, you will only have 28 days remaining in the interest-free period, meaning your daily repayments will increase to $54 ($1,500/28), or around $380 per week, for example.

Note, if you are also using the same credit card for your daily expenses and want to make sure that the money which you are repaying (for the computer), doesn't get absorbed and spent elsewhere, save the required amount into a bank account first. Then, when the credit card due date nears, you can use the saved funds to make a lump sum repayment of $1,500 on the card.

How to Avoid Missing Repayments

To avoid missing repayments (and paying costly fees), try this:
- Diarise the due date
- Use an automatic repayment plan

DIARISE THE DUE DATE

If you miss making the repayment by the due date, you may be charged a 'Late Payment' fee. The fee varies between card issuers. To avoid paying unnecessary fees, try diarising the due date each time you receive a statement (paper or online).

If you elect not to receive paper statements (save the trees) and your card issuer doesn't automatically email your statements you will have to log on to your online banking to view the statement. Find the due date and diarise it—make it a couple of days earlier to be on the safe side. The due date will usually be around the same time each month. This can change depending on the number of days in the month. At least it will remind you that the payment is coming up soon, prompting you to log in and check the statement for the exact date.

USE AUTOMATED PAYMENTS

Automating your repayment is a simple way to ensure that you meet the due date on time each month and avoid fees. You simply set up an automated payment to come from a nominated bank account each due date. Your card issuer can arrange this (via phone or online banking) and may offer you the choice of repaying:

◆ The minimum repayment
◆ A percentage of the closing balance
◆ A set amount of the closing balance
◆ The full closing balance

**Knowing what you know now,
you only ever select the last option.**

It still helps to diarise the approximate due date to ensure you have sufficient funds in your nominated bank account for the payment to lodge successfully.

You must also note that if you have partially repaid your credit card since receiving the statement (made repayments after the billing cycle 'end date'), the card issuer's automatic repayment system will not take into account those repayments and will still debit your account for the full closing balance shown on the statement, meaning you will pay over and above the closing balance (not a bad thing).

You will not 'lose' the extra money transferred into the card; the funds will simply reduce next month's closing balance (or sit in credit if no purchases are made the next month).

Be careful if you wish to transfer the 'funds in credit' back into your bank account however, as a card issuer will usually treat it as a Cash Advance and charge you extra fees. It's best to contact your card issuer in that instance so they can assist you.

Cash Advances = bad idea, don't do it.

If you withdraw cash from a credit card using an ATM, it's called a Cash Advance. The problem with making Cash Advances is that the majority of card issuers will charge a handling fee, usually around 3% of the amount withdrawn and start charging interest straight away. Also, the rate of interest charged is usually higher than the rate for purchases, and there is rarely an interest-free period for cash advances.

Say you are charged an interest rate of 26.90% per year for Cash Advances plus 3% fee, the following table shows how much it would cost you to withdraw $1,000 in cash from an ATM using a credit card.

TABLE 5: Cash Advance Cost (Example)

	10 days	20 days	30 days	50 days
Interest 26.90%	$7.37	$14.74	$22.11	$36.85
Plus, Fee 3%	$30.00	$30.00	$30.00	$30.00
Total Cost	**$37.37**	**$44.74**	**$52.11**	**$66.85**

As a comparison, for a $100 cash withdrawal with 20 days taken to repay in full, you will pay the handling fee of $3 plus approximate interest of $1.47. Total fees $4.47.

Although $4.47 may not sound like a lot, it can really start to add up over multiple transactions or the longer it takes you to repay the amount in full. Cash Advances are not the intention of credit cards—credit cards are for purchases (using credit) and then repaid, which is why card issuers charge additional fees for cash advances.

Online banking systems can treat the transfer of money from a credit card and into a bank account as a Cash Advance, even if the transfer is done online and no cash is withdrawn from an ATM. If you wish to transfer any extra funds that are sitting in credit from your card back to your bank account, it's best to contact your card issuer so they can assist you (and avoid extra fees). Paying unnecessary fees is like throwing money away.

Rewards Programs—Are they worth it?

Some credit cards link to Rewards Programs, whereby you collect points for every dollar spent on the card, which goes towards flights and other rewards, services or money vouchers that you can claim over time. Accruing enough points to be able to redeem a reward takes time (a lot of time) for someone spending an average amount on their card each month, especially to redeem a larger reward such as airfare. The more you spend on the card, the more points you accrue and the quicker you can claim rewards. However, collecting points mustn't be the driving factor for racking up credit card debt if you can't afford to repay it because collecting enough points to claim a reward takes time—it can be years. Some cards will offer a greater number of points per dollar than others or better/more useful rewards. However, card rewards are getting harder and harder to achieve—the card issuers keep changing the number of points accrued per dollar, so you spend more, but claim fewer rewards.

Credit cards with reward programs will generally charge a higher annual fee compared to a 'no frills' card which offers less 'bells and whistles'. The better the rewards program, the higher the annual fee in many cases. The cards will have names such as 'Silver' and 'Gold' or 'Ultimate' and 'Platinum', selling you on the idea that you are getting a lot of added value. But are you?

You need to weigh up the risk vs. reward, i.e. for the cost of the annual fee (which may be $30 to $400 per year or more), what do you get for that cost? If you are unlikely to be able to claim a reward for several years, i.e. a flight, then consider the annual fees you will pay over those years. Often, you can simply pay the cost of a flight in less time than it takes to accrue enough points. Most card issuers will have online calculators available so you can calculate how many points you will need for a particular reward, to give you an idea of the time that it may take you to accrue enough points (using your average monthly card spend for example).

When reward programs can work...

If you use a credit card successfully (repay the full balance each month) and you will be doing so for the foreseeable future as part of your money management, then a reward program can play a part in that, especially if the card charges a low annual fee (or better yet NO annual fee). If you are going to be using the card regularly anyway, perhaps you can reward yourself over time with smaller rewards or benefit from the other services that may be included (travel insurance or airport lounge access etc). Reward programs don't suit everyone. When a rewards program is 'worth it' some people will charge every expense possible to their credit card to maximise the accrual of points and refrain from paying bills with cash wherever possible. However, if you don't fly often and will not use the lounge access enough to 'get your money's worth', why sign up for a card with such a high annual fee? Instead, just pay for lounge access when you actually fly. You need to read what the rewards program is offering and determine what 'value' it will be to you. If there is no significant value to you (or break even and not very exciting) then go for a no annual fee card and instead pay for the extras/rewards that you actually want and need in life vs. aiming for extras/rewards that you never actually achieve.

Whilst living abroad, I had a credit card which cost $400 per year in annual fees, however I had chosen that particular card for specific reasons; the card provided me with (1) airport lounge access, (2) travel insurance (decent coverage for what I needed at the time—yes, I checked the policy terms to be sure, you need to be that thorough) and (3) points for airfares with a major airline (which I was using frequently).

I was travelling a lot at that time, so paying $400 per year was much more cost effective at the time, compared to paying for the lounge access each time and a separate travel insurance policy for the basic coverage that I needed. Also, the points accrual was generous, and I had calculated (before applying for the card) that enough points for an airfare in less than two years was possible.

Therefore, two years x $400 = $800 in annual fees for two years' worth of lounge access, multi-use travel insurance, and the potential of a 'free' flight that I was very likely to receive. As I was flying a lot, it was a good deal (for me), for the value that I received.

If you are not prepared to crunch the numbers don't bother with rewards programs. Likewise, if you are struggling with managing your cash flow or with credit card debt then keep things simple and don't bother with reward programs. Chopping up your card and getting your finances in order is much more important and deserves more of your time than fiddling with Reward Programs.

Credit Cards vs. Debit Cards

Debit cards are an alternative to credit cards and are great, especially for people who struggle to manage credit card debt or simply don't want the temptation to overspend. Most major institutions now offer debit cards—they don't offer any 'credit limit' and instead customers can only spend the money in their bank account which is linked to the card (like an ATM card for example), the difference is that you can use the debit card for online and telephone payments and other situations where normal ATM cards won't suffice.

Note that credit cards can be safer for online purchases as the anti-fraud systems are much more stringent (a debit card will link straight to your bank account, and purchases are made in real-time, meaning funds are immediately debited from your account at the time you make a purchase), therefore if you suspect fraud, disputes with card issuers can be more difficult to resolve with a debit card compared to a credit card. However, if the temptation to overspend (on credit) is there, then online fraud is not your biggest concern. Debit cards are a 'happy medium' for when you need credit card type features (e.g. online purchases) but don't want the temptation of spending money that doesn't belong to you.

Simply stay away from credit cards if you are unsure of how you will afford to repay the full balance by the due date, and especially if you already have existing credit card debt. Ditch the credit card. Instead, use only your income to fund purchases.

Switch to a debit card which gives you many of the same features, but without borrowed money. Make the debit card your new best friend.

Interest-Free Shopping Plans

Some larger department and home appliance stores offer 'Interest-free Shopping Plans' or '0% Interest Payment Plans' as they are also known.

Simply put, the store offers you credit so that you can shop as you like now and repay the amount you spend, in an agreed time-frame (with an interest-free period).

Some plans will not even require you to make payments until a certain period of time has passed.

The minimum spend may be as low as $300 up to $1,500 and the interest-free period may be anywhere from six, 12, 18, 50 or 60 months, for example.

Sounds like it could be a great deal. So long as you repay the balance (and fees) within that interest-free period, you will pay no interest.

Interest-Free Shopping is there to entice you to shop.

The agreement you sign works very much like a personal loan or credit card—your application for credit will be lodged by the store with a lender. The lender will assess and approve (or deny) your application (usually whilst you wait in the store). The lender may be a separate company to the store but affiliated in some way e.g. commission share. Interest-Free Shopping Plans are not all the same, so you must read the Terms & Conditions to know what you are signing up for (as with any loan). However, it's hard to do that adequately if you are standing in the middle of a store.

Harvey Norman, one of Australia's largest department stores, has had huge success over the years partly because it made finance (credit) readily accessible to the masses with Interest-Free Shopping Plans. Note that Harvey Norman and other stores that offer shopping plans are not 'out to get you' or purposely trying to send you broke, but they are in the business of making money. It's your choice as to whether you take up those offers.

Whenever you are offered an interest-free period be aware that the cost is built in. The store would have already paid for those goods in one way or another, so there is a cost to the store to give you goods without paying for a period of time. Someone has to pay for it. That someone is you.

Here are two examples of actual Interest-Free Plans offered by Harvey Norman, as an example of the types of plans available in the marketplace.

The plan in Figure 2 on the following page states that no payments are required from you for 18 months. You do not have to do anything for 18 months except enjoy the goodies you purchased—how generous of the store.

However, the Terms & Conditions clearly states: 'If there is an outstanding balance after the interest-free period ends, interest will be charged at 29.49%'.

If the interest-free period is 18 months, but you have not made any payments (because you didn't have to), then the full amount borrowed will still be outstanding at the end of 18 months and you will start paying interest of 29.49% per year.

That's a significant interest rate. If you borrowed $500, $1,000 or $1,500, your interest costs for the next year would be around:

$500 = interest costs of $147

$1,000 = interest costs of $295

$1,500 = interest costs of $442

FIGURE 2: 18 Months Interest-Free Plan. No Payments (for 18 months)*

*http://www.harveynorman.com.au/customer-service/finance-options/interest-free. February 2017.

Those interest costs are just for 12 months. The interest will then compound over time, just like a credit card. If you want to avoid interest costs, then you must divide the amount borrowed (plus fees) by 18 months—that's the amount you need to repay each month from the start. Establishment and Account Service Fees will be around $114.10 over 18 months. Be sure to start making payments straight away (use the amount that you calculated), even though you are not required to do so just yet. If the plan will not accept payments straight away (some may not), then make sure to save that regular amount into a separate savings account, ready to make the full payment before the 18 months is up. Either way, make sure 100% of the balance is repaid within the 18 months.

Remember, personal short-term debt is there to entice you to shop and pay interest—it's how the credit providers (lenders) make their money. Harvey Norman and other stores that offer Interest-Free Shopping Plans want you to spend more.

It's all business.

FIGURE 3: 60 Months Interest-Free Plan. Minimum Payments (until Feb 2022)*

*http://www.harveynorman.com.au/customer-service/finance-options/interest-free. February 2017.

This plan does require minimum payments to be made over the 60-month interest-free period (2017 to 2022 = 5 years).

For this plan, the Terms & Conditions clearly states:

'Minimum monthly payments must be made during the interest-free period, and interest and payments are payable after the interest-free period. Paying only the minimum monthly payment will not pay out the loan balance before the end of the interest-free period. If there is an outstanding balance after the interest-free period ends in Feb 2022, interest will be charged at 29.49%.'

The minimum payments will be set by the loan agreement and will depend on the amount borrowed. But, by making only the minimum payment—you will still have debt owing after the 60 months and you will start paying a high amount of interest.

If you want to avoid interest costs, then you must divide the amount borrowed (plus fees) by 60 months—that amount will be higher than the minimum. Establishment and Account Service Fees would be around $322.00 over 60 months.

Be sure to make higher than minimum payments (use the amount that you calculated), even though you are not required to do so initially. If the plan will not accept higher than minimum payments, then make sure you save the difference into a separate bank account, ready to make the full repayment before the 60-month term is up.

It is best that these Interest-Free Shopping Plans are not used, especially if you are already having some trouble managing your finances. They are there to entice you to shop.

Instead, take control of your savings beforehand. Give yourself time to save the amount needed to be able to buy the items and don't risk the temptation of shopping plans. It doesn't take much to accidentally miscalculate and not have the funds available to clear the loan in full at the end of the interest-free period.

Be sure to set up a 'Just in Case' Account as soon as possible, with continuous, regular savings. Then, when the time comes to make a substantial purchase in the future, you will not have to 'wait' to go shopping or pay more than you need to because of debt.

Buddy's real-life story

I have a friend, let's call him Buddy. Buddy told me about an experience he had at a department store trying to buy furniture to set up his first 'living away from home' experience—fridge, washing machine, TV, microwave, couch etc. The purchase was substantial. Buddy didn't have enough savings available at the time, so he agreed to use the Interest-free Shopping Plan offered by the store.

Whilst sitting with the salesperson and going through the paperwork, Buddy was informed of the interest-free period and the minimum repayments that would be payable. The salesperson was talking fast whilst having Buddy sign various forms and agreements, with not much time for him to sit and think about the loan terms he was agreeing to. Buddy took it upon himself to stop and do a quick calculation to work out what he would repay (approximately) over the interest-free period by just repaying the minimum.

Minimum Repayment x Number of Months (in the interest-free period)

Buddy realised it was nowhere near the full amount that he was borrowing. Buddy questioned the salesperson as to what would happen at the end of the interest-free period, knowing full well there would still be money outstanding and was advised by the rather now uncomfortable salesperson that the interest rate would kick in and be **back-dated** to the start of the agreement. Buddy enquired about making repayments over and above the minimum throughout the interest-free period and was told that it wasn't allowed. The minimum payments were set at the start of the term and it was up to Buddy to pay the balance owing on the final day of the interest-free period or pay the interest costs.

Buddy proceeded with the shopping plan (he needed the furniture right then and there) and made the choice to save the extra amount needed each month into a separate bank account, ready to be able to repay the full balance of funds owing at the end of the interest-free period—and avoid all interest costs. The furniture was costing enough already. He didn't then want to also pay extra for it.

*Buddy's experience was a few years ago. The current Harvey Norman Interest-Free Shopping Plans no longer backdate interest. Agreements vary between stores—**always read the fine print.***

Chapter 8 summary

- Credit card debt is one of the worst kinds to owe.
- Don't just pay the minimum amount shown on the statement.
- You must repay the full closing balance to avoid interest costs.
- If debt is left unpaid, you pay interest on top of interest!
- Use automated repayment plans so you never miss a due date.
- Never withdraw cash from a credit card.
- If struggling with credit card debt, switch to a debit card.
- Keep things simple, avoid rewards programs.
- Avoid Interest-Free Shopping Plans.
- A simple rule of thumb: don't buy things on credit!

CHAPTER 9

Erase Credit Card Debt (In 3 Easy Steps)

D o you have more than one credit card with money owing on each? Perhaps you have realised that you can't afford to repay all of the card balances in full by the due date. You now know that you will be charged interest. So, what to do? Is it better to repay the card with the biggest balance first, or the smallest balance, or a little on each one? Repay the card with the highest interest rate first, or the lowest interest rate, or a little of each one? Is it best to combine the card balances? This is what I would do...

1. Stop creating new debt.
2. Assess what you owe.
3. Start a repayment plan.

STEP 1: STOP CREATING NEW DEBT

If struggling with credit card debt, you need to cap the 'problem' to tackle it. Cut up the cards so you stop increasing the amount owed. If you have credit card debt, it means you are not using credit cards correctly—stop using credit cards—simplify things by cutting them up. If for some reason you won't, then at least put the card somewhere under lock and key. Try the freezer! By the time you access the card from the ice or behind some frozen meat in the heat of the moment, you may just cool off and think about the purchases you were wanting to make 'using credit'.

STEP 2: ASSESS WHAT YOU OWE

The aim is to repay the debt as quickly as you can, so you pay as little interest as possible. This has to become your main debt repayment priority because credit cards have high interest rates attached—usually much higher than a personal loan or home loan. Ring each card issuer and tell them that you are considering moving your card balance to another institution (whether you do or not—in reality—is irrelevant). Request a reduction in your interest rate right there and then over the phone. Most card providers will offer some discount to keep your business. This does work, and it never hurts to ask. If you don't ask then you don't receive. Any rate reduction, even if just a small one, will help you to reduce your interest costs and repay the debt faster.

TABLE 1: Multiple Card Example

Card	Balance Owing	Interest Rate
1	$2,500	10.99% pa
2	$500	16.99% pa
3	$4,000	23.00% pa

STEP 3: START A REPAYMENT PLAN

List the cards and rank them from highest to lowest interest rate. It makes the most 'financial sense' to repay the card with the highest interest rate first, which is card number 3 ($4,000) in this example.

TABLE 2: Cards Ranked In Repayment Order

Card	Balance Owing	Interest Rate
3 (repay 1st)	$4,000	23.00% pa
2 (repay 2nd)	$500	16.99% pa
1 (repay 3rd)	$2,500	10.99% pa

Make minimum repayments on cards 1 and 2—you must repay at least the minimum on each card, otherwise you will be charged additional fees and tarnish your credit history. If you are currently making **extra repayments** on cards 1 or 2, stop those and reduce to just the minimum for now. Use all available surplus income to make the extra repayments on card 3—over and above the minimum repayment. Throw everything you have at it. Focus on that card. When card 3 has been fully repaid 'snowball' the extra repayments to the card with the next highest interest rate (card 2 in this example) and so on.

Now breathe.

Some finance gurus will tell you to direct the extra repayments to the card with the lowest balance first—that works too—it's more of an 'emotional strategy' and will suit some personalities better. You end up paying more interest and so it's not the most optimal financial strategy. If you want a sense of achievement by quickly clearing at least one card, to motivate yourself to keep going and clear the rest—then by all means switch the order. The important part is that you direct your extra repayments to one card first, clear it, then snowball to the next card (remembering to continue making minimum repayments on all cards).

This strategy works for all personal debt (credit cards, personal loans, car loans etc). A credit card will usually have a much higher interest rate compared to a car loan, and a car loan will usually have a much higher interest rate compared to a home loan. List all loans in order of interest rate.

Focus on getting rid of any credit card debt first as it will likely have the highest interest rate, then snowball your extra repayments afterward to a car loan for example (including the 'freed-up' money used to repay credit card debt)—all of that which goes to the car loan. Finally, when the car loan is repaid in full, snowball the extra money to repaying a home loan faster.

If you have any existing credit card debt, it's best to also clear that first so cut back on your Just In Case savings. Credit card debt is expensive and one of the worst kinds to owe, so you need to clear that first (because it costs you money and drains your cash flow), before treating yourself to non-essential luxury items (iPads, holidays etc).

Balance Transfer Cards

A Balance Transfer Card allows you to move existing credit card balance(s) to a new card with a lower rate; usually interest-free for a period of time. Having a 0% interest rate means you remove the interest costs and can then repay the actual debt faster. By consolidating multiple card debts into one Balance Transfer Card, your paperwork also reduces as the 'old' cards are replaced and cancelled by the Balance Transfer Card. The low/nil rate will run for a fixed time (usually 6–24 months), after which time the rate will revert to a significantly higher rate (may or may not be higher than your original cards). The aim of a Balance Transfer Card is to repay the balance in full in the interest-free period and never carry the debt past that time.

A low/nil interest rate can be attractive; however, it means that the card issuer is losing out on missed revenue and that lost revenue needs to be recovered somehow—usually by charging you higher fees and charges (including annual fees). Therefore, you may pay a one-off Balance Transfer Fee (a percentage of the balance transferred) to set up the new card. That fee can be negotiated (reduced) or waived in full—ask the card issuer.

TABLE 3: Consolidated Debts Example

Card	Balance Owing	Interest Rate
1	$2,500	10.99% p.a.
2	$500	16.99% p.a.
3	$4,000	23.00% p.a.
Transfer to 'Balance Transfer Card' (existing cards will be cancelled)		
1	$7,000	0.00% p.a. for 18 months then reverts to 15.99% pa

In this example, if you consolidate the three debts into one Balance Transfer Card (total $7,000) and repay the full $7,000 owing within the 18 months 0% interest period, then you will not pay any interest at all. That can work wonders to repay your debt faster. Repayments needed to clear the debt in time are = $389 per month ($7,000/18 months). If for some reason you don't repay the full amount within the interest-free period, then interest reverts to 15.99% p.a. in this example. You will still be better off paying 15.99% p.a. interest with the new Balance Transfer Card, compared to the original interest rates on cards 2 and 3 (16.99% p.a. and 23.00% p.a. respectively), however worse off than if you had kept card 1 (10.99% pa).

There is a fine line between using a Balance Transfer Card correctly, or not. Even though your debts are consolidated, you have to maintain disciplined repayments to repay that consolidated debt. Before you consider a Balance Transfer Card, start with Steps 1–3, which are simply a redirection of existing repayments and simpler to start with. With a Balance Transfer Card, you are essentially applying for new credit ($7,000 in this example). So, if a Balance Transfer Card isn't available to you, stick to Steps 1–3.

When using a Balance Transfer Card, you must cut it up so you are not tempted to accrue more debt. If you make any new purchases on a Balance Transfer Card they have to be repaid first and you will incur a higher interest rate on those purchases, which defeats the purpose.

Chapter 9 summary

- Avoid all personal debt, including credit cards.
- There are 3 steps to getting out of credit card debt:
  1. Stop creating new debt (cut up cards)
  2. Assess what's owed (rank highest to lowest interest rates)
  3. Start a repayment plan (make extra repayments on one card at a time)
- Balance Transfer Cards only work if you cut up the card and repay 100% of the consolidated balance by the end of the interest-free period.
- Having savings to access gives you more options in buying what you want now, without debt.
- If you can't afford to save a regular amount each week now, how will you be able to afford to repay a credit card debt?

CHAPTER 10

Are You Wasting Money?

E very dollar that you don't spend is another dollar that you can save or invest. Every dollar that you don't pay in fees, charges and interest costs or wasted on unnecessary expenses is another dollar in your pocket. Life is here to be enjoyed, so the key is to be frugal in your spending by making deliberate choices as to where you spend every dollar, rather than never ever spending a single dollar. Don't be stingy with money—be selective. Live deliberately.

Even billionaires are frugal with their money.
Warren Buffett, the chairman, and CEO of Berkshire Hathaway,
still lives in the same home he bought for $31,500 in 1958.
Net worth: $60.7 billion.

Mark Zuckerberg, the founder, and CEO of Facebook drives
a manual-transmission Volkswagen hatchback.
Net worth: $42.8 billion.

Carlos Slim Helú, the founder of Grupo Carso (richest man in
Mexico), has lived in the same six-bedroom house for more than
40 years. Net worth: $23.5 billion.

Charlie Ergen, the chairman of Dish Network, still packs a brown-bag lunch every day. Net worth: $14.5 billion.

Ingvar Kamprad, the founder of IKEA, flew economy and often rode the bus. Net worth: $39.3 billion.

EXERT FROM ARTICLE WWW.BUSINESSINSIDER.COM,

TANZA LOUDENBACK,

7 FEBRUARY 2016.

I am not saying you need to go as far as these billionaires. If I had the same wealth as Ingvar Kamprad, I guarantee you that I wouldn't fly economy, ever. Different people value things and experiences differently. Some people value things over experiences. Some value experiences over things.

A problem arises when you don't pay attention as to where your money is being spent or how it's being wasted and sending you financially backwards—regardless of whether you spend on things or experiences. Spending is spending! One of the best ways of keeping money in your pocket rather than someone else's pocket is not to waste money in the first place.

No one can rightfully judge what you choose to spend your money on and what you value compared to someone else. Buying more and more stuff will not make you happy, it will only make you poor. Spend money on experiences (rather than things); experiences create life-long memories whereas things only provide short-term happiness. Cut down the amount of things you fill your house with and instead go on a day trip somewhere.

We all place value on the stuff we buy, otherwise we wouldn't buy it in the first place. However, if the stuff that you buy is stopping you from having enough money available when you really need it, or your house is filling up with more and more 'non-money-making possessions', then you are placing too much value on that stuff. Are you spending and buying low-value items regularly, for short-term happiness?

By cutting down on your everyday spending, you will have more money available for the things you really want in life and for investing (to create more money). The more money you save and make from investing, the further in life you can get. Sure, we all still buy some stuff here and there, but it needs to be a deliberate decision each time, rather than an impulse purchase. Remember, it's okay to consume, but not to 'compulsively consume'. You are not going to get happier by consuming more stuff. Instead, reconsider the value of stuff vs. financial security and being able to afford other things in life. What's really important to you? What do you crave in life?

Regardless of whether you spend on things or experiences, your first step in having more money is to cut down on spending. After all, spending is still spending.

Here are strategies to help curb your spending on 'stuff'—you know, the things that you don't really need but buy anyway.

STRATEGY 1: DO I REALLY NEED IT?

An 'impulse purchase' is one made on impulse/spur-of-the-moment/on-the-spot. Something purchased right then and there, which you were not planning or intending on purchasing (until you saw it), such as:

- Clothes and Accessories that you had to have, but which now sit in your closet with price tags still attached (or barely worn).
- Sporting Equipment that you swore you were going to use, but now sits in the garage collecting dust.
- A Pay TV or Gym package.
- An Insurance Policy or Donation you paid for when a telemarketer phoned you.
- A credit card (or store card) a bank teller sold you on whilst you were in a branch (for some other completely unrelated reason).
- Any item you purchased for the promotional item attached.

When considering making a purchase, particularly for non-necessity lifestyle items such as new clothes, household appliances or furnishings, tech gadgets, etc, stop and ask yourself 'Do I really need it?' You have probably heard of this one before, that's because it's an oldie but a goodie that works. However, for it to work, take a few extra seconds whilst standing in the shop (or with the salesperson) to really consider the question and your answer. Don't rush through it or you will easily talk yourself into the impulse purchase.

Take the thought process a step further and also ask yourself:

◆ 'Have I gotten along fine so far without it?'
◆ 'Do I have something at home which is still good enough?'
◆ 'What will I throw out (to make room for the new item)?'
◆ 'Where will the money come from?' Does something else have to be cut from your budget?
◆ 'Can I come back to the new item in a week or so?' You are likely to have forgotten about it by then unless you really need it.

By the time you have this 'little chat with yourself', the excitement you felt when first wanting to buy the item (the rush of instant gratification) will usually wear off. Instead, you will be content with not purchasing right then and there and to save your money for something else. When considering buying items such as new gadgets and electronics, do your research first. Go home, away from the high energy shop environment and read online reviews—this is another way to redirect the chase of instant gratification into something more productive. Then, if you are still very interested in a particular item and have budgeted accordingly, you can make a well-informed purchase and appreciate it more.

Have a look around your home and be honest about the stuff you own. Did you need it all? Did you plan each purchase, especially the larger-cost items? Of course not, no one is perfect. The aim is to reduce bad habits which don't help your financial situation.

It's easy these days to spend on impulse, especially online. Online shops are only a click away and you are constantly over-stimulated by marketing campaigns. The feeling of instant gratification that comes from buying can be addictive. If struggling to control your online shopping, give yourself and the checkout button some space.

Often, it's the fun of browsing and selecting items that's most appealing with online shopping, rather than the actual process of imputing credit card/debit card details. Try browsing online and adding what you want to the cart, but then put your smartphone down or step away from your computer, rather than going straight to the checkout page. Give yourself time to 'cool off' and then close the website. Don't jump into completing an online purchase.

STRATEGY 2: INSTEAD OF THIS, I REALLY WANT THAT

If you have a particular thing or experience in mind that you really want, keep it in mind to help talk yourself out of making other, more frequent impulse purchases which see you buying other stuff in place of what you really want. The money that you spend elsewhere on stuff will only take away from that particular thing or experience which you really want. Regardless of the amount, even if it's only $10 or $20, that $10 or $20 can go towards what you actually desire. It all adds up. It all 'buys milk' as a friend of mine says.

If you have no particular thing or experience in mind right now, nothing better to aim towards, make it up or just keep your options open. You never know what the universe may throw at you in the future. It's just a matter of saving money 'for something better' that no doubt will come along, as it always does.

STRATEGY 3: DON'T SHOP WHEN HUNGRY

Have you ever been grocery shopping whilst hungry? Did you end up buying more groceries than you intended or bought items not on your list? Staring at all that food on the shelves whilst hungry is enough to drive anyone crazy, and it only makes sense that you end up grabbing extra food from the shelves because your brain naturally thinks you will be eating it straight away. I am sure that our brains don't register the fact that we still need to finish shopping and pay at the checkout. The desire to have an immediate food fix is generally over by that time. Shopping when hungry doesn't work for me. What about you?

STRATEGY 4: SHOP WITH A LIST

Simple and effective. Whether it be a paper list or an online app using your smartphone, if an item is not on your Shopping List then don't put it in the trolley. Tick items off as you move around the shop. Whilst not foolproof, items can still slip into the trolley especially if 'shopping hungry' or you legitimately forgot to put some items on the list, it sure does help. Having a list will help you to make a conscious decision about each item that you pick up and know when you are buying extras—you will also reduce the extras. Use a list of groceries, clothes or any other items you need/want. For example, having a list of clothes that you want, gives time to think about each item, plan your wardrobe and then search for the perfect item.

STRATEGY 5: CHOOSE THE BEST VALUE

There is a lot of product choice available in supermarkets these days. So much so that it can be quite confusing as to which size bottle/packet/can/jar you select. However, the quantity (amount) you buy and whether you select the smaller size or, the larger size of a product each time can make a difference to your expenses over a year. My Grandfather taught me an invaluable strategy when buying groceries, or any item for that matter, when different quantities are available choose the best 'value'.

TABLE 1: Product A Price Comparison

Size	Price
250ml	$5.00
500ml	$8.50

Which is better value? In this case, the bigger bottle is exactly twice the size of the smaller bottle. If you buy the 500ml bottle, it will cost you $8.50, but if you were to buy 2 x 250ml bottles (also 500ml in total), it would cost you $10.00 (2 x $5.00)—that's more expensive than buying the larger bottle at $8.50. Therefore, it is better value to buy the larger 500ml bottle and save $1.50 for the same quantity. When two package sizes are not exactly double, it's simply a matter of comparing the price per 100ml (or 100g whichever is relevant), to compare 'apples with apples':

TABLE 2: Price Per 100ml Comparison

Size	Price	Price per 100ml
250ml	$5.00	$2.00 ($5.00 / 2.5)
500ml	$8.50	$1.70 ($8.50 / 5)

The bigger bottle is cheaper per 100ml. Some supermarkets are even providing these figures to you for price transparency. You just need to look for at the price tag. I am surprised more people don't do this and instead simply grab the same size product each time, depending on their habits. Make these comparisons often enough, and it becomes second nature and takes a couple of seconds to calculate whilst in the shop.

If a product is a perishable item and you know that you will not use up the larger size before the expiry date, then it makes sense to buy the smaller size. Otherwise, you will end up throwing away the unused product, which is the same as throwing away money.

STRATEGY 6: BUY LESS BUT BUY BETTER QUALITY

It took me a long time to figure this one out. Sounds simple, but it can be a challenge.

I was brought up to appreciate the value of money, but also how scarce it can be and hard to come by. The answer to that for many years was to simply spend less. To always buy a cheaper item instead of a more expensive one (why spend $10 when I could spend $5?)

That way I had 'more' to spend. Sound familiar? Do you buy a lot of low-value items? However, I now also understand that some of those family members who I watched whilst growing up and who passed on their knowledge of money to me had a different relationship with money largely because of their own childhoods (growing up in war-torn Eastern Europe with no money or choice but to spend as little as possible). Spending less meant that money went further in that situation, but living in Australia, my environment is different and I am lucky to have more choices and options available to me. For years I bought cheaper clothes, shoes, and electronics for example, especially in my early 20s and in line with my earnings then (which wasn't much), so that I could buy more stuff and get more 'bang for my buck'. That habit carried through in later years, even as my earnings increased over time.

I have since learnt that in some cases, not all, but definitely some, buying better quality can actually save money in the long-run and that cheaper is not always better. Buying cheap may cost less initially, however cheap items may not last as long, fit as well or work as well as they should. Buying better quality means spending more initially. If the clothes look better, fit better and last longer, or electronics per-form better and are built to last, then it's worth it (and you will not need to buy as often). Assess each item for its own merits. Consider cost vs quality. Price vs value.

The aim is not to spend more than you have to, especially when not necessary, and buying expensive doesn't always mean better quality or that you buy lots of expensive items. Be smart about it. Look for quality and value, not just an expensive price tag. Why pay $50 for a white t-shirt made of the same materials as a $30 white t-shirt? If a product is truly like for like, then why pay extra? That's crazy and missing the point. Compare materials. Compare ingredi-ents. Compare brand history. Buying less, along with buying better quality is a happy medium between buying cheap and wasting money.

STRATEGY 7: DON'T 'LIVE GUCCI', DON'T 'BUY GUCCI'

A hairdresser I know has a 'handbag fetish' and spends most of her surplus money on handbags. Not just any handbags, very expensive designer handbags. Nothing wrong with buying luxury items such as designer handbags, if that's what you like, however the problem was that the hairdresser also often complained to me about 'never having any money' or 'not being able to buy her own home'.

Now I love a good handbag as much as the next girl. To buy designer handbags or other luxury items that cost hundreds of dollars, sometimes thousands, when you earn an income that's not in line with that level of non-essential spending is crazy. The hairdresser knew that I am 'good with money' so asked me one day how to stop herself from buying luxury items and have more self-control to get ahead financially. I answered:

'You don't 'live Gucci' so why buy Gucci?'

What I meant by that was, if your house, car, and suburb don't correspond with walking around with a very expensive designer handbag on your arm then why do it? Why give off the image of someone with lots of money (who can afford those types of items) if in fact you can't and don't spend that kind of money in other areas of life? If wanting to 'walk the walk' then be sure to have the total lifestyle to match. If those luxury items are holding you back from progressing financially and mean that you don't also have the car or home you desire, then you cannot afford the bags.

Now I don't mean that you must spend an exactly equal amount in all areas of life before indulging in a designer handbag or luxury item from time to time—if that's what you desire—just consider your overall lifestyle before spending significant money on luxury items, especially at the cost of your financial happiness. If you have no savings or investments but have a closet full of luxury items, expensive restaurant bills or other things that you really can't afford (whatever your spending fetish may be), then you cost yourself money now and in the future. Hold back on the luxury for a while and create a comfortable financial situation for yourself, which in turn will help you afford more of those luxury items in the future. To drive a crappy car, live in a dodgy suburb and live payday to payday without savings, investments, and security, with a fabulous bag on your arm, doesn't match up. You need to make deliberate choices as to what you spend your money on and live within your means. Remember, don't be stingy with money—be selective. If you want to be able to afford luxury items then put away a regular amount of savings each payday and when you have the money you need treat yourself. If those luxury items are getting in the way of, say, your 10% Savings, then reassess the value that you are placing on those luxuries. Leave the bags for a while, until your finances are in order.

STRATEGY 8: CHECK EVERYTHING... YOUR BILLS, RECEIPTS ETC

This is so simple to do, yet so overlooked. Whenever you are billed or invoiced for money, from anyone, you must check the bill to ensure that it's correct. Check for errors or overcharges—whether you are standing in a shop reaching for your wallet or sitting behind your computer. Even if you pay some bills using automated payments or direct debits, you will still receive a copy of the bill in the mail or email—check it. This includes café and restaurant bills, household bills, bank account statements, credit card statements and rental property statements. Waiters make mistakes. Shop Assistants make mistakes. Bank tellers make mistakes. Rental agents make mistakes. We all do. Companies make mistakes, especially big companies. If anything looks 'off' in your bill, or you can't quite work out how the charges were calculated or what a particular amount is actually for—query it with the company, taking the time to ask a question, make a phone call or send an email (and follow it up) can save you big time. Be sure to check all charges made to credit cards and debit cards. Are there any double-ups? Did you authorise each purchase? Do you have any recurring charges that perhaps you forgot about and need to cancel? A magazine subscription that you don't even read anymore? Or beauty product reorders from telemarketers? Or ongoing donations you forgot that you agreed to?

On the flipside, if money is due to you, say a refund from a company, then make a reminder in your diary for a couple of weeks' time to check that you received it—if not, contact the company (again) to follow up and make another diary reminder.

I can't tell you how many times I've avoided being overcharged or missing out on money simply by checking my bills. It takes a matter of seconds. Don't just hand over money.

To be time effective, limit the checking and paying of household bills to once per week—nominate one day a week (Thursday works well) to check/pay everything at once—that's much more productive than devoting a little time to it each and every day. Be different. Be in control—it's your money at stake. This year, become a Financial Pitbull. Don't allow anything to get past you—it's your money.

Chapter 10 summary

- Don't be stingy with money—be selective. Live deliberately.
- Stop wasting money.
- Reducing your expenses will create immediate surplus cash flow.
- Be in control of your money—don't be financially lazy.
- Check everything—bills, statements, receipts etc.
- Become a Financial Pitbull. Nothing should get past you—remember it's your money.

CHAPTER 11

How To Increase Your Income

t doesn't matter how much you earn, you can still get ahead financially and create more with what you have, even if you earn just an 'average' income. Two people earning the same income can have vastly different lifestyles and financial situations. It all depends on how they choose to spend.

What's important is that you:

- **Regularly Save**: 10% of income for your future (home loan deposit or other investments), plus an extra amount for emergencies and 'just in case'.
- **Spend Wisely**: make deliberate choices every time you spend money and don't waste money. Spend less on everyday expenses so you have more to invest.

Consistency is the aim of the game. Remember, when I started working full-time 20 years ago at age 17, I was earning the grand sum of $230 per week. At that time it wasn't a lot. Today, it's not a lot, but it's what I had to work with. The choices I made with that money enabled me to lay a solid foundation and achieve great results, even with a meagre income. However, if you can also increase your income, why wouldn't you? Earning a higher income can help speed up your financial progress and enjoy a few extras along the way.

Consider the following ways to increase your income:

- Pay Rise: Just ask. If you don't ask you don't receive.
- Training and Education: Undertake further education or training to increase your skills set and make yourself more valuable to an

employer and therefore able to command a higher salary. Some education costs that are in line with improving your current occupation may be tax deductible (check with an Accountant). Your employer may have a budget available for staff education and training and cover some or all costs (if you ask).

- Change Careers: What do you enjoy? What other work are you able to do for money? It might be as easy as applying for an alternative job and moving on. You never, never know if you never, never go. (www.seek.com.au)
- Change Employment Type: Become a freelancer or contractor— stay in the same line of work as you are now however change the way you are paid. Becoming self-employed by doing the same work on a freelance basis can significantly increase your income.

In today's world, more and more companies are getting used to the idea of outsourcing tasks to freelancers and contractors, rather than employing more full-time staff. Outsourcing can often be more cost-effective for companies and is becoming increasingly accepted and utilised. Whether tasks are outsourced for a limited time during busier periods or permanently on an ongoing basis, there are options available for many different occupations to do some freelance work on the side or to replace a full-time job.

Benefits of becoming a freelancer or contractor (vs. employee):

- **Higher Pay**: set your own hourly rate or price per job, usually significantly more than an 'employee' doing the same work.
- **Unlimited Earnings**: no salary cap. You can be paid more for doing the same (or less) amount of work, in less time.
- **Flexible Hours**: start out small and build up with minimal risk.
- **Work from Home**: be in the comfort of your own home.
- **Efficiency**: fewer interruptions compared to some workplaces, no phones ringing, colleagues interrupting you or endless staff meetings.

- **Save Time**: no commute to a workplace. Use that time to get more work done, go to the gym, be at home with children or work on other projects/businesses.
- **Tax Benefits**: additional tax deductions are available when working from home.

Things to consider:
- **Variable Income**: this can be inconsistent although it will average out over a year.
- **Time**: takes time to develop a long-term, reliable client base.
- **Discipline**: you must be disciplined to get work done quickly and efficiently. The beauty is, the more efficient you are, the more profit you can make.
- **Distractions**: working from home is not for everyone—stay out of the fridge and turn off the TV!
- **Accounting**: greater responsibilities for self-employed people, the need for a business number and to keep adequate records for your accountant at tax time.
- **Staff Benefits**: Superannuation Contributions, Annual Leave and Sick Leave are usually your responsibilities, but earning a significantly higher hourly rate is meant to compensate you for the loss of those types of 'employee benefits'.

Working as a remote freelancer/contractor may not be available to every occupation, especially if your occupation is site-specific, meaning you must be in a specific setting to do your job tasks, whether it's a mine site, shopfront, factory or medical lab/clinic, etc. However, if you are experienced in any sort of administration, personal assistant, executive assistant, secretary, teaching/tutoring, programming and tech, web design, graphic design, digital marketing, writing and translation, video and animation, music and audio or other consultation services, then look into it—in addition to your regular job (for extra money), or with the aim to eventually replace your job.

Speak to your employer about outsourcing certain tasks to you (outside of office hours working from your home). You can earn more but also create more time during office hours to get on with other tasks, which the business may be struggling to complete because of the day-to-day (more mundane tasks) that keep getting in the way, for example. Be creative. Or, suggest to your employer that you work one or two days a week from home in order to increase your efficiency by not having the distractions of the office. This can be a good way of testing the water and opening the conversation in the future about changing from employee to full-time freelancer/ contractor. Even though it may not change your hourly rate at first, you can complete work quicker and more efficiently, plus reduce commute time and other workplace stresses, all of which result in more time for you and a better lifestyle.

If your current job will not agree to any kind of freelancing or contracting possibilities or working from home at all, then consider sourcing work that's separate from your 'day job' using online advertisements (www.gumtree.com.au or Facebook Communities) or specific freelancing sites such as:

VIRTUAL ASSISTANT

Freelancer www.freelancer.com.au

A Virtual Assistant is just as a personal assistant but works from home, normally for a small number of different clients. Clients benefit because they get the help they need to run their business without the cost, risk and hassle of employing someone. You benefit because you get to work from home, choosing your hours to suit you.

FREELANCE PROJECTS

Up Work www.upwork.com

If your occupation has you complete 'jobs' or 'projects' for clients, consider growing your own freelance business.

◆ Freedom to work on ideal projects: you run your own business and choose your own clients and projects. Just complete your profile and Up Work will highlight ideal jobs. Also, search projects and respond to client invitations.

- ◆ Wide variety and high pay: clients are now posting jobs in hundreds of skill categories, paying top price for great work.
- ◆ More and more success: the greater the success you have on projects, the more likely you are to be hired by clients that use Up Work.

Fiverr www.fiverr.com
Work Your Way. You bring the skill. Fiverr makes earning easy.

Whilst you may work more hours initially by taking on extra freelance work around your day job, it's possible to increase your freelancing income to the point where you can quit your day job if that's something you aim for. Working from home as a freelancer may not be for everyone. It is definitely a wonderful way to potentially earn more money whilst staying in the same type of work.

> *Full-time income from freelancing is definitely possible and realistic. I know, because I am a full-time freelancer. I changed from a full-time employee role to freelancing over 10 years ago and because of the flexibility and the income have never looked back. The rate I earn per job (for numerous Financial Planners) is more than I can possibly earn per hour sitting in an office all week writing those same plans for one Financial Planner.*
>
> *Plus, I love working from home, with minimal distractions and stress, meaning I complete work more efficiently (and therefore earn more money) without wasting time commuting to an office. It takes discipline. The anticipation of being paid only after completing a job sure is motivation enough for me.*
>
> *Can this also work for you?*

Jessica's real-life results

I have a friend, let's call her Jessica. Jessica worked in an office as a full-time employee working 40 hours per week in an administration role. She earned $40,000 ($19.23 per hour) for that year of work and had the normal inconveniences of commuting to work, paying for parking, being away from her home and children during the day and childcare costs/worries.

To earn some extra money on the side, Jessica listed herself on various websites as a Virtual Assistant, offering her administration and secretarial services. Depending on the jobs Jessica was hired for, the payment was calculated as 'per job' or 'per hour'. The work was very flexible and Jessica was able to do it from the comfort of her own home (around her existing job and children).

The main difference was the hourly rate that Jessica was paid for that freelancing work was over $30.00 compared to $19.23 per hour in her day job (for the same work). Jessica also saved time and money by not having to commute to a second job location or pay additional childcare costs.

Chapter 11 summary

- First, create immediate surplus income by reducing expenses.
- Second, consider ways to increase your income—pay rise, training/education, change of career or employment type.
- Become a freelancer or contractor.
- Consider working from home—virtual assistant/freelance projects.

CHAPTER 12

Why You Must Invest

What is 'investing'?

It is to put money into financial schemes, shares, property or a commercial business venture with the expectation of achieving a profit.

Money isn't everything, but it sure does give you choices in life. There are only two ways to make money:

1. Work for your money (be paid for every hour of work you do)
2. Invest your money (make money work for you/passive income)

Saving money is the first step to creating wealth and means more money in your back pocket. It's the fundamental basis of all successful money management. Unfortunately it doesn't mean that your money is working for you. Without also investing, you will never have any more money than what you can save.

The purpose of investing is to make money; more money than what you physically earn from a job. To create real wealth, you need to save first and invest second. By investing your money properly, your money will earn 'interest' (income) and go up in value over time (capital growth).

Whether you want to be able to send your children to a tertiary school of their choice or to retire early to the south of France, you need to invest. Maybe you are young, don't have children and are not even thinking about an early retirement, however you definitely want to afford the nicer things in life (well before retirement)—those nicer, more costly things such as a house, car, boat etc will take more than just saving up your salary.

The kind of investing I am referring to is when cold hard cash is used to buy financial assets such as property and shares—even term deposits—with the view that they will go up in value. Investing doesn't need to be complicated. Some people will invest in businesses or 'collectibles'—jewellery, valuables, art, etc which they collect with the hope of the value going up over time, or gold bars/different currencies, which they may trade for profit. Those are speculative and specialised investments and outside the scope of this book. Let's talk about the types of fundamental investments which you have access to and can all use to make real life money—term deposits, shares, and property. Let's get 'old school' because it works.

Risk vs. Return

The 'return' you make on an investment is your 'reward' for investing (the reward you receive for risking your money)—calculated risk though, not casino risk. The risk is the possibility of losing your money. Whether an investment is worthy of risking your money depends on the return you may make and of course how likely you are to actually achieve that return, otherwise known as the 'risk vs. return' trade-off.

There are five main different types of investments (asset classes): cash, fixed interest, property, Australian shares and international shares. Each has its own level of risk as well as a potential return. The following graph demonstrates the higher the risk (changes in investment value) then the higher the potential return (money you make).

GRAPH 1: Risk vs. Reward*

Risk vs return – trade off

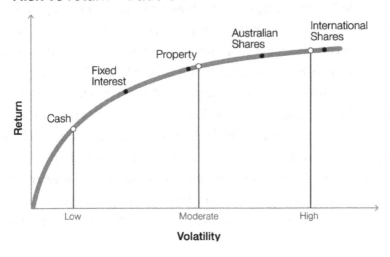

*Provided by Financial Professionals.

The aim of investing is not to take as much risk as possible but to take enough risk to justify the return. If you can achieve a suitable return (to help you reach your goals) by taking on a lower level of risk then why risk your money and take on more risk? All investments carry some risk. By making quality investments, preferably smaller investments for a longer period (just like your savings), you can reduce your risk further and make the return worthwhile. For example, lower-risk investments such as high-interest bank accounts and term deposits may return you say 1%–3% per annum (p.a.), whereas higher-risk investments such as property and shares might return you anywhere from 7%–10% p.a. and so much more. Compare those to everyday bank accounts, which may offer only 0.1% p.a. (if that). You must diversify away from only keeping money in the bank. The cost of living increases each year. That's called 'inflation'. The cost of inflation is around 2.5% p.a. So earning just 0.1% p.a. from your bank account actually means that your money is going backwards over time. What's riskier than investing is to not invest at all!

Note that cars and homes (a property that you live in) are not included in the property asset class, that's because they are not investments (assets that make you money), they are liabilities (things that cost you money). 'Property' means investment properties—a property which is rented out for income.

The secret of the rich is to buy assets which go up in value and which make more money, to then afford the nicer things in life, whilst also having money left over. The more you invest, the more money you make.

Income vs. Growth

The return on an investment can be 'income' (dividends or rent) or 'growth' (the increase in the value), or a combination of the two.

◆ **Income Investments** generally lower-risk and pay a rate of interest (income) e.g. bank interest. Includes Cash (bank accounts) & Fixed Interest (term deposits).

◆ **Growth Investments** aims to grow the original amount invested (the capital) as much as possible and outperform the cost of inflation (living). A higher-risk compared to income investments and should be held for a longer time. Includes Property (residential and commercial) and Shares (Australian and international). Growth investments can also earn income such as share dividends or investment property rent.

Whether you choose income or growth investments, or a combination of the two, depends on what you want to achieve with your money.

Types of Investments (Asset Class)

Type	Description
Cash (Income)	Bank Accounts, High Interest and Cash Management Accounts are most common. Low risk, very secure, at-call access to funds. Income only, no capital growth. Returns depend on interest rates at the time. As they are low risk, the returns are quite low and may or may not outperform inflation i.e. bank accounts may pay 0.1% p.a. but Higher Interest & Cash Management Accounts may pay 1.0% p.a.
Fixed Interest (Income)	Term Deposits are the most common, whereby you deposit an amount of money with a bank or other institution for a set term (time), such as 3–12 months or more and in return you receive a specific amount of interest income (at the maturity date). Low risk, very secure, funds locked away for a set time. Income only, no growth. Higher returns than bank accounts, but still quite low in the scheme of things. The longer the term (and the more you invest), the higher the interest paid to you should be. Penalties may apply for breaking the term early e.g. forfeit the income promised. Other fixed interest investments include bonds, mortgage trusts, and loans.

TABLE 1: Example of Term Deposits Rates: Investment of $5,000–$499,999*

Term	Interest at Maturity/ Annually
3 months	2.10% p.a.
6 months	2.10% p.a.
9 months	1.80% p.a.
12 months	2.40% p.a.
24 months	2.60% p.a.

*Current at time of writing. National Australia Bank 'Blackboard Specials' (shown as example not a recommendation to invest).

In this example, if you invested $10,000 into a Term Deposit for 6 months, you receive interest of around $105 at maturity, as payment for leaving your money with the bank (for the bank to use) for 6 months (without you withdrawing it).

Type	Description
Property (Income and Growth)	• Residential Property: for many people it may be their first and most significant investment and may be purchased for housing rather than as an investment to make a profit, whereas some buy property to rent out as an investment solely. • Commercial Property: includes offices, shopfront and industrial properties such as warehouses and factories) and generally held for higher rental income compared to residential property (but also higher cost and risk). • Earns rental income (paid by a tenant) and capital growth (increase in the property value). Can be a wonderful, medium-risk investment. • Provides good tax advantages as well as allowances offered by the government for people to borrow money to invest (into property). • However, with the upside come risks such as poor suburb selection, lack of tenant, maintenance costs. Usually, a property is purchased with borrowed money (loan), so if you pick a poor performing suburb, you can lose money and even end up owing more money to the bank than what the property is worth. • Poor liquidity: you can't sell the front door if you need some cash, you have to sell the whole property. So, it's very important to have a good amount of emergency cash saved up, i.e. for times when the property is vacant. • Higher risk compared to cash and fixed interest but also much higher returns, especially over the long term. Still considered relatively 'safe' by many ('as safe as houses'), provided that a 'good quality' property was selected.
Australian Shares (Mainly growth with some income)	• When you buy shares, you become a partial owner of the company and therefore share in any profit and capital growth that the company makes. Australian shares are for companies listed on the Australian Stock Exchange. • Earns income through dividends (distribution of the company profit) and capital growth (increase in the company value). Can have tax benefits attached such as Franking Credits (imputation credits) which help to reduce the amount of tax you pay. • Good liquidity, meaning you can sell part of your shares if you need cash, but the sale price will fluctuate daily and differ to what you originally paid (the aim is to sell for higher than you paid of course). Risks like with owning any business such as cost increases, regulation changes, and competitors. If the company doesn't do well, then your shares won't either. • Higher-risk compared to cash and fixed interest but also much higher returns, especially over the long term. Lower risk than International Shares.

International Shares (Mainly growth)	• Allows you to become a partial owner of an international company, the same as with Australian Shares. Offers opportunities not available in the Australian share market and provide good diversification as the economy of different countries grow at different rates. The Australian share market only represents about 2% of the world market. • Australian shares are relatively easy to buy and sell, whereas investing directly into International shares can be more difficult for the general investor. You may need an international share broker or access to international trading platforms. Most Australians will hold some international shares through pooled investments, such as managed funds through their superannuation. • Considered to be the highest risk asset class and price fluctuations can be volatile, but returns should also be the highest over the long term.

Spreading your money between different asset classes can reduce investment risk because each asset class performs differently over time. Holding different types of investments can help to achieve more consistent overall returns, because when one asset class is 'down', another asset class may be 'up', for example when bank interest rates are low, the Australian share market is usually higher (increasing and performing well) and vice versa. It's global economics.

Investment Timeframe

The length of time you invest for (investment timeframe) is critical to improving the likelihood of achieving a good return. Each type of investment has a minimum timeframe over which it needs to be left to perform (deliver your return). Generally, higher-risk investments should be held for a longer period, to reduce the impact of short-term price fluctuations. Usually, the longer you hold an investment, the less your overall risk will be, even if a particular investment is quite volatile in the shorter-term.

◆ Short-term (up to 3 years): cash and fixed interest
◆ Medium Term (3–5 years): mixed portfolios of short and long-term assets
◆ Long-term (5 years +): property and shares

Trading investments are the art of buying and selling investments over shorter periods of time for profit and can include share trading and even flipping properties, i.e. buying, renovating and selling relatively quickly. Trading is a learnt skill, takes more time and is not for everyone, whereas most people can find comfort in buying and holding good quality investments over the long-term, which is more of a passive approach to investing (rather than active) but has its benefits.

It's the low fuss approach to making money in the 'background' of life.

GRAPH 2: Asset Class Value Fluctuations

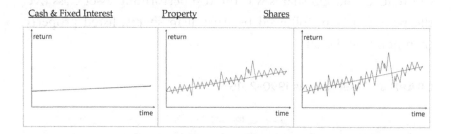

Here you can see that the cash and fixed interest investment didn't fluctuate in price at all, the only increase in value was because of the interest income earned.

The property investment fluctuated more, and the shares fluctuated even more. Yes, property values also fluctuate, quite a lot in fact. The difference is that property prices are not valued daily, whereas share prices are easily advertised on the stock exchange in bright shiny lights and reported in the nightly 6pm news. Even with the price fluctuations, over the long term, the value of the property and shares still went up and outperformed the cash and fixed interest investments. The investment returns 'smoothed out' over the long-term because of **time in** the market, rather than **timing** the market and because of 'compound interest'—we'll discuss that soon.

Holding good quality investments is important—holding a 'bad' investment for the long-term will not necessarily turn it into a 'good' investment. If unsure whether to sell or hold an investment you have then it's best to seek advice from an Investment Adviser such as a Financial Planner, Stockbroker or Real Estate Agent, etc.

The chart below shows the performance of various asset classes over the last 25 years. All asset classes increased over that long-term. There can be a benefit in diversifying a portfolio of investments across each asset class, to help reduce volatility and smooth out returns over time. Blending asset classes over longer time periods can reduce risk. US shares was the top performing asset class over the period shown, followed by Australian shares, listed property, then bonds and cash.

GRAPH 3: Asset Returns 1990-2016*

*Graph provided by AMP.

Compound Interest—The Game Changer

'Compound Interest' is the real power of investing—when the interest (income) from an investment is reinvested and earns more interest. The interest earns interest on top of the interest, which earns more interest. Compound interest is incredibly powerful.

The longer you invest for, the better you can take advantage of compound interest.

If you invest $10,000, which returns 5% p.a. and you reinvest those earnings back into the investment as you go along, it may be worth $12,762 after five years. If you leave that same investment to grow for 10 years, it may then be worth $16,288. The higher the return, the higher the compound interest. Instead, if the investment returns 7% p.a., it may be worth $14,025 after five years or $19,671 after 10 years. The secret is 'time in' the market, rather than 'timing' the market.

GRAPH 4: The Power of Compound Interest: Three Different Investors, earning 7%*

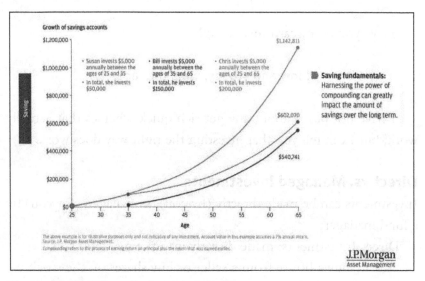

*Graph provided by JP Morgan Funds, www.businessinsider.com

The graph shows three investors Susan, Bill and Chris. Each invested $5,000 per year (that's less than $100 per week). Bill (lower line) invested $150,000 over 30 years and ends up with $540,741 at 65.

Susan (middle line) invested $50,000 over 10 years and ends up with $602,070 at 65. Susan ends up with more money than Bill but invested less money. Why? It's because although Susan invested less money, she started earlier. By leaving her 'smaller' investment to grow for longer, Susan benefited more from compound interest.

In comparison, the third investor Chris (top line) is the ideal scenario—Chris started investing even earlier than Susan and added to his investment for more years. Chris invested $200,000 over 45 years (still $5,000 per year) but had $1,142,811 by 65.

Just like putting away your regular savings, a little goes a long way if done consistently. Imagine what you can achieve over your lifetime if you start today. Regardless of your age or financial position, it's never too late to start saving or investing.

Aim to save and invest consistently, for as long as possible.

Have you ever heard this saying?

'Slow and steady, wins the race.'

I have not heard about any get rich quick schemes that actually work, but I can tell you that investing the right way does work.

Direct vs. Managed Investments

Investments can be made directly (by you) or managed (for you) by a fund manager:

- Direct Investments: made directly into the markets. You literally buy a house from a seller or buy shares on the stock exchange or place a term deposit with a bank. This can require large amounts of money and may need borrowed funds (especially for direct property). To invest directly, you need to take the time to learn about the asset class. You need to do research accordingly as to what investment to buy or seek advice from other professionals (Real Estate Agent, Stockbroker, Financial Planner). Direct investments also take time afterwards to monitor and manage—you make the decision on what to buy and sell, so you have to keep an eye on market trends and changes to tax and law.

◆ Managed Investments—allow you to pool money together with other investors, even though you don't know the other investors. Professional fund managers offer 'managed funds' into which you deposit money and buy units (shares) in the investment. The fund manager administers and manages your investment with the aim of making you profit (buys/sells on your behalf), whilst monitoring economic and legislative changes which affect your money. The fund manager charges a percentage fee for their expertise (for you to be part of the fund). You receive help to select and manage the investment and pay a fee for that service. Managed funds can remove the guesswork from investing if you don't know where to start.

Benefits of Direct Investments include:

◆ Profit: you are on your own with direct investments so to speak, but that also means that you keep all of the profit as well.

◆ Control: you decide on everything—what you invest in, when you invest, how much money you invest, for how long you invest, etc. You have total control and ownership over the transactions made, whereas a fund manager will make the decisions for a managed fund.

◆ Transparency: you know exactly what you are invested in. Fund managers must disclose what approximate investments will be held in a fund (percentage ranges), but will not disclose their exact portfolio holdings, so their competitors don't know. That can make it more difficult to analyse exactly what investments you hold in a managed fund, whereas you know exactly what you hold with direct investments because you place the direct investment yourself.

◆ Fees: direct investment fees can be lower than managed investments, i.e. shares purchased on the stock exchange have no ongoing management fees attached whereas a managed fund does. That management fee can be quite high for some managed funds (generally range from 0.25% up to 4% p.a. +), especially if the fund is a specialised, boutique type portfolio. When share markets are low, some share-based managed funds can find it tough to outperform the market after taking into account their management fee, i.e. if the management fee is 4% p.a. then your fund needs to return you at least 4% p.a., for you just to break even.

Benefits of Managed Investments include:

◆ Start Small: to invest in a managed fund, you need a much smaller amount of money (minimum $1,000). That small amount can give you exposure to the various sectors of the market and dozens of individual shares. Managed funds also allow you to add a regular amount to your fund. Adding as little as $100 per month can add up over a long period of time, and you can stop and start the additions.

◆ Diversification: enables you to invest in different asset classes, companies, industries, sectors and even countries, which can reduce risk by minimising the impact of poor performance in a particular area. To diversify direct investments in the same way requires larger amounts of money.

◆ Access: can provide access to assets which may otherwise be difficult to access due to factors such as financial limitations (shopping centres), market access (international markets) or where it's difficult to gain research or information (small micro-cap stocks in emerging markets).

◆ Cost Effective: investing directly in shares or property comes at a cost. Expenses such as brokerage, stamp duty, and agent's fees can have a significant effect on the value of your investment. Managed funds allow you to access certain investments at a fraction of the usual cost (albeit higher costs than holding direct shares for example). This is because you share these costs with other members of the fund, rather than paying all fees on your own.

- Expert Managers: managed by professionals who have the education and skill to make appropriate investment decisions. These experts have access to investment research and information, which may not be easily available to individual investors.
- Good Liquidity: you don't need to sell an entire portfolio to access money from a managed investment. You can generally access your money within 5-10 days. Accessing money in direct investments, particularly property, can be very difficult, costly and time-consuming (you can't just sell the front door of a property if you need some quick cash).

One of the main reasons that people choose a managed fund is the skill of the fund manager. If a fund manager can outperform its benchmark (the rest of the market), net of management fees, then it's worth paying management fees. For others, direct investments may be much more profitable or enjoyable—depending on how active you wish to be in your own investing. A combination of the two = magic.

Types of Managed Funds

Managed funds can be used as a means to invest in one (or a combination) of the major asset classes. The types of funds include:

CAPITAL GUARANTEED (LOW RISK)
- Guarantees that the capital you have invested will not fall in value.
- Tend to be heavily weighted in cash and fixed interest type investments.
- Investors may pay a fee or premium for the guarantee over their investment.

CASH & FIXED INTEREST (LOW RISK)
- Usually invest in securities (such as bills and bonds) issued by financial institutions including banks, Government, and semi-Government authorities. Known as 'defensive' funds.

- Cash funds are suitable for short-term liquidity requirements and emergency needs, while fixed interest funds are good as a source of regular interest income.
- Focus on generating an income stream with a lower risk of capital loss.

CAPITAL STABLE (LOW RISK)
- The majority is invested via cash and fixed interest. A smaller proportion is usually held in shares and property to provide some growth to the fund.

BALANCED (MEDIUM RISK)
- Invest in all asset classes, usually weighted towards growth assets.
- Generally subject to a higher level of volatility than defensive funds yet long-term performance is expected to be higher.

GROWTH (HIGHER RISK)
- Focus on long-term capital growth rather than income and are generally suited to people who don't need to access their money for at least five years.

SECTOR SPECIFIC
- Generally invest in only one asset class, with a small holding of cash to meet liquidity requirements. Allows an investor to be 'overweight' in an asset class, so there is the potential to achieve a higher level of return and in-turn, a higher level of volatility.

> *Did you know...?*
> *Your superannuation fund is likely to be invested in managed funds; you are already an investor. The investments will generally have been selected on your behalf by the superannuation fund trustee according to your age unless you select a*

portfolio of your own. Your superannuation statement will show you how your retirement savings are invested. If you are young with many years before retirement, then you generally hold more growth investments (shares and property), for long-term capital growth. If you are in your 50s or 60s and close to retirement, you generally hold a mix of defensive and growth investments (with a more balanced portfolio). If unsure, seek professional advice—after all, it's your money.

Listed Investment Companies (the cousin of managed funds)

There are many, many different types of investments available in the world markets. I can't cover them all in a single chapter, nor is it necessary. This chapter aims to increase your understanding of what investments are available to you from the beginning, not advanced investment strategies.

I have discussed direct vs. managed investments. Another type of investment which is worth mentioning is Listed Investment Companies (LICs), which have some similarities to managed funds, but also some differences.

LICs are another way of accessing exposure to a range of assets in a single transaction. LICs are a type of investment, actually set up as a company and listed on a stock exchange—in Australia—usually the Australian Securities Exchange (ASX). LICs are bought and sold on the ASX, through a broker or online trading account just as you buy or sell ordinary direct shares. As LICs are companies, dividends are paid to investors and can have tax benefits attached such as franking credits (imputation credits), just like direct shares. Those franking credits can be used to reduce the amount of income tax you pay. Like managed funds, LICs have an external or internal manager who is responsible for selecting and managing the company's investments. The underlying assets can vary between the different LICs, so it's important to understand how the company is investing your money. There are four broad categories:

- Australian Share funds: invest in listed Australian shares.
- International Share funds: invest in shares listed on overseas stock exchanges.
- Private Equity funds: invests in unlisted companies (Australia or overseas).
- Specialist funds: invest in special assets or particular sectors such as wineries, technology companies, infrastructure or property.

The investment approach will be different, ranging from conservative to aggressive. Aggressive funds can have higher returns, but they can also be much higher-risk. The timeframe needed for this type of investment is usually long-term, because of the potential for volatility of the underlying assets.

A major benefit of LICs compared to managed funds is that the management fees of LICs can be much lower than managed funds. Also, you can place the investment direct using your broker or online share trading account to have a hands-on approach to your investment selection if you desire.

Exchange Traded Funds (ETFs)

Another type of investment that has become incredibly popular for both active and passive investors alike are exchange traded funds (ETFs).

ETFs are baskets of securities that track an index, sector, commodity, or other asset, but which can be purchased or sold on an exchange the same as a regular share. ETFs are a low-cost way to access diversified investments and can earn a return similar to an index or a commodity, with a dividend investment plan.

Units in ETFs can be bought and sold through a stockbroker, or online trading platform, the same way you buy and sell shares. ETF prices fluctuate all day as the ETF is bought and sold just like shares; this is different from managed funds.

A major benefit to ETFs is that they offer lower management fees compared to managed funds and fewer broker commissions than buying the shares individually.

Dollar Cost Averaging (adding regular amounts)

Money can be invested either as a lump sum amount or at regular intervals. Whilst not everyone will have a sizeable amount of cash to make a lump sum investment, most people can instead afford to invest a much smaller, fixed amount of money over a regular period of time, known as 'dollar cost averaging'. A fancy name, which simply means adding to your investment—regularly.

Consider it as a 'savings plan' if you will. Instead of saving into a bank account, you save into an investment. This strategy provides a disciplined way to invest for the future, as it gets you into the habit of investing on a regular basis, the same as you save money on a regular basis—after implementing what you have learnt from this book.

Dollar cost averaging also reduces the chance of investing your money at a bad time as your money is invested in smaller, regular intervals, rather than on one single day. If you invest on a regular basis rather than investing all at once, you can minimise the effect of a market downturn. Investing regularly, regardless of whether the market is up or down, means that you achieve an 'average' unit price over time (buy some high and some low), rather than a single price for all your money.

Jim and Jane both have $12,000 to invest for the long-term (5-plus years). Jim invests $12,000 once-off in January, at a unit price of $1.00. Jane invests $1,000 regularly each month, at various unit prices each time as follows:

TABLE 2: Dollar Cost Averaging Example

Month	Investment unit price	Jim's Investment	Units purchased	Jane's Investment	Units purchased
January	$1.00	$12,000	12,000	$1,000	1,000
February	$1.02	-	-	$1,000	980
March	$0.97	-	-	$1,000	1,031
April	$0.92	-	-	$1,000	1,087
May	$0.95	-	-	$1,000	1,053
June	$0.89	-	-	$1,000	1,124
July	$0.95	-	-	$1,000	1,053

Month	Investment unit price	Jim's Investment	Units purchased	Jane's Investment	Units purchased
August	$1.10	-	-	$1,000	909
September	$0.96	-	-	$1,000	1,042
October	$1.03	-	-	$1,000	971
November	$1.02	-	-	$1,000	980
December	$1.07	-	-	$1,000	935
Total Invested	-	**$12,000**	**12,000**	**$12,000**	**12,165**

Assuming a unit price of $1.07 at the end of the year, the portfolio return is as follows:

Assumed Price $1.07 per unit	Jim	Jane
Market value	$12,840 (12,000 x $1.07)	$13,016 (12,165 x $1.07)
Total return	7.00%	8.47%
Dollar cost averaging benefits	-	**$175 (1.47%)**

The unit price went up as well as down. By investing each month, Jane was able to purchase more units when the unit price fell and made $175 more than Jim, even though they invested the same amount of $12,000. Jim, on the other hand, didn't benefit during the period the unit price dropped. By investing each month, Jane achieved a greater investment return (+1.47% more than Jim).

ADDING TO MANAGED FUNDS

Managed funds provide an easy way to use Dollar Cost Averaging as you can set up a managed fund with a small initial amount (of around $1,000) plus an ongoing monthly amount as low as $100 per month, with no additional fees charged for the monthly direct debit from your nominated bank account. This is a major attraction for managed funds when you are starting out with investing.

ADDING TO LICs AND ETFs

LICs and ETFs can be a little trickier to add to on a frequent basis as they are bought and sold on the stock exchange (ASX), and therefore brokerage fees are payable each time you add to the investment. To limit brokerage fees, it can be advantageous to save regular amounts into a bank account first and then add quarterly amounts to an LIC or ETF. This may reduce the benefit of dollar cost averaging a little, in turn though you will reduce brokerage costs (which immediately eat into your net return).

....

CASE STUDY

Real-life 'Dollar Cost Averaging' results

I am a huge fan of direct property investing, but I also have some managed funds for diversification and to access markets that I otherwise wouldn't know how to or know enough about to be able to make a good investment decision. The managed funds are easy to set and forget in the background and tick along nicely in a 'passive' way with a monthly amount being added by me, directly debited from my nominated bank account, whilst I spend my time 'actively' investing in property. The power of adding a small amount to an investment over a long time must be realised and not dismissed.

When I first started working in Financial Planning 20 years ago at age 17, I learnt about managed funds and after a short time made a choice to start investing as they 'seemed like a good idea'. After all, my boss was advising his clients to invest in managed funds and he himself was investing in managed funds (so I followed along). I saved $1,000 cash and invested in my first managed fund, plus I also added $100 per month (I saw the difference that adding a small amount for a long time could make to a portfolio). Soon after I saved another $1,000 and invested in a second, different managed fund plus $100 per month, for a bit of diversification. I kept those funds going for about a year, and as my salary increased a little, I was able to save more and invested in another couple of managed funds. (Remember I was only earning $230 per week net when I first started working, so it was a gradual process over time.) By the time I left that job six years later, age 23, I had kept the managed funds going (and the monthly additions) and had accumulated over $40,000. A great home loan deposit for anyone of any age, even with today's property prices. I didn't know any other 23-year-olds that had $40,000 to their name, built from zero.

Some of the managed funds performed well and some not so good. Throughout that time I had also experienced my first market crash with the burst of the 'Tech Bubble' and yes, I lost some money and made some money. Investing has risks. The important part was that I saved $100 per month into each of the funds ($100 per week spread across the four funds), consistently and without stopping (started small and built up). I got my first taste of being able to have more choices in life, thanks to regular savings and investing—what was I able to buy with $40,000... a new car? Nah, I was more than happy with the one I had (why cash out a growing investment to buy something that goes down in value?). An over-seas holiday? Well, I had already been on my first European holiday (which I saved for in cash using my Holiday Account). I didn't want anything for the time being. Very soon after, I bought my first property at age 23.

....

Money and Children

SAVING FOR A BABY

A couple without children living together in today's modern world is most likely a 'double-income household', meaning both partners work. Both earn an income. In most cases, one partner will stop work after having a baby (at least for a while). Generally, most couples will continue to use both incomes for living expenses throughout the pregnancy. Nothing changes **until** the baby arrives.

Drop to one income NOW, sooner rather than later.

Switch your thinking and instead, start living off only one income now, straight away, from the day you find out you are expecting (or as early as possible). Start saving one income. After all, in nine months, you will be living off only one income for a period of time, that's guaranteed. It might be a few months or a few years. You may as well get used to it now and avoid a monetary shock when you welcome your little bundle of joy into the world. Whilst you can't control everything throughout pregnancy and childhood, you can control your finances and reduce the money-stress for you and your new family. If you can't meet your expenses with just one income now, then you need to reduce your expenses as a couple NOW and get ready for how it WILL BE after the birth.

Whether one or both partners receive any Maternity Leave or not is irrelevant; treat Maternity Leave income as a bonus.

CHILD EDUCATION

Educating children can be one of the most expensive costs. How much money you need to be able to send them to a school of your choice will depend on whether you want your children to go to public or private school and whether they plan to go to University.

For example, if you send two children to a private high school which costs $10,000 per year per child (that's a modest fee example, some can be $20,000 per year or more), then by the time they both finish school, you would have spent over $100,000 on school fees. And that doesn't include the extras for uniforms, books and school camps etc, or the increase in school fees over time (inflation).

Even if you earn a good income, to be able to save $100,000 ready in time for high school, you need to start early. The earlier you start, the less you need to save each month. For example, refer to the following graph, if you start an investment with $2,000 and earn 5% p.a. (reinvested for compound growth), you need to add $437.11 per month to reach $100,000 in 13 years (high school start age).

GRAPH 5: Child Education Savings Example*

Results

After 13 Years	
Starting balance	$2,000
Regular savings	$68,189
Interest	$29,811
Total	$100,000

Savings

Years

You need to save
$437.11 per month
to reach your goal of $100,000 in 13 years

*Money Smart Calculators www.moneysmart.gov.au

The lighter portion represents your investment earnings ($29,811 over 13 years). You contribute (invest) a total of $68,189 + investment earnings $29,811 = $100,000. If $437.11 per month is unaffordable for your budget then you need to increase the time-frame, increase the investment earnings or choose a cheaper school.

If you save a lesser amount, the outcome in 13 years may reduce to:

- Invest $2,000 plus $100 per month = balance of $25,828
- Invest $2,000 plus $200 per month = balance of $47,830
- Invest $2,000 plus $300 per month = balance of $69,833

Even if you don't save the exact amount you need, by the time you need it, something will be better than nothing. Remember, it's your choice to have children. So, if you do decide to go down that expensive road, don't be financially reckless.

One thing you must definitely do is to start a savings account for baby as soon as possible, preferably when you find out that you are expecting. If not, then start when the baby is born. If you are past that point in time then start now. Whether the savings are ultimately used for baby's education or another purpose—such as baby's first car or home loan—the important thing is to have some savings on hand.

Remember, the earlier you start, the less you save each month (fortnight or week). When baby is old enough, and you proudly show baby that you have been saving 'X amount' for nearly as long as baby has been alive, you will pass on the knowledge of just how powerful long-term savings can be and will pass on, I believe, one of the most important lessons in life that is so often overlooked. Be conscious of money. Be conscious of the money lessons you teach a child. Successful money management isn't taught in schools (or many homes), it needs to be, however sadly, it isn't.

Managed funds can be a great way to save for long-term goals such as Child Education. The longer you leave the investment, the better. Whilst there are specific 'Child Education Savings' investments available, I am not a huge fan of such products if they lock you into anything, e.g. how long you must invest for, the amount you must invest or what you can ultimately use the money for. You need to check carefully the Terms & Conditions for fees and minimum lock-in periods (when funds will be released to you).

I much prefer Index managed funds for child savings as they offer excellent flexibility such as low initial investment amounts, low monthly contributions (which can be altered over time) and low management fees. Managed funds also give you access to the funds when needed and most importantly the choice to use the money for things other than just education fees, i.e. say your child doesn't wish to go to University and instead you use the money to help out with their first car or first home loan deposit.

A managed fund can provide flexibility and returns higher than bank interest—so don't rely on a bank account (even a high-interest account) for child savings. Generally, you will be investing for a long time (10 years plus), so look into investing in more growth assets (shares and property funds) and aim for higher long-term 'capital growth' returns.

The important part is to start early with your child saving (especially if you are saving a small amount each month) and be consistent. Then don't touch it.

Gearing (Borrowing Money to Invest)—the next level

Borrowing money to invest is known as 'gearing'. Borrowed money can be invested in direct property, direct shares and also managed funds, for example. It isn't generally used to invest in cash or fixed interest (term deposits), as the returns of a geared investment need to outweigh the cost of borrowing (the loan interest rate) for you to make a profit. If used correctly, gearing can propel your wealth creation and make a substantial difference—mainly because you will have more money to invest from day one (and some tax benefits along the way, which reduces tax and helps pay for the cost of the borrowings).

Gearing can be risky business and is not for everyone, usually higher-income earners (benefit more from the tax breaks), who are prepared to take on higher-risk and with a long-term investment timeframe (5 to 7 years plus). In saying that, there are plenty of people who may not necessarily feel comfortable borrowing money to invest in shares, although have no hesitation to borrow for an investment property… or their own home.

BENEFITS OF GEARING:

- Access to Funds: provides more money to invest now, rather than relying only on savings, i.e. to save enough to buy a property in cash is not realistic for most.
- Increased Returns: borrowing to invest can increase returns when markets rise although it can also increase losses when markets fall. Earning 10% compound interest on a $100,000 share portfolio will grow your investment faster than having only $1,000

invested. Conversely, losing 10% from a $100,000 investment will be a 'bigger loss' compared to 10% from a $1,000 investment— both losses are 10%, but the dollar loss is $10,000 vs. $100.

◆ Tax Efficient: if you have a high marginal tax rate (37% or 45% for example in Australia), gearing can have tax advantages. The interest payable on the loan is tax deductible if the investment earns incomes (share dividends or rental property income, etc). The tax deductions help to reduce the income tax an investor pays.

RISKS OF GEARING:

The more money you borrow the greater the risk, as you need to repay the borrowings regardless of how the investment performs. You need to have a plan for each risk.

◆ Investment Income risk: the income you receive from an investment may be lower than expected. Can you afford the borrowings if you don't receive rental income or share dividends for a period of time?

◆ Interest Rate risk: the interest rate payable on the borrowings can increase. Will you be able to afford the interest costs if the rate rose by 2% or 4% p.a.? What if you have several other loans as well, i.e. home, car, credit card and all those interest rates increased across the board at the same time?

◆ Income risk: what if your income stops because of sickness or injury or you lose your job? Do you have adequate Income Protection insurance? Job security?

◆ Capital risk: What if the investment value falls or the property sells for less than the size of the loan? How will you repay the loan?

Chapter 6 talked about the difference between good vs. bad debt. Gearing is considered 'good debt' because of the tax advantages, whereas loans for cars, holidays or credit card debt etc are 'bad debt' (no tax advantages). Home loans are also considered to be bad debt.

Although we might live in our own property which can increase in value over time, a home is not usually rented out to earn income, so the interest paid for a home loan isn't generally tax deductible (no tax advantages). Do you see the difference? Investments made using good debt can make money. Buying things with bad debt only costs you money.

Gearing an investment is a higher-risk strategy and requires that you always seek professional financial advice to make sure the strategy is right for you. Let's ignore gearing into shares and managed funds for now...

Instead, gearing into a property will be discussed in the next chapter, as most people will undertake a home loan at least once in their lives. Borrowing to buy a home is a form of gearing... the difference is it's done for lifestyle and not investment purposes.

Chapter 12 summary

- Investing is the secret of the rich; earning compound interest is a game changer!
- Saving money is the first step to creating wealth but without also investing you will never have more than what you can save up.
- Investing doesn't need to be complicated.
- Understand risk vs. return and income vs. growth.
- Understand investment timeframe.
- There are five main assets classes: cash, fixed interest, property, Australian shares and international shares.
- Investments can be direct or managed (on your behalf).
- Dollar Cost Averaging is powerful.
- Time in the market vs. timing the market.

CHAPTER 13

Buying Your
First Property

S o, you have made the decision to buy a property. Good on you. Do you actually know how much money you need to buy a property? How much can you actually borrow? How much deposit is required? What other costs are payable? Whether or not you earn enough salary? What your loan repayments will be? What amount of Government assistance is available as a first-home buyer?

Or do you dream of being able to buy your own home but think that it's 'too expensive' and that you will never be able to 'afford it'? Well, that's a limiting belief and is not true. Anyone can, it all depends on how expensive your taste is and what timeframe you allow.

As with anything in life, if you don't investigate what's actually the true situation, then you can't be certain as to whether you can (or can't) afford something you want. You may miss out because what you think is true is not actually the case at all. Some things in life can be easier to do than you think... you need to investigate.

Whether you intend to live in the property (as your home) or rent it out (as an investment), your first step is the same—put together a sufficient loan deposit. The more deposit you save and the higher your salary, then the more you can generally borrow. The more you borrow however, the higher your repayments will be.

Buying Within Your Means

If you are overwhelmed by the concept of having to save thousands of dollars towards a deposit and have no idea as to how one person is meant to do that, then take the pressure off yourself by firstly limiting the amount you spend on a property. The cheaper, less expensive, more affordable, lower-priced the property is, the less deposit you will need and the smaller your loan repayments will be. Yes, you will still need to save a deposit of 5%–20% of the property value. At least 5%–20% of $300,000 (for example) is much less than of $600,000. That's a start—the dollar amount to save up will be less, even though the percentage is the same.

Even if you can save a good deposit or earn a high salary, or you will be buying with a partner (and your combined financial position is much better than buying alone), doesn't mean you have to borrow the maximum amount. Leave a buffer. Buy something at the cheaper end of things to start with and get into the market. Something 'middle of the road' regarding price. Why? because things change in life. Whilst interest rates are low now (right now the lowest they have been in Australia for many years), repayments can seem afford-able—but rates do rise.

Currently, the economy is at the bottom of an interest rate cycle, and they will go up from here—when and by how much is any-one's guess—a possible 2% rise in rates over a period of time may not seem like much but it's deceptive. Increase your interest rate by 2%–4%, and it equates to a 20% increase in repayments. Ouch! Plus, jobs end, health changes, relationships break up, children are born—give yourself some breathing room. Just as you wouldn't (shouldn't) buy a luxury car for your first car, it's also very okay for your first property to be a 'starter home' and not your 'dream home'. If you spend around $250,000–$400,000 on your first home, then yes, it will probably be an apartment (unit, flat or villa) and that's okay. Most people move homes every few years. You will likely live in other homes throughout your life. Don't overextend your budget and spend $500,000–$600,000, even if you are eligible for that size loan.

Property prices vary in the different suburbs of Australia, and yes, some are more expensive than others, much more expensive. One million dollars doesn't buy you much in some parts of Melbourne and Sydney—but I am talking about buying your first home. It's unrealistic for many people to buy a house right in the heart of Melbourne or Sydney to start with. However, with a budget of $250,000–$400,000, you will get a one- or two-bedroom apartment in those locations. If you want a three- or four-bedroom house, then you will need to look at suburbs further away from the main CBD to stay within a budget of $250,000-$400,000.

First home buyers today seem to have very expensive taste right from the start and an ego to match. Don't try to impress anyone. Be smart. There is nothing impressive about struggling financially because you 'bit off more than you can chew' and borrowed too much (just because you were able to at the time).

Spending less doesn't mean buying a crap home that you hate living in. It may be smaller than you would have hoped for, or next to the suburb you really love, or a place that you live in just for a few years before moving on. That's okay. Most people can't buy their dream home at the beginning of their working lives; it's something they work towards over time as they can afford it. To be able to afford a nicer property over time doesn't mean you have to save a larger and larger deposit each time—although it can help. There are other ways to upgrade where you live over time.

The beauty of property ownership is that most properties increase in value—by how much and how soon depends on various factors including the type of property, the location, the price you paid and the timeframe you hold it. That increase in value from your first property can then be used to fund a nicer property in the future, for example (or a second property). Using the gain made from one property towards the next property can be much quicker than trying to save a larger deposit each time you wish to upgrade or buy more properties.

The important part is to get into the market—just get started. Remember, time in the market, rather than always timing the market.

The sooner you start saving towards a deposit, the less you need to save each month, and the sooner you can buy that first property. The sooner you get started, the sooner you are 'invested' and the sooner you can benefit from property value increases, which will far outweigh your savings ability.

Crunching the Numbers

Working out a suitable size home loan for your first property is about finding a balance between the lifestyle you want and the lifestyle you can comfortably afford. If you are currently renting, look at how much rent you pay and what it might possibly increase to, before it would become unaffordable to you—that will give you a good indication of what maximum loan repayments you can afford. However, bear in mind that with property ownership comes extra ongoing costs that you will also have to pay (in addition to loan repayments), which you don't pay as a renter, such as:

◆ Council Rates and Water Rates
◆ Strata Levies (common with units, flats, apartments, etc)
◆ Pest Control
◆ Property Building Insurance
◆ Other Repairs and Maintenance

When you rent a property, the landlord pays those costs. When you own a home, you pay. Factor those extra costs into your total affordability (and leave a buffer). Spending too much on housing (rent or mortgage) is a major reason why people struggle financially. Whilst there is no definite rule, your aim is to spend no more than 25%–35% (approximately) of your gross income on housing and that amount needs to include all related expenses such as utility bills (electricity, water, gas), any property taxes, insurances, etc.

If you are a double-income household, an awesome scenario is to borrow only as much as one salary can afford to repay—just in case. Even if your circumstances don't change or tragedy doesn't strike, doing this will give you much more breathing space to use more of the second salary towards repaying the loan faster or investing elsewhere.

Dip your toes in the water regarding affordability and loan repayment commitment. You can always upgrade the property later, you have time on your side, but it's hard to downgrade quickly if you get into financial strife. Learn from other people's mistakes. I have seen the consequences where people take on too much financial responsibility, and it isn't pretty when things go bad—of course, those people never thought it would go bad... for them. Don't say I didn't warn you! Now, let's get stuck into the nitty-gritty of how many dollars you need to get started.

The Deposit

When speaking to a bank about taking on a home loan, the first two questions you will be asked are:

1. How much deposit have you saved?
2. Do you have a solid employment history?

Without both, it will be difficult to secure a loan. You need to show that you have saved a deposit over time, with true-savings and that you can hold down a steady job (no jumping between employers or changing jobs regularly).

Use your 10% Savings towards a deposit.

The minimum you will need to save is 5% of the property value, as the maximum you can generally borrow is 95%. The ideal deposit to have is 20%, so you borrow only 80%. If you borrow more than 80%, you will need to pay extra fees and charges such as Lenders Mortgage Insurance (LMI), which protects the bank, not you, and can mean thousands of extra dollars added to your loan. Whilst it's not the end of the world to have less than a 20% deposit, it's a case of having the 'more the better'. It will be cheaper for you, with fewer fees and charges, and a smaller loan (less for you to repay and less cost).

In addition to the deposit, there are other costs involved in buying a property. They equate to about an extra 5% of the value, so if you only have a minimum 5% deposit and no other funds for the buying costs, then you won't have enough. So, really you need:

Minimum Deposit = 10% (5% for the loan + an extra 5% for costs)
Ideal Deposit = 25% (20% for the loan + an extra 5% for costs)

As a first-home buyer, aim to save at least 10% of the property value (or more). There are Government grants in place to help fund some of the extra costs.

TABLE 1: Deposit Examples

Property Value	5% Deposit	10% Deposit	20% Deposit
$300,000	$15,000	$30,000	$60,000
$400,000	$20,000	$40,000	$80,000
$500,000	$25,000	$50,000	$100,000

The less you spend on a property, the less you need to save (even though the percentage is the same) and the quicker you can get into the market.

If your heart just sank a little at the thought of having to save $30,000 to afford even a $300,000 property (middle of the road price point), then take a deep breath, it's possible, it's done all the time. It's normal to buy property. It's normal for it to take some time. Plus, these days, there are other ways to put that money together (quicker than you think) as not all of it needs to be true-savings, however the majority must be. It just takes some forethought, some action, and some patience. Keep reading.

Throughout this chapter, let's follow the example shown above— buying a $400,000 property.

Lenders Mortgage Insurance (LMI)

LMI is the insurance premium you pay when borrowing with less than a 20% deposit, as the risk to the bank is higher. It protects the bank (not you) in case you default on the loan and the bank has to sell your home to recover the money, but the sale price is not enough to cover the full loan amount—in that scenario, the LMI pays the shortfall to the bank. However, you are still then liable to repay the shortfall to the LMI insurer. It's important to understand that LMI doesn't protect you and must not be confused with Loan Cover, which protects the loan and repayments (protects you) in the event of death, disability, unemployment, etc (more in Chapter 17). They are very, very different.

With LMI, you pay the premium (to protect the bank) as follows[*]:

Property Price: $300,000
$285,000 loan (5% deposit) = LMI cost $7,211
$270,000 loan (10% deposit) = LMI cost $3,672.
$255,000 loan (15% deposit) = LMI cost $2,117.
$240,000 loan (20% deposit) = LMI cost $0.
The greater your deposit, the less LMI cost to you?

Property Price: $400,000
$380,000 loan (5% deposit) = LMI cost $12,578.
$360,000 loan (10% deposit) = LMI cost $6,336.
$340,000 loan (15% deposit) = LMI cost $3,536.
$320,000 loan (20% deposit) = LMI cost $0.

Property Price: $500,000
$475,000 loan (5% deposit) = LMI cost $15,723.
$450,000 loan (10% deposit) = LMI cost $7,920.
$425,000 loan (15% deposit) = LMI cost $4,420.
$400,000 loan (20% deposit) = LMI cost $0.

[*]Premiums current as at time of writing www.yourmortgage.com.au.

The extra cost to you (the LMI premium) is usually added to the loan balance, so you may not necessarily 'feel' the extra cost upfront. Any extra fees and charges that increase your loan means it will take you longer to repay. In many first-home buyer situations, paying some LMI can be the difference in being approved for a loan (or not) and therefore can have its place at times. Your aim is first to avoid LMI costs and secondly to at least limit the amount of LMI payable.

Other Buying Costs (the extra 5%-ish)

When buying property, there are other costs to pay which vary from state to state. Using a $400,000 property as an example and assuming it's located in Victoria, Australia and that a 10% cash deposit has been saved ($40,000), the other fees to consider are:

TABLE 2: Extra Costs to buy a $400,000 Property in VIC (10% deposit)

Who	What	Amount
Government Fees (total $17,631)	**Stamp Duty:** a state Government tax and your biggest upfront cost, which is payable at settlement. May be added to the loan or discounted for first-home buyers *(Settlement: the official meeting between the lender and conveyancer to exchange ownership from the existing seller to the buyer)*	$16,370
	Registration of Mortgage: a state Government fee to register the mortgage on the title of the property	$115
	Registration for Discharge of Mortgage: a state Government fee to remove the seller's existing mortgage from the property title	$115
	Registration of Transfer: a state Government fee to transfer the property's title from the seller to the buyer	$1,031
Conveyancing Fees (total $1,500 est.)	**Settlement Agent/ Solicitor Fee:** a fee for the conveyancer (settlement agent) or solicitor to prepare the documentation for the property purchase (varies but generally $900-$1,500)	$1,500

Who	What	Amount
Bank Fees (total $800 est.)	**Bank Settlement:** a fee your lender charges to attend settlement (varies)	$200
	Loan Application or Establishment Fee: a fee your lender charges to set up your loan (varies and can be removed if you ask.)	$600
TOTALS	**Fees & Charges**	**$19,931**
	Deposit Saved (10%)	**$40,000**
	Remaining Actual Loan Deposit (5%)	**$20,069**
	Loan required $379,931 **Add LMI payable $12,576** **Total Loan $392,507 (including LMI)**	

Total extra costs for a $400,000 property may be $19,931.

As a comparison:

Extra costs payable for a $300,000 property = $14,697

Extra costs payable for a $500,000 property = $25,765

This list is not exhaustive, and fees will differ depending on your state/territory/country and lender. You don't need to be an expert in knowing all the fees and charges payable, your lender or settlement agent will help you. You just need to be aware of the extra costs and to save as much deposit as possible. It pays to save. Saving a 10% cash deposit will generally cover the extra costs (5%) and then leave a 5% deposit for the actual loan. That means only an absolute minimum deposit remains for the loan (those figures can be tight). If the remaining deposit after extra fees is less than 5% of the property price, you will need to save more.

Other costs payable may also include:

◆ Building & Pest Inspection Fee ($300–$400): always get these done, particularly if you are buying an existing property. A Pest Inspector will check for pests such as termites. A Building Inspector will check for internal defects to the property, which only a trained specialist can spot. You don't want to buy a house with serious internal structural damage, do you?

- Council & Water Rates ($500–$1,000): you are required to pay the remaining yearly or quarterly rates, such as water and land (council), from the settlement date.
- Home Building Insurance (cost varies between insurers): some lenders require this before they will book settlement.

Government Help: Grants, Exemptions & Concessions

Government grants, exemptions and concessions are there to help first-home buyers enter the market (to stimulate market activity in the economy). They help by providing an additional amount (which can be thousands of dollars) towards boosting your deposit and covering costs, or even by removing (or discounting) major costs such as stamp duty. It means that even with a deposit of only 5% saved, the extras you receive from the Government could mean you still have enough overall funds to secure a loan, which you otherwise wouldn't have had enough deposit for.

FIRST HOME OWNER GRANT (FHOG)

*http://www.sro.vic.gov.au/first-home-owner/apply-first-home-owner-grant-fhog

The First Home Owner Grant (FHOG) was introduced on 1 July 2000 to offset the effect of the GST on home ownership. It's a national scheme funded by each state and territory. A one-off grant is payable to first-home buyers who satisfy the eligibility criteria. The grant can provide thousands of dollars towards those extra costs, leaving more of your cash deposit for the actual loan. The amount of grant varies depending on the state or territory in which the property is located and whether the property is a new build or established (existing property). Some states offer larger grants to those willing to build a new home, to promote just that, new home builds, usually in newer suburbs, spread further away from congested cities. The available grants change from time to time (each financial year), depending on what outcomes the Government is trying to achieve for the economy.

EXAMPLE: FHOG IN VICTORIA

Currently, a $10,000 First Home Owner Grant (FHOG) is available when you buy or build your first home in Victoria, Australia. The property can be a house, townhouse, apartment, unit or similar. It must be valued at less than $750,000, built new, and be the first sale of that property as residential premises. It can't be an investment property or a holiday house.

The FHOG has been increased to $20,000 for new homes built in regional Victoria and valued at less than $750,000. The FHOG may be paid in addition to other exemptions or concessions for eligible home buyers. You (or your spouse) must also meet the following eligibility criteria:

◆ Not received the FHOG before.
◆ Not owned residential property (jointly or separately) before 1 July 2000.
◆ Intend to live in the property, as your home, for at least 12 continuous months, commencing within 12 months of settlement date or completion of construction.
◆ Be over 18 and an Australian citizen.

Penalties apply if you receive the FHOG when not entitled to it.

FIRST HOME BUYER DUTY EXEMPTION

Some states are also offering an exemption from land transfer duty (stamp duty) for first-home buyers (or at least a concession/discount) for homes up to a specific value. In Victoria for example, you need to buy a home costing under $600,000 to receive a full exemption. In New South Wales, Australia you need to spend under $650,000 to receive a full exemption, etc. That's a huge deal and can save you thousands of dollars! Meaning more of your deposit is left for the actual loan (rather than just covering fees).

EXAMPLE: FIRST HOME BUYER DUTY EXEMPTION IN VICTORIA

First home buyers buying a home for less than $600,000 will not pay any stamp duty. First home buyers buying a home worth $600,001–$750,000 will pay a concessional rate of stamp duty, calculated on a sliding scale. (Not that you need to worry about that as it is wise to never consider buying a property that expensive as your first home. Agree?)

To be eligible for the full duty exemption:

◆ The property needs to be valued at less than $600,000.
◆ You need to meet the FHOG eligibility.
◆ At least one purchaser must live in the property as their home (principal place of residence) for 12 months, starting within 12 months of settlement.

Additional Government exemptions and concessions are available. To see if you are eligible or for more information about the First Home Owner Grant and other Exemptions (such as the Duty Exemption), contact the revenue department in the state or territory in which you intend to purchase your home (http://www.firsthome.gov.au/).

With the $400,000 example property that you are following in this chapter (purchased as your home), it is possible that you can receive an FHOG of $10,000 and stamp duty might reduce from $16,370 to $0.

Essentially, that means your $40,000 cash deposit just grew to $50,000, and most of the extra fees will be paid for you (you pay fees of $3,562 instead of $19,931).

That's a massive advantage to first-home buyers right now (and one which definitely didn't exist when I purchased my first property).

TABLE 3: Buying a $400,000 Property (with FHOG and Duty Exemption) in VIC.

Who	What	Amount
Government Fees (total $1,261)	Stamp Duty	Exempt
	Registration of Mortgage	$115
	Registration of Discharge of Mortgage	$115
	Registration of Transfer	$1,031
Conveyancing Fees	Settlement Agent/ Solicitor Fee	$1,500
Bank Fees	Bank Settlement	$200
	Loan Application or Establishment Fee	$600
TOTALS	**Fees & Charges**	**$3,561**
	Deposit Saved (10%)	**$40,000**
	FHOG	**$10,000**
	Remaining Actual Loan Deposit (11.6%) Loan required $353,561 Add LMI payable $5,834 Total Loan $359,395 (including LMI)	**$46,439**

Result with concessions:
- The extra costs you have to pay are less.
- More of your deposit goes towards the loan, you pay less LMI.
- Loan reduces to $359,395 (compared to $392,507 without FHOG and Stamp Duty Exemption).
That's a $33,112 saving!

Even if you miss out on the full Stamp Duty Exemption, the effect of the FHOG alone gives you a greater deposit and reduces your loan (and LMI) to $381,029 compared to $392,507 without the FHOG.

SHARED HOME-OWNERSHIP SCHEME

Shared Home-ownership is a Government initiative which allows you to purchase a home from the Government Housing Authority with a SharedStart loan through Keystart (the Government's lending agent). Newly-built homes and off-the-plan properties are offered across metropolitan and regional areas. You own 80% of the property, and the Housing Authority owns 20%. You aim to buy the final 20% as your financial position improves (subject to review).

Advantages include:

- Low deposit of $2,000 or 2% of the purchase price (whichever is greater) for first-home buyers (stamp duty and fees only payable for non-first-home buyers).
- No savings history required.
- No lenders mortgage insurance.
- No monthly account keeping fees.
- FHOG can be used towards the deposit.

Disadvantages include:

- Limited property locations (you buy where the Government allows).
- Undesirable property locations (public housing dwellings, ex-housing commission units, flats villas, apartments, etc).
- Restrictions on selling the property in the future.
- Limited resale market (reduced number of potential buyers).
- Limited loan features and flexibility.
- Inability to rent out the property (the owner must live in it).

This scheme is not my first choice to acquire a property. I wouldn't let the Government dictate where I invest my hard-earned money and wouldn't buy a property with restrictions attached. I am not opposed (at all) to investing in 'ugly duckling' suburbs (so long as they are in the process of turning into 'better looking' swans), but when doing so, the type of property you buy is very important and unlikely to be one which is offered in this scheme.

It might be 'better than nothing' to get into the property market—although I don't believe you need to do it. There are many restrictions and after all, the Government doesn't usually offer something unless they also benefit—perhaps by getting people to buy their 'dud' ex-Housing Commission properties by offering 'sounds good' deals with much smaller deposits. Instead, plan your deposit, plan your purchase and buy a better-quality property.

Parental Help: Guarantees/Equity Sharing

FAMILY GUARANTEE

A family member, such as a parent, can use the equity in their home (the difference between the property value and their own home loan) as security for your home loan. They become the 'Guarantor' of your loan. Becoming a Guarantor has risks and mustn't be taken lightly, nor should you expect a parent to automatically be comfortable with taking on the responsibility of becoming a Guarantor. After all, they are risking their own home, which they worked hard to pay for, for you to buy one with little or no deposit of your own. If you as the borrower miss any of your loan repayments, they as the Guarantor are obligated to make those missed payments. They guarantee the loan and therefore become equally responsible for the loan. If you default on the loan, the Guarantor's home may well be seized by the bank and sold to recover lost money. A very bad scenario for all involved!

A less risky arrangement for a family member would be to lend cash if possible, rather than equity (with a written financial agreement). That way, if the borrower defaults, the family member only loses cash, rather than being responsible for another loan, and risk losing their own home and tarnishing their Credit History.

A NOTE TO PARENTS:

Ideally, don't gift your child a house deposit (cash or equity). It's a very generous offer, but unfortunately teaches nothing—no savings commitment and no appreciation for money. Instead, offer to 'match dollar for dollar' what your child saves towards a deposit.

That motivates and rewards more so and will give your child a sense of achievement. The same can be used if helping to buy their first car.

If you prefer to lend money towards a deposit (to be repaid to you over time), then put in place a Financial Agreement. Yes, seriously. A basic, written legal contract will clarify how the money is to be repaid and when. If the terms of the loan are documented, then there is less risk to parents, and the child also understands the gravity of the situation more seriously. It's a perfect lesson on how loans work in the real world.

Other ideas, instead of giving money upfront:

◆ If the child is still living in your home, charge them 'board' but secretly save that money (without them knowing) to put towards a future deposit. They get to experience the responsibility of paying a regular amount (warms them up to future bills in adulthood). What a wonderful surprise to then be rewarded for their consistency.

◆ If the child has moved out, offer to pay a particular bill, so they can save extra money towards a deposit (keep an eye on the deposit, however, to make sure it is, in fact, building up quicker).

The Property Affordability Crisis… or just an excuse?

I don't buy into the argument that young people of today are disadvantaged because of high property prices and therefore unable to save the required loan deposit—anyone can do it—it does take time. Remember, I was earning only $230 per week when I first started working at 17, so it was a gradual process for me to be able to save $40,000 which took me several years of consistency—something that perhaps many young people of today don't have (or are not taught).

Whilst property prices were lower then than they are today, saving an amount of $40,000 (even in today's dollars) was a big achievement and is still a decent deposit and a relevant amount today. If it was possible to achieve that whilst earning a low income, then imagine what can be achieved with today's higher salaries. Plus, there are more government incentives now and more loan sharing programs available for first-home buyers to afford a home.

The disappointing thing is that even though salaries are a lot higher now, when I chat to people who are wanting to buy their first home and who complain about 'affordability', I ask them how much deposit they have saved so far. The response (most times) is zero, regardless if they are 20, 25 or 30+. It's hard to save 'enough deposit' (ever) if you don't make a start. They either don't save at all or have saved only $1,000–$2,000 and expect to be able to borrow a large sum of money with that level of deposit, the moment they decide to buy a home. Well, let me tell you, for most people, it isn't going to fall from the sky. It doesn't work like that. You need to be prepared and give it some forethought. For the Government and/or parents to 'chip in' towards a deposit, one expects the person who is wanting to buy the home to make a significant start and show a big effort towards the process. Remember, all excuses are created equal.

The key is to start saving a deposit as early as possible and to be consistent. A small amount saved regularly will go a long way. Be patient. Be consistent.

EXAMPLE: HOW TO SAVE FOR A $400,000 PROPERTY
If Buying Solo
Say you finish high school at age 17, you take a year off to travel and then settle into University studies for the next four years. You are 22 when you graduate and start working full-time. You secure a decent paying job (considering you just studied for four years for it). You start saving $100 per week into an ordinary bank account (earning nil interest let's assume) = you would have $31,200 by 28 (six years). Plus the FHOG of $10,000, your total deposit could be $41,200. By 28, you could be buying your own home worth $400,000 (with a better than 10% deposit). There's nothing wrong with buying your first home at 28! You can also speed things up if you save more, start earlier, buy a cheaper property or come across extra money from

time to time that you put towards the deposit instead of spending elsewhere (bonuses/tax refunds).

If in doubt that you will secure a job which will earn enough to be able to save $100 per week, then rethink your choice of career path.

I started working full-time at 17 (studied at University part-time via correspondence) and started saving earlier, whilst I was still living at Mum's house. Even though I didn't know exactly what I was saving for at that stage other than for 'my future', after six years I bought my first property at age 23.

If Buying Together

There are a lot of double-income households these days. Perhaps you buy a home with a partner, and you save $100 per week each. Together, you could save the same deposit quicker and be buying at 25 (three years of saving). Or keep saving until 28 and have a larger deposit of $31,200 each + $10,000 (1 x FHOG) = total deposit $72,400 (18.1%).

Consistency will pay off. It may not be possible to afford a property purchase after only one year of saving, with time however, and effort, you will be rewarded when the time is right.

Buying a property is a costly decision and probably the biggest one you will ever make, so don't expect it overnight.

The Loan (Mortgage)

With a budget sorted and loan deposit in hand, you are ready to take the plunge. Now what? Talk to your bank or a mortgage broker to arrange the loan application. Your lender/mortgage broker will do the sums and confirm if you are eligible for a loan based on your income and expenses, assets and other debts, plus the amount of deposit you have saved and price of the property you wish to buy.

Securing a home loan is a five-step process:

1. Application
2. Verification

3. Valuation
4. Approval
5. Settlement

It can be advantageous to use a mortgage broker as they have access to different lenders (not just a single bank) and will look at the best deals on offer, plus help with the paperwork and other requirements. Another major benefit of using a broker is that they understand how banks operate and what information is preferable for the bank to see (and what's not). A broker can also do preliminary calculations to give you an idea of your loan eligibility, rather than you applying for and possibly getting declined, which is then recorded on your Credit History and may hinder the success of future loan applications.

APPLICATION

When applying for a home loan, you need to supply documentation:

◆ Identification: one primary photographic form of ID (passport or driver's license) and one secondary form (such as Medicare card, recent utility bill, etc)
◆ Proof of income (from all sources)
◆ Details of other assets and debts (if any).

A home loan is a big commitment, so there will be many questions asked of you.

Conditional pre-approval is an indication from a lender that you are eligible to apply for a home loan up to a certain amount. You are under no obligation to take the loan, and the lender has no obligation to lend you that amount, but it can give you the confidence to know that you are on the right track to securing a loan (can afford the property in mind) and shows sellers that you are serious about buying. Getting conditional pre-approval can be done fairly quickly and helps you focus your property search by giving you a clear idea of what you are likely to afford based on what a lender is prepared to loan you. Conditional pre-approval differs from formal approval, which happens at a later stage.

VERIFICATION

The lender will assess your application to determine whether you meet their serviceability and credit requirements. This process includes confirmation of your income, employment, and a credit history check. Your supporting documentation is also assessed at this time.

VALUATION

The lender will order a valuation of your chosen property from a professional Valuer. The Valuer will either inspect the property (including the inside) or by do a 'desktop/curbside' valuation (based on the value of similar properties in the area). The bank valuation allows the lender to use the property as security for the loan. It's the price the lender believes they could sell the property for if you default on the loan and they need to recover their money.

A bank valuation may not be the same as a real estate agent's appraisal. Bank valuations protect the lender and you. If a bank valuation doesn't agree with the purchase price of the property, the loan will not be approved—if that happens, it means there was a significant difference in the purchase price and the valuation (not good), which in turn, can save you from significantly overpaying for a property.

APPROVAL

Formal approval (also known as unconditional approval) is when you have been officially approved for the loan. All conditions and criteria to assess the loan application have been supplied, assessed and approved. It's only when a home loan application is formally approved that the borrower can feel comfortable that they have obtained a loan. The lender will then issue a formal Letter of Offer. Mortgage documents will be prepared and will be sent to the borrower for signing.

It's not advisable to exchange property purchase contracts until such time that your loan has been formally approved.

In fact, when making an offer for a property, a Finance Clause must be included (by you the buyer), stating that purchase is 'Subject to Finance'. That way, if your loan application is declined, you are not legally bound to still buy the property (somehow). Finance Clauses don't generally apply to purchase of property via auction.

SETTLEMENT

A meeting is arranged by the lender together with your solicitor/ conveyancer (settlement agent) to 'settle' the transfer of ownership of the property from the current owner to the new owner. The settlement date is the official date that you take possession of the property (and the front door keys). The lender may request confirmation that a Building Insurance policy has been purchased by the borrower before settlement occurs. The first repayment of your home loan is usually required one month after settlement.

Loan Repayments

Just like with a personal loan, a home loan is an agreement to repay the loan balance (principal) over a period of time (term). The term of a home loan is usually 25 or 30 years (much longer than a personal loan). Only after you repay the loan in full do you take ownership of the property and the lender will release the Land Title (ownership papers). Until then, the lender technically owns the property.

The longer the term, the lower the repayments will be, but the more interest (costs) you pay to the lender. For example, a $300,000 loan with an interest rate of 5.5% paid over 30 years will mean P&I repayments of around $1,703 per month. Reduce the term to 25 years, and repayments increase by $140 per month (to $1,843 per month).

The interest paid on that 25-year home loan will be around $252,000. Repay the same loan over 30 years, and you will pay $313,000 in interest. That's an extra $61,000 in interest costs!

In the $400,000 property example (used throughout this chapter), purchased with a $40,000 cash deposit and $10,000 FHOG (assume no stamp duty exemption as a worst-case scenario), your loan would be around $381,029 (including LMI). With a 4.5% p.a. interest rate, the repayments are:

TABLE 4: Repayments for a $400,000 Property

Loan Term	Repayment @ 4.5%
25 years	$2,118 pm ($489 pw)
30 years	$1,931 pm ($446 pw)

Remember interest rates do rise. What does that mean to repayments with a rate rise of 1%, 2% or 3%? The repayments then increase as follows:

Loan Term	Repayment @ 5.5%	Repayment @ 6.5%	Repayment @ 7.5%
25 years	$2,340 pm ($540 pw)	$2,573 pm ($594 pw)	$2,816 pm ($650 pw)
30 years	$2,163 pm ($499 pw)	$2,408 pm ($556 pw)	$2,664 pm ($615 pw)

I've also shown the weekly equivalent of the repayments for comparison purposes. You can see that to buy a $400,000 property is quite costly to an average salary, when rates rise. The lower your loan, the more breathing room you have when circumstances change ('when' they change... not 'if').

PRINCIPAL & INTEREST REPAYMENTS VS. INTEREST ONLY

Most home loans have Principal & Interest (P&I) repayments, meaning your repayment is divided into two portions. Part of the repayment pays off the interest due on the outstanding loan amount, whilst the remainder repays the actual loan amount. Unfortunately, at the beginning of a loan, most of your repayment goes towards interest costs and only a small amount will go towards repaying the principal. As the loan principal reduces (slowly) over time, less interest is payable, meaning more of the repayment goes towards repaying the principal. However, even as your principal gets smaller and you pay less interest, your repayments will not get smaller. That's because your lender has calculated exactly how much you need to repay each time, to repay the loan by the agreed term.

Interest Only loans are a type of loan whereby the borrower pays only the interest costs (and doesn't repay the loan principal). As the borrower is only required to pay the interest costs, the major benefit lies in having lower monthly costs to meet, which is why these loans are primarily used to purchase investment properties. The loan is not repaid (generally until the property is sold), so long as interest is paid.

VARIABLE VS. FIXED INTEREST RATE

The interest rate attached to a home loan can also be variable or fixed. Standard variable home loans are the most popular loan type in Australia today, and generally consist of a good degree of flexibility and allow home buyers to make additional repayments on the loan early without being slapped with an extra fee. Standard variable home loan interest rates fluctuate depending on the cash rate set by the Reserve Bank of Australia. When interest rates rise, so do your repayments. The same applies to rate cuts—if interest rates go down, so do your repayments (pay less interest).

Conversely, fixed rates stay the same for the agreed fixed term (usually 1, 3 or 5 years for example). Fixed rates provide comfort and security in knowing exactly what the repayments will be for the fixed term. On the downside, if a rate cut is announced, those with fixed-rate loans will not benefit from any reduction in interest (these are locked into the agreed rate).

How to Repay a Loan Faster

EXTRA REPAYMENTS

It is important to repay a home loan as quickly as possible to reduce interest paid to the lender. The quicker you repay, the lower the 'real cost' of the loan and the property. Home loans are considered a form of 'bad debt' as the interest payable is not tax deductible (no rental income is earned from your home). There are usually no ongoing tax benefits in owning your own home (excluding any home-businesses, which are outside the scope of this book). Using a 30-year term the following table shows the 'real cost' of a loan.

TABLE 5: The Real Cost of Borrowing @ 5.5% p.a. interest (30-year term)

Loan Size	Monthly Repayments	Total Interest 5.5%	Total Cost
$300,000	$1,703	$313,212	**$613,212**
$381,029	$2,163	$397,810	**$778,839**
$400,000	$2,271	$417,616	**$817,616**
$500,000	$2,839	$522,020	**$1,022,020**

The second line is our ongoing property example. The real cost of a $400,000 property (with a loan of $381,029 over 30 years) is $778,839—Ouch!

Use your ongoing 10% Savings to make extra repayments.

Did you know that by making extra repayments on that loan of just 10% ($50 per week) you could save around $82,900 in interest and repay the loan six years faster?

Focusing on repaying a home loan faster is a good start to wealth creation as you create more equity, which then increases your personal wealth and opens up future investment opportunities, i.e. the equity created can be borrowed to invest elsewhere. Plus, the extra repayments you make creates an extra emergency fund (cash buffer) for times when property prices are falling or unemployment hits, so you are not always 'borrowed up to the eyeballs'. You don't ever want to be in a negative equity situation—that's when property prices fall and the amount borrowed ends up being more than the property value. That is a scary situation, because if you sell the property for less than the loan balance, you still owe the difference to the bank.

If you are a double-income household, then the ideal scenario is to live off one person's income and use the second person's income to make extra loan repayments. In doing so, it's possible to fully repay the loan and be mortgage free in a few years!

> *Always make extra repayments on a loan with the highest interest rate first, which is usually a credit card, followed by a personal/car loan and then a home loan, in that order. Clear any personal debt before making extra home loan repayments.*

FORTNIGHTLY VS. MONTHLY REPAYMENTS

Repayments are usually set to monthly, although often you can select weekly or fortnightly repayments. Ask your lender. Interest is calculated daily and therefore it makes sense to make repayments on a more frequent basis rather than monthly, to reduce interest costs (same with personal loans—Chapter 7).

Making monthly repayments is not as effective as fortnightly because you must wait a whole month to make a repayment, meaning your principal loan balance was higher for an entire month, and interest was calculated on that higher balance, compared to if you had made fortnightly repayments and reduced the balance a little quicker. Also, there are only 12 months in a year, but 26 fortnights—so by making fortnightly repayments you effectively make an extra repayment each year. Fortnightly repayments help to repay a loan faster, as the principal reduces more frequently and therefore is more advantageous compared to monthly repayments. Weekly repayments will reduce the loan balance even faster and can save you more interest.

OFFSET ACCOUNTS

An offset account is a type of bank account which is attached to a home loan (mortgage). The advantage is that funds held in the account offset the loan balance, so interest is calculated on a lower loan balance. This reduces interest costs and means you repay the loan faster. Every dollar saved in interest is another dollar in your pocket, rather than the bank's. Effectively, funds held in an offset account earn a 'rate of return' equal to the loan interest rate (tax-free and without any investment risk).

What do I mean by that? Say $20,000 of savings is held in a High-Interest Bank Account and earns 1.5% p.a. = $300 per year. The interest earned is 'income' and therefore is taxed at your Marginal Tax Rate + Medicare Levy. Using a tax rate of 34.5% as an example, you will lose $104 in tax. However, if that $20,000 is instead held in an Offset Account and the loan interest rate is say 5% p.a., your interest costs will reduce by $1,000 per annum. That $1,000 'saving' is money you keep in your pocket, it's not income and therefore not taxable.

TABLE 6: Offset Account Example

Savings in Offset Account	Home Loan	Interest Charged On
$20,000	($381,029)	($361,029)
If you have money in an Offset Account	The savings balance will offset the home loan	Then interest is only charged on the difference

Using an Offset Account to hold your Long-term Savings (10% Savings) is a great strategy to reduce interest costs whilst your savings are 'not in use'. Offset Accounts also provide flexibility as the funds in the account can be withdrawn, if needed. So, you need to be disciplined if you make extra repayments into an Offset Account. Don't be tempted to withdraw those extra repayments (to spend elsewhere). If you are, then ask your bank to apply the extra repayments straight onto the loan balance.

Some very disciplined people will have their salary paid directly into an Offset Account, then use a credit card for all living expenses so that their full salary sits in the Offset Account for as long as possible to reduce interest costs, before being withdrawn (just enough to repay the credit card). This is an advanced strategy and can knock years off a home loan, but only works if the credit card is repaid in full and a budget is maintained. I mention it here only to expand your knowledge of what's possible.

CASE STUDY

Real-life 'Power of Property' results

I love investing in property and seeing the results that ordinary people can achieve through the power of property. I didn't know anything about property investing when I started out, however over time, I learnt about it and enjoyed it all—the research, the purchase, and the sale.

Recently, I sold an investment property for $771,000, which was purchased for $420,000 only two years and eight months beforehand ($351,000 gain in a relatively short timeframe of only 32 months). To be able to 'save up' that kind of money over the same timeframe would require saving $10,969 per month—this is just not possible with most average salaries. That shows the power of investing and how $351,000 can propel you forward into a nicer, bigger, fancier home (or to buy more investment properties). Think about living in an 'okay' property for two years and eight months before moving into a 'much better' property without the need for extra debt.

Not all properties perform so well in that amount of time. That gain was achieved by selecting a particular suburb and type of property, which I believed to have a high likelihood of increasing in value (quickly), according to my research and which paid off very nicely (but wasn't guaranteed). It may not represent a typical first home gain over the same timeframe—or could it? There is nothing stopping you from achieving the same result, after all, I only spent $420,000, and the property was in fact located 8km from the heart of Melbourne.

Another property which I owned for nearly 10 years (my first investment property, purchased in my mid-20s), located 20km from Melbourne in 'the burbs', originally cost me $345,000 and was recently sold for $615,000. That's a $270,000 gain made over a much longer timeframe and is even more achievable. Again, to be able to 'save up' that amount of money in the same timeframe requires saving $2,250 per month for 120 months—possible for some people, however not possible for most.

Chapter 12 talked about investing money over time, into quality investments, to grow wealth—you can only 'save' so much of your salary. Good investment gains though, can be limitless. Investing can help you to have the lifestyle (or home) that you want.

Chapter 13 summary

- Buy within your means—don't overextend yourself.
- The more you borrow, the higher your repayments will be.
- Start saving for a property deposit as soon as possible in case you wish to buy a property (or some other investment) in the future (10% Savings).
- It can take several years to save a deposit—that's normal.
- Get into the property market (home or investment)—but don't buy an undesirable property just for the sake of it!

CHAPTER 14

Home vs. Investment Property (Which is Best?)

To buy or not to buy, that's the question... Actually, it's not even the question at all. Many of the wealthiest people in the world have made their fortunes through property. Investing in property has been good to me, and I have experienced firsthand the power of property. The question is, do you buy a home or an investment property? The answer depends on what you want to achieve... lifestyle, wealth or both?

'Rentvesting'

The Australian dream of home-ownership seems to be changing, at least for some people who are becoming more interested in owning investment properties instead of their own home (me included)... but why?

1. For the numbers (profit & tax benefits)
2. For the lifestyle (affordability)

From a tax perspective, it makes more financial sense to own an investment property and to rent where you live—coined as 'Rentvesting'. It can also be cheaper to rent where you want to live (for the lifestyle you want) than to buy a home in that same suburb. Some people Rent-Invest forever, others just for a few years until they can afford to own where they want to live.

TABLE 1: Owning a Home vs. Investment Property

	Advantages	Disadvantages
Renting	• Limited financial obligation • Little or no responsibility for maintenance • Low move-in costs • Location choices (near work or school) • May include extra amenities (pool etc) • More mobility (easier to move) • More liquidity • Less expensive than owning a home	• No equity (increase in property value) • Lifestyle limitations (pets, smoking) • Decorating/ renovating limitations • Less predictable housing expenses (rent increases) • Less stability (landlord may sell the property or not renew a lease)
Owning	• Possible equity growth • Lifestyle choices • Decorating/ renovating choices • Not dependant on a landlord to maintain a property • Pride of ownership • A sense of community, stability & security • More predictable housing expenses	• Substantial financial obligation • Significant annual expenses • Less liquidity • Less mobility • Interest rate rises can affect loan affordability

THE NUMBERS: PROFIT AND TAX BENEFITS

The major difference in owning your own home or an investment property from a tax point of view is that all costs and expenses related to an investment property (rented to a tenant for income) are tax-deductible to you (the landlord/owner), whereas, with your own home, none of the expenses are tax deductible. (Unless you run a business from home, but that can be a complex scenario and outside the scope of this book.)

Think of property investment as a business. Your property generates rental income, which is taxable income, so you get to offset that income by claiming all associated running costs as a tax deduction. Tax deductions reduce the amount of tax you pay on the rental income. Those tax savings help you to afford the investment property (or to buy additional properties). The government allows those deductions to promote property investment.

TABLE 2: Tax Benefits Comparison: Own Home vs. Investment Property

	Scenario 1	Scenario 2	
	If you own a home (where you live)	If you rent where you live...	...and own an investment property
Expenses	You (owner) pay all expenses such as loan repayments (P&I), council rates, water rates, strata rates, repairs and maintenance.	You (tenant) pay rent to the landlord and very limited maintenance costs. The landlord pays for everything else, relating to the property.	The tenant pays rental income to you. You (the landlord) pay all other costs. Loan repayments are less as you usually switch to Interest Only payments (don't repay the loan until you sell the property).
Tax Benefits	Nil	Nil—but, your overall expenses are usually much less than to own that same home.	Yes—expenses **are tax-deductible** to you. You can also claim Depreciation costs, which are 'on paper' expenses, but not actually paid from your pocket.

The government allows you to claim an extra expense known as 'Depreciation' which is the decrease in value of the house building due to wear and tear. Land increases in value, whereas the actual building gets older and decreases in value (like with a car) and includes things attached to the house (carpets, blinds, air con units, ovens, etc). You don't actually 'pay' Depreciation from your own pocket, it's an 'on paper loss' that you are still allowed to claim as a deductible expense in your annual Tax Return, which further reduces your income tax and helps you to afford to maintain the investment property.

THE LIFESTYLE: AFFORDABILITY

To rent a property is usually a lot cheaper than to own the same property. Mainly because you pay minimal expenses towards the upkeep of the property as the tenant, none of the council rates or insurances, nor do you pay for the loan repayments. In cases where someone bought a home a few years ago (for a lower price than it's worth today), their property maintenance costs and loan repayments may be less than the cost of renting a similar property in today's market, however that's not a fair comparison. It's important to compare the cost of renting a property vs. buying that same property (at today's prices). Compare apples to apples, not apples to oranges. Renting a property for less than it costs to own can be a huge advantage in being able to afford the lifestyle you want (by living in the suburb or type of property that you desire), without the associated costs of home ownership.

> *Throughout this chapter, let's follow this real-life example: Amanda rents a beautiful 1930s Art Deco apartment, 2 bedrooms, with wooden floorboards and a fireplace, fully renovated with modern interior, located in a trendy inner-city suburb of Melbourne, with shops, restaurants, and cafes all within walking distance, plus access to multiple tram lines, trains, and bus routes. It's a fabulous apartment and a great suburb to live in. It's not cheap. Rent is $550 per week. (The property itself was recently valued at $950,000.)*

Amanda lives in the suburb she wants, in the type of property she wants and has the lifestyle she wants for $550 per week ($28,600 per year). She isn't responsible for any other costs such as property maintenance, council rates or insurance. However, Amanda is curious as to how much money she would need to buy such a property:

TABLE 3: Deposit Needed: Buying A $950,000 Property

Who	What	Amount
Government Fees	Stamp Duty, Registration of Mortgage, etc	$54,618
Conveyancing Fees	Settlement Agent/ Solicitor Fees etc	$1,500
Bank Fees	Bank Settlement, Loan Establishment, etc	$800
TOTALS	Total Fees & Charges	$56,918
	Loan Deposit (5% absolute minimum)	$47,500
	FHOG ($0 as the property value is over $600,000)	Nil
	Total Deposit Needed (from Amanda)	**$104,418**
Loan	Loan	$902,500
	Add LMI	$40,161
	Total Loan (including LMI)	**$942,661**
	P&I Repayments (30 years @ 4.5% interest rate)	**$1,102/ week**

Amanda needs minimum cash of around $104,418 for the deposit and costs.

◆ With only a minimum 5% deposit remaining (after costs) a large amount of LMI will be payable; it's an expensive property with a large loan.

◆ Amanda also needs to earn a high income to be approved for that size loan. Let's assume she does earn a high income because she is already affording relatively high rent.

However, even if Amanda can come up with the deposit, the principal and interest loan repayments will be around $1,102 per week ($57,304 per year), which is much higher than her current rent costs of $550 per week ($28,600 per year). In fact, it's double!

Plus, as the homeowner, Amanda will be responsible for all other related costs such as maintenance, council rates, insurance, etc, which means a further $5,000 per year or more to pay. Amanda will not receive any tax benefits, as the property will be her own home (owner-occupier).

Outcome: It is much cheaper for Amanda to rent the apartment than to buy it.

She may not be able to afford the lifestyle she wants if she buys the property, as her overall housing costs would increase substantially (more than double with mortgage repayments + property running costs), which would put significant pressure on her budget.

Even if Amanda earns a good salary, say $100,000 per year, which is possible considering she is already renting an expensive apartment herself, after deducting income tax, mortgage repayments and other property costs, she may only have around $200 per week left over to pay all other savings, groceries, bills, and fun. That won't be enough. It's unaffordable.

Amanda can't afford to buy the property (even if she could come up with the deposit). It's likely the bank wouldn't approve the loan in the first place, based on these numbers.

Rentvesting in Action

What if Amanda keeps renting where she wants to live (keeps her lifestyle) and then buys a more affordable investment property to invest her money into? The investment property would need to be in a cheaper suburb to make the numbers work and be a better investment opportunity. Not all expensive suburbs make good investments—yes, the capital gains made over time and the type of tenant attracted can be good, but the rental income return (yield) is actually usually quite low because of the high property prices. It can cost a lot from your own pocket to hold an expensive property.

> **Just because you live in a particular suburb doesn't mean you should invest there.**
> **Just because you invest in a particular suburb doesn't mean you want to live there.**

For Amanda's landlord, earning a rental income of $550 per week equates to an income yield of only 3.01% p.a. (gross, before running costs). The net return will be even less after deducting expenses. That is not a great rental yield. I usually look for properties with a gross rental yield of at least 5.0% p.a. or more.

The lower the rental yield (rental income), the more expenses to be paid from the landlord's own pocket (which is costly). The aim with property investing is to select a property that (1) increases in value over time and (2) earns high enough rental income to pay as much of the loan interest and other expenses as possible. Otherwise, a landlord has to pay the difference in expenses from their own salary, which puts a strain on budgets and limits the number of properties the investor can afford to hold at any one time.

> *What if Amanda does the following:*
> *Continues to rent where she lives at $550 per week. Amanda doesn't buy the apartment. Instead, she buys an invest-ment property somewhere else; a 1-bedroom apartment in a different inner-city suburb. Still a trendy and desirable suburb, but more affordable than where Amanda rents. There are more apartments in the suburb she chose to invest in, plus a large University nearby, meaning more renters (more competition and therefore property prices are more affordable). Price of the investment property is $395,000 (plus buying costs). Expected rent is $400 per week (gross rental yield 5.26% p.a.) = tick. Other annual running costs include Council & Water Rates $2,500, Strata Levies $1,200, Landlord Insurance $700, ad-hoc Maintenance $850 & Real Estate Management Fees 10% of rent + plus $100 Inspection Fees.*

Let's see the outcome of Amanda's new Rentvesting strategy.

TABLE 4: Deposit Needed: Buying A $395,000 Investment Property*

Who	What	Amount
Government Fees	Stamp Duty, Registration of Mortgage, etc	$17,369
Conveyancing Fees	Settlement Agent/ Solicitor Fees etc	$1,500
Bank Fees	Bank Settlement, Loan Establishment, etc	$800
TOTALS	Total Fees & Charges	$19,669
	Loan Deposit (5% absolute minimum)	$19,750
	FHOG ($0 as the property will be rented out)	Nil
	Total Deposit Needed (from Amanda)	**$39,419**
Loan	Loan	$375,250
	Add LMI payable	$12,421
	Total Loan (including LMI)	**$387,671**
Cash flow	**Income** Rental Income @ $400 per week	$20,800
	Expenses Less Interest Only Loan Payments (@ 5.5% p.a.) Rates can be higher for investment loans Less other running costs (rates, insurance, etc) Less agent's fees & inspections Negative cash flow (paid by Amanda)	-$21,322 -$5,250 -$2,180 **-$7,952** ($153/ week)

*Real-life numbers taken at the time of writing, sourced from www.realestate.com.au.

Amanda needs to save up cash of $39,419 to buy the investment property, which is much more affordable (and faster) for most people, compared to $104,418 in the previous example.

◆ LMI payable would be less.

◆ Loan repayments would be less (Interest Only instead of P&I).

Negatively vs. Positively Geared

When rental income is not enough to cover the loan interest and other running costs of an investment property, the property has negative cash flow, and is 'negatively geared'. It's very common to have a negatively geared property initially. After a few years (as rental income rises), the property should become 'positively geared', whereby the rental income eventually starts to cover all costs. Whilst a property is negatively geared, it costs the investor money from their own pocket to hold the property (they pay the difference in costs) —the investor will be hoping for good capital gains (increases to the property value), to offset the income losses, so they still make a profit in the long-term.

Generally, if a property earns high rental income then the capital growth may be low and vice versa, if a property earns high capital growth, then rental income may be low. A good mix of rental income and capital growth makes the perfect investment.

Positively geared properties (from day 1) are possible, however they are not easy to find, can take strategic work to locate, and often don't earn good capital growth. Let's exclude those types of properties and concentrate on the most common occurrence—negatively geared property (in the early years).

The aim is to buy an investment property which is not too negatively geared, so that it's still affordable to hold until becoming positively geared (otherwise it's too much strain on an investor's budget).

So, in our example, Amanda has to cover the negative cash flow of $153 per week. That's a sizeable cost. How will she do it? With the tax benefits, of course. We assumed that Amanda is earning a salary of $100,000 per year, but what if she is earning less, say $70,000 per year? (Maybe she is sharing that fabulous two-bedroom apartment with someone. Otherwise it's unlikely that Amanda could afford rent of $550 per week.) Let's calculate both scenarios.

TABLE 5: Amanda's Cash flow (Tax Benefits)

Cash flow & Tax	Example: Salary $100,000		Example: Salary $70,000	
	No investment property	With investment property	No investment property	With investment property
Salary	$100,000	$100,000	$70,000	$70,000
Rental Income	N/A	$20,800	N/A	$20,800
Total Income	**$100,000**	**$120,800**	**$70,000**	**$90,800**
Less Loan Interest	N/A	-$21,322	N/A	-$21,322
Less Property Costs	N/A	-$5,250	N/A	-$5,250
Less Agent's Fees	N/A	-$2,180	N/A	-$2,180
Less Depreciation	N/A	-$2,500	N/A	-$2,500
Taxable Income	**$100,000**	**$89,548**	**$70,000**	**$59,548**
Income Tax/ Medicare	-$26,632	-$22,555	-$15,697	-$11,984
Net Salary	**$73,368**	**$77,445**	**$54,303**	**$78,816**
Tax Savings		**$4,077/year**		**$3,713/year**

By having the investment property, Amanda will pay around $4,077 per year ($78 per week) less tax whilst it's negatively geared. That $78 per week goes towards covering the negative cash flow ($153 negative cash flow less $78 per week tax refund = $75 per week), still to be covered by Amanda (using some of her surplus income). Paying $75 per week towards the investment is more affordable than $153 per week. The tax benefits associated with the investment property make it more affordable.

The theory behind Rentvesting is that paying $550 per week to rent where Amanda lives, rather than $1,102 per week to own it, Amanda is then able to afford $75 per week towards an investment property, whilst also having the lifestyle that she wants. Paying $75 per week towards an investment property is not a bad result. It's a realistic outcome and quite achievable and affordable for a new property investor and even similar to some of the properties that I have owned. I used real property values and rental income figures in this example (taken at the time of writing from www.realestate.com.au).

Someone earning $100,000 per year salary should be able to pay $75 per week towards a property. However, if Amanda can't for some reason, but understands that real wealth can be made from investing in property and that the strategy will benefit her financial future, then a wise alternative is for Amanda to rent a cheaper place to live in (say $450-$500 per week instead of $550); rejig her life-style and budget a little, so she can get ahead and propel her finances. Or she can select a different investment property (lower cost or with higher rental income).

Rentvesting is all about crunching the numbers to get the best result.

TABLE 6: Amanda's Rentvesting Example (salary $100,000)

	Home-ownership	Rentvesting
	Amanda buys the $950,000 apartment (no investment property)	Amanda buys a $395,000 investment property (and rents where she lives)
Income		
Rental Income Received	N/A	$20,800 ($400/week)
Less Expenses		
Loan Repayments	$57,304 (P&I)	$21,322 (switch to I/O)
Other Costs (rates, maintenance etc)	At least $5,250 +	$5,250
Agent's Fees @ 8%	N/A	$2,180
Add-back Tax Refund (above table)	N/A	$4,077
Total Cost	**$62,554($1,202/week)**	**$3,875 ($75/week)**
Add cost to rent where Amanda lives	N/A	$28,600 ($550/week)
Total Cost	**$62,554($1,202/week)**	**$32,475 ($625/week)**
Extra Cash flow from Rentvesting, instead of buying a home (to use towards other goals, debt repayment or second investment property)		**$30,069 ($578/week)**
Loan Deposit Needed	**$104,418**	**$39,419**

In this example, Amanda will be $573 per week better off by Rentvesting (difference in extra cash flow) and will own a $395,000 investment property with a 5.26% p.a. rental yield, all whilst also having the lifestyle she desires (living where she wants to).

Whilst the property is negatively geared in the initial years, Amanda will benefit from some income tax savings which she can put towards the property cash flow. As the rental income increases over time, the cash flow will become positive, and the property value should also increase (and create a capital gain). That is how you increase your wealth with property investing. As the property value increases, Amanda can then use some of that increase as a deposit for a second investment property (Chapter 15) —she doesn't need to sell her first investment property to be able to buy another.

For Rentvestors, it's about making the deliberate choice to rent where they live, to improve lifestyle and cash flow. Rentvestors live where they want and can then afford an investment property.

Note that you don't always have to rent where you live to be able to afford an investment property. A lot of homeowners also have investment properties. There is an emotional element in owning your own home, instead of renting, which you need to consider. As a renter (tenant), you may not be allowed to paint the house walls a colour you like and may be limited to a 12-month lease each time for example, but on the plus side, you have more flexibility in the suburb and type of property you live in and much lower costs—more money you can then put towards investing.

The traditional thought that paying rent money is 'dead money' (paying for someone else's investment) is not relevant to Rentvesting, so long as the Rentvestor invests in property themselves. If you choose to rent, however don't use your extra cash flow towards increasing wealth, and you don't buy an investment property, instead you spend your money at the pub each week, then you are not Rentvesting at all—you are in fact paying 'dead money' and paying off someone else's investment, which will not increase your own wealth. If you are currently renting due to affordability and feel that you don't have any other choice—then reread this book, start saving regularly (towards an investment property deposit) and change your reality.

'If you don't like where you are, move. You are not a tree.'

Rentvesting is becoming more and more popular, especially for first-home buyers who struggle to afford to buy the type of property that they want to live in. They may afford a lower-cost investment property, which may not necessarily be in the suburb they want to live in themselves.

Renting Out An Existing Home

What if you already have a home that you own (with a mortgage)? What if you also want to buy an investment property to grow your wealth? Does it make sense to stay in your current home and buy a second property to rent out, or are you better off renting out your current home (turning it into an investment) and moving into the second property as your new home? Once again, there are two deciding factors:

1. The numbers: what's the best financial decision?
2. The lifestyle: where do you want to live?

If you love your current home and don't want to move, then don't. No investment is worth giving up something you truly love in order to make money. Instead, ask your lender if you can use some of the equity in your current home as a deposit for the investment property (Chapter 15). This would help you to become a property investor without having to rent where you live. You stay in your current home and grow your wealth at the same time.

If you are looking for a change and want to move homes, then move. Simple. Decide to rent your next home, so you can reduce your expenses and free up cash flow to put towards an investment property—you then become a Rentvestor.

If you don't mind either way and will move depending on which scenario gives you the best financial outcome, then that's when it gets interesting. Read on.

Samantha's rentvesting result

Samantha owns a two-bedroom unit worth $350,000, which she lives in (owner-occupier). Her loan balance is currently $280,000 and the P&I repayments are $347 per week (5% p.a. interest). Samantha pays all other expenses (insurances, maintenance) with no tax benefits. Samantha works full-time and earns $75,000 per year.

Samantha is unsure if it's best to stay in her current home or move out, turn it into an investment property and then rent a newer, bigger place for herself (preferably with a dishwasher and lock up garage) which she doesn't have now. Which is the best strategy?

Samantha expects that she will be able to rent out her unit for around $340 per week. Samantha researches online and finds a place she likes, which will cost $365 per week—a brand new villa with all the extras that Samantha wants for her lifestyle (including the dishwasher and lock up garage). Bigger and nicer than her current unit.

To move, or not to move? The rent Samantha will pay for the bigger place will cost more than she can rent out her current unit for. Is it a good deal? Samantha crunches the numbers and comes up with the following outcome...

TABLE 7: Samantha's Numbers: Own or Rent Comparison (annual figures)

Samantha's Tax Benefits	Salary $75,000	
	No investment property (living in her own unit)	Turning her unit into an investment property (renting out her home)
Salary	$75,000	$75,000
Rental Income	N/A	$17,680
Total Income	**$75,000**	**$92,680**
Less Loan Interest	N/A	-$14,000 (Interest Only)
Less Property Costs	N/A	-$4,050
Less Agent's Fees	N/A	-$1,414
Less Depreciation	N/A	-$1,500
Taxable Income	**$75,000**	**$71,716**

Samantha's Tax Benefits	Salary $75,000	
	No investment property (living in her own unit)	Turning her unit into an investment property (renting out her home)
Income Tax & Medicare Levy	-$17,422	-$16,289
After Tax Salary	$57,578	$58,711
Tax Savings from Rentvesting		$1,133/year ($22/week)

Samantha's Cash Flow	With Home-ownership	With Rentvesting
	Amanda's Current Unit $350,000 (owner-occupier, no rental income)	Amanda's Unit Rented Out (earning income of $340/week)
Income		
Rent Received	N/A	$17,680
Expenses		
Loan Repayments	$18,044 (P&I)	-$14,000 (switch to I/O)
Other Costs: Insurance, Rates etc	$4,050	-$4,050
Agent's Fees	N/A	-$1,414
Add-back Tax Refund (above table)	N/A	$1,133
Total Cost	$22,094 ($424/week)	$651 ($13/week)
Add cost to rent where Samantha will live	N/A	$18,980 ($365/week)
Total Cost	$22,094 ($424/week)	$19,631 ($378/week)
Extra Cash flow from Rentvesting, instead of living in her own unit (use towards other goals, debt repayment or second investment property)		$2,463 ($46/week)

Outcome: By turning her home into an investment property (and then renting where she lives), Samantha will live in a bigger, nicer property with the features she wants (better lifestyle) and achieve tax savings of around $1,133 per year ($22 per week). The total increase to Samantha's cash flow is around $2,463 per year ($46 per week), which can be used towards other goals, debt repayment or the cost of holding another investment property. Is it a good deal for Samantha to become a Rentvestor? Yes, I think so.

The key when renting out your own home (turning it into an investment), is to switch the loan repayments from principle & interest to interest only—you want to reduce your expenses to the minimum to increase cash flow. Also, you don't necessarily want to repay an investment loan ('good debt'), especially in the initial years. Instead, you repay the loan if and when you one day sell the property. Of course, if you have no other personal debts to repay first and can afford to maintain P&I repayments then by all means, repay the investment debt!

As a rule of thumb, if your current home rents for a certain amount and you find a place to rent yourself for around the same amount each week, then you will generally be better off by becoming a Rentvestor. You will benefit from being able to claim expenses as tax deductions (to reduce income tax) and also reduce your housing expenses (the landlord will pay most of the costs at your new home). The less your personal expenses are and the less income tax you pay, the more cash flow you have available to afford additional investments, whether they be property(ies), shares or businesses.

It's all in the numbers and of course... the lifestyle.

Chapter 14 summary

- Rentvesting can be a great way to have the lifestyle you want whilst also being able to invest (to grow wealth in a tax effective way).
- The key parts to Rentvesting are:
  1. Rent where you live
  2. Invest the money you save (by renting instead of owning)
- Renting where you live, however, without also investing is not Rentvesting.
- Even if you have no interest in buying a property right now— one day you may. Start saving for a deposit just in case.
- It's all in the figures. If unsure, seek professional advice.

CHAPTER 15

The Secret To Buying Multiple Properties

S ome of the wealthiest people in the world have made their fortunes through property. Owning a single property may not
make you rich but owning multiple properties can.

Owning multiple properties is very achievable—how do I know?
Because I did it. I am still doing it. It's a work in progress throughout
life. Investing in more properties as I go. No inheritances. No handouts. No windfalls. Just time, effort and determination.

You too can have a slice of the property pie and become wealthier,
however only if you take action—if you invest smart—and if you are
consistent. As with anything in life, you start with one (property)
and accumulate more over time. One brick at a time (pun intended).
How many properties you own is up to you. Aim for one or two to
start with and see how you go. Everyone is different. Not everyone
has a desire to become a property magnate, although most people
wish to be wealthier. Either way, have you ever wondered just how
some people are able to buy multiple properties? Well, for starters,
they definitely don't save up a 20% cash deposit every time they want
to buy a property. Instead, they buy one property to start with, then
use the 'equity' from that property as the deposit for the next property. And repeat...

What Is Equity?

Equity is the difference between the value of a property and how much is owed on it (loan amount). It's the portion of the property that you own. Not the bank. As your equity increases over time, you can draw out (borrow) part of that equity to use as you please. Smart people will use their equity to fund the deposit for more properties.

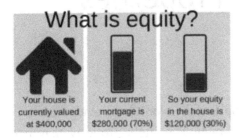

Your house is currently valued at $400,000
Your current mortgage is $280,000 (70%)
So your equity in the house is $120,000 (30%)

With most lenders, you need to leave 20% equity in a property as security for the loan, meaning you can access up to 80% of the property value, less any existing loan of course. In the above example, the owner can draw out $40,000 equity, which is calculated as:

$400,000 property value x 80% = $320,000
Less existing loan $280,000 = $40,000 available equity

Drawing out equity means that you are borrowing more money against that property, so you still need to qualify for the loan and meet the lender's requirements. Also, interest is payable on the extra borrowings, so you must only ever draw out equity to buy assets which will make more money (investment properties and shares for example) and outperform the interest rate. By doing that, the interest costs also become tax deductible and reduces the tax you pay.

In the past, banks have pushed TV commercials enticing people to take out 'Equity Loans'; draw equity from homes, to spend on lifestyle items—cars, boats, etc. After reading this book, you now know that it doesn't make financial sense to borrow money to buy things that go down in value over time (costs you money = liabilities).

Don't take out equity loans to buy lifestyle stuff.

Adding Value (Increasing Equity Faster)

The consensus is that property values will roughly double every seven to ten years. Not always and not every property. That period is known as a 'property cycle' and refers to the swing in house prices through phases of boom and bust. So, if you buy a property at a fair market price and then simply wait for the property to increase in value through normal market conditions, you could be waiting some years before having enough equity to buy another property, and if you overpay for a property at the time of purchase then you will be waiting a lot longer to see any available equity. The key for me in being able to buy multiple properties quicker than waiting years between purchases has been to 'add value' to each property to increase the value faster and therefore create more equity—to manufacture my capital growth, to fund the next property purchase quicker.

> *Choosing a property which can be changed/altered to create an immediate increase in value can allow you to move onto the next property a lot quicker. In doing so, I have bought/ built one property every two years for the last handful of years—which is by no means aggressive and is quite conservative. Increases in property values through normal economic conditions (property prices rising) is then 'cream on the cake' and a backup plan.*

Add value to a property (to increase equity faster) by:

◆ **Renovating:** improving the look of an existing dwelling. This can be a 'cosmetic renovation' (basic improvements such as painting walls, new carpets or flooring, updating the kitchen and/or bathroom, gardens etc) or a 'structural renovation' (major changes such as knocking down walls, changing the shape of the dwelling, adding an extra room which may or may not need council approval).

◆ **Building:** putting a new dwelling on a vacant block of land (e.g. buying a block and hiring a builder to build the dwelling or buying a pre-packaged house and land package from a developer).

◆ **Developing:** demolishing an existing dwelling to create a new one, usually with the aim of fitting more dwellings onto the same block to better utilise the land and increase the overall value e.g. knocking down an old house to build medium-high density dwellings (such as units, apartments or townhouses for example etc). The number of dwellings allowed depends on local council zonings.

Developing property is more advanced and is outside the scope of this book, however, it has played a part in my overall property journey. It's best learnt over time and more suitable for future property strategies, rather than your first one or two investment properties. Start out buying an existing property for basic renovation, perhaps do that a couple times or complete a few 'new builds' here and there to gain experience and knowledge about property investing, before worrying about developing property.

Let's follow the example at the end of Chapter 14—Samantha's $350,000 existing home (2-bedroom unit).

TABLE 1: Example of Equity

Property Value	Loan	Equity
Year 1 $350,000	($280,000)	$70,000 (20%)
Year 2 $364,000	($280,000)	$84,000 (23%)
Year 3 $379,000	($280,000)	$99,000 (26%)

See how the equity increases over time (in this example I have assumed a modest growth return of 4% p.a.)?

Most lenders require 20% equity to remain as security for a loan, so in this example, Samantha has no available equity to access right now which means that she either needs to save up cash as the deposit for a second property or think smarter about what other options are available to manufacture an increase in the existing property value (and speed up the normal process).

Samantha is an existing property owner and therefore no First Home Owners Grant (FHOG) is available (it's not available when buying an investment property anyway). However, what if Samantha's property could do with a basic cosmetic renovation, such as fresh paint and perhaps some upgrades to the kitchen, bathroom, and flooring to increase the value immediately? As an example, even if you spend just 1% of the property value on renovations, if done well, it can add thousands to the end value.

In Chapter 13, I mentioned a property that I recently sold for $615,000. Prior to the sale, it was valued at only $560,000–$580,000. To increase the value, around $5,000 was spent on new carpets, internal painting, driveway painting and front garden. To keep the costs low, some work where possible was done personally, rather than hiring tradies. A few weeks later, the property sold for $615,000 = an increase in value of up to $55,000 (less renovation costs of $5,000 = $50,000 net). Definitely worth the time, energy and money.

TABLE 2: Example of Equity (after Samantha spends say $5,000 on renovations)

Property Value. (after renovation)	Loan	Equity
Year 1 $385,000	($280,000)	$105,000(27%)
Year 2 $416,000	($280,000)	$136,000(33%)
Year 3 $433,000	($280,000)	$153,000(35%)

After completing the renovations, Samantha gets her bank to revalue the property. Let's assume the bank feels that the property is now worth $385,000. That's an increase of up to $35,000 (less renovation costs of $5,000 = $30,000 net) simply because of the renovation. Samantha's equity will then compound greater over time, as she will have more money (value) invested in the property market (compared to table 1) and that's without relying on the suburb increasing in value through normal market conditions for example.

For Samantha to be able to spend $5,000 cash on the property, she needs to have her 'Just In Case' savings in place and ready to go. You always need to be financially prepared, especially when investing in property.

In this example, Samantha has immediately increased her equity from $70,000 (20%) to $105,000 (27%). Of that $35,000 increase, 80% can generally be borrowed, which equates to $28,000 equity to use as a deposit for another property:

$385,000 property value x 80% = $308,000
Less existing loan $280,000 = $28,000 available equity

Samantha doesn't have to sell her existing property to be able to buy another, she can leave the first property invested as is and simply use the available equity as deposit for another loan. That then avoids all the extra fees and taxes which may be payable to sell an existing property (this will eat into the available equity) and means that Samantha has more money invested in the property market.

Whether a property is suitable for renovation and what likely difference it makes to the end value is easily researched by speaking to a few local real estate agents and searching for similar properties (before and after renovation) on sites such as www.realestate.com.au and www.domain.com.au.

A note of caution: renovating doesn't guarantee an automatic increase in value. The bank might disagree with your efforts and the valuation may not stack up with your estimations, so don't overcapitalise by spending too much money renovating areas of the property that are unlikely to add significant value. Stick to improving the general aesthetics of a property, a cosmetic update. Don't knock down walls or install a pool. There are many websites and books devoted to the subject of renovating for profit, many of which suggest that fresh new kitchen and bathrooms are what attracts buyers and renters.

If you have an existing property which is not suitable for a quick cosmetic renovation (i.e. newly built or already renovated), then you may be limited in how you can add value. You may need to wait a while until the value increases, over time, through normal market conditions to see any available equity or come up with other entre-preneurial ways to put together a deposit for the next property—save up good old cash (surplus income) or buy with a family member/ friend to share the commitment.

However, if you are looking to buy a property soon, whether it be your first property or an additional property, then look for one which is a good candidate for renovation. Adding value isn't limited to renovating of course—use your imagination. Speak to local real estate agents for other possible ideas. Google it. Research it.

The worst-case scenario is you start saving the deposit for your next property (which can have value added) whilst you wait for your existing property to go up in value. A slower approach, but it's a matter of doing what needs to be done, however long it takes and learning in time for the next property purchase.

Buying Multiple Properties Using Equity

Table 3 at the end of this chapter is a real-life example of adding value (to increase equity) to buy multiple properties over time using various strategies.

Note that the loans for property 2 onwards equal 100% of the property value, as the deposits were funded by using equity (bor-rowing) from the other properties.

When searching for an investment property, being able to add value in some way is extremely important, so that you can manufacture growth in the property value, without having to only rely on normal property market conditions. However, it's still only one aspect of picking a winning property.

◆ Follow Property Cycles: Property values go up and they go down. Normal economic conditions will see to that, such as supply and demand. There is no single property cycle in Australia, they vary from state to state, so that when one region is booming, another may experience a downturn. Knowing where the property market is in its cycle is important to help reduce the risk of buying in a hot market and overpaying. Investing in the different Australian States can help to take advantage of the different property cycles, e.g. the Perth and Melbourne cycles quite often seem to be in opposite directions; when the Melbourne market booms, the Perth market often seems to soften. This adds another level of diversification, so all your eggs are not in the one basket.

◆ Choose Growth Suburbs: Buying in your own neighbourhood doesn't always make the best investment. You need to buy in suburbs which appeal to renters, which will also grow in value over time. Look for areas of demand, often next door to the more popular suburbs. Check areas that the Government has sizeable spending planned for the near future. 'Ugly Duckling' suburbs, or those that are not that desirable right now, are benefiting from Government spending and gentrification (improvements) can be a goldmine. Steer clear of problem suburbs with high crime rates or too many renters vs. owner-occupiers. Usually if the Government is spending money in a particular suburb, it can be a good sign of things to come.

◆ Buy Right: Overpaying for a property can be disastrous and means you have to wait even longer to see any available equity. Do your research and be confident in the value of a property. Always negotiate on the price and be prepared to leave a property alone if the asking price is too high (seller won't negotiate) or you are outbid on your offers. Don't buy in a 'sellers' market' and vice versa, don't sell in a 'buyers' market'.

If unsure, hire the professional services of a Buyer's Agent to do the searching and bidding on your behalf (for a fee). And of course, always be sure that you can add value to a property you are looking to buy.

Successful property investing takes time. Not just time in the market but time to research and to select a suitable property which stacks the odds in your favour. It's a journey. Not a race. Take it slow.

Start researching well before making a move. Research takes time. Becoming a successful property investor doesn't need to become a second full-time job, however, you do need to give it the time that it deserves. After all, the decisions you make will risk hundreds of thousands of dollars, however when done correctly can reward you for life.

TABLE 3: Buying Multiple Properties (Real-life example) using actual figures

Property	Description	Location	Date of Purchase	Total Cost	Loan	Current Value
1	Renovation: 2 bed, 1 bath villa, 1 car, a complex of 8. Lived in as a home (owner-occupier) until July 2009, then became a rental.	Perth	Jun 2004	$178,000 (includes renovations)	($152,000)	$365,000
2	New Build: Purchased a block of land, then hired a builder to build a 4 bed/2 bath house	Melbourne	Dec 2007	$345,000	($345,000)	$615,000
3	Development: Purchased a triplex size block of land, then hired a builder to build 3 x 3 bed/2 bath villas	Perth	Mar 2009	$306,000	($306,000)	($400,000)
4				$306,000	($306,000)	($400,000)
5	New Build: Purchased a block of land, then hired a builder to build a 4 bed/2 bath house	Regional Perth	Nov 2011	$427,000	($427,000)	($450,000)
6 Becomes 8 properties when the project is completed	Development: Purchased an old house on a suitable block of land, with the view to build 3 x townhouses.	Melbourne	Feb 2015	$420,000	($420,000)	$771,000
	Totals			**$1,982,000**	**($1,955,000)**	**$3,001,000**
	Gross Profit					**$1,046,000**

Chapter 15 summary

- You don't need to sell one property to be able to buy a second.
- Use an increase in the value of one property as the deposit for another property.
- Adding value to a property can increase equity faster.
- The suburb you live in doesn't always make the best location for investment.
- Research is key to picking a winning suburb.

CHAPTER 16

Understanding Superannuation

What's superannuation?
Superannuation (super) is money you set aside throughout your
working life to provide you with income after you retire. Super is
made up of employer contributions, your own personal contributions
and sometimes additional Government contributions. When you
retire, your super balance can be converted to a pension
to provide you with money to live on.

In the past, older Australians have relied on the Government Age Pensions for income in retirement. As the Baby Boomer population ages and puts pressure on Government funding, there is more and more focus on super—saving for your own retirement!

Over time, the government is extending the general retirement age and making the Age Pension harder to qualify for. A common thought is that by the time most younger Australians reach retirement age, the Age Pension may be gone! The Age Pension isn't very much at all. Even if you do qualify, it's not an ideal retirement income, it's simply a safety-net.

Whilst younger, it's easy to pass off super as something you don't need to 'worry about' because your retirement is 'too far away' however, as you enter your 30s and then your 40s, you need to be aware and know that it only becomes harder and harder to save enough for when you are in your 60s. As with any savings, the longer you wait, the higher the amount you have to save. The earlier you start, the less you need to save each time. Plus, super is changing as the Government introduces programs for some people to be able to access their super before retirement for things such as buying a first home. Now that's something of more interest to younger Australians!

When you start work, your employer makes contributions into a super fund for you as a legal requirement—those payments are known as super guarantee contributions. Your employer must contribute an amount equal to **9.5%** of your salary (minimum) into your fund which is an **extra** payment on top of your salary. Most employees can choose the fund that their employers pay into. If you don't choose your own then your employer will choose one for you (which you can change at a later date if you wish).

In addition to employer contributions, you can also top up your super by making personal contributions to your fund. If you earn a low income, you may also be eligible for Government contributions. Actually, you **need** to top up your super fund to have enough money for retirement! The 9.5% contributions that your employer makes on your behalf won't result in you having enough super by retirement age. It's a good start, but not nearly enough. You need to increase your contributions to around 15% of income.

The good thing is super is a very tax effective investment. When you make contributions yourself, you can also reduce the tax you pay. The amount you 'sacrifice to super' reduces your taxable income so you pay less income tax each year. Also, earnings made within your super fund are taxed at only 15%, instead of your personal tax rate, which is usually a lot higher (up to 45% in Australia), and later, when you retire and start a pension with your superannuation, the tax reduces further to 0%. That's pretty good!

Those tax concessions are Government incentives for you to save for your own retirement. However, to benefit from those tax incentives, you have to leave the money you have in super until retirement.

Generally, you can't access super until you reach 'preservation age' and retire (age 55-60 depending on birthdate) or when you reach age 65 (regardless if you have retired or not).

Note that preservation age is not the same as the Age Pension age, which is currently age 65.5 however increasing to 67 by 2023.

How Much Super Do You Need for Retirement?

Depends on when you retire, how much income you need (want) and how long you live! Do you want to live a low-income lifestyle in retirement or afford luxuries such as travel? Will you want to upgrade your car or repay any remaining home loan balance that you may have? After working for your entire life, you don't want to be poor in retirement—do you?

Assuming you are debt free by retirement, in order to maintain a comfortable lifestyle, you will generally need a minimum income of around $45,000 p.a. (single) or $60,000 p.a. (couple) in today's dollars. Currently, the life expectancy age of a man is around age 80 and for a woman is around age 84. If you retire at age 67, that means you need to have enough money saved in super to generate income for 13–17 years... or longer! So, what does that mean in dollar terms?

TABLE 1: Super Needed (for 18 years in retirement, excluding Age Pension)

Retirement Age	Desired Income (to age 85)	Super Balance Needed (without Age Pension)*
Single - 67	$45,000 p.a.	~ $750,000
Couple - 67	$60,000 p.a.	~ $1,100,000 (combined)

* Assumes an investment return of 5.5% p.a. and investment management fee of 1.0% p.a. as an example. The results take into account many different variables and ignores the Age Pension or other investments you may have separate to super.

If you are single, retire at age 67 and want an income of $45,000 p.a. you need to save around $750,000 in super. If you are a couple, both retire at age 67 and want an income of $60,000 p.a. you need to save around $1,100,000 in combined super. If you receive some

Age Pension in retirement or have other investments, then you may not have to save as much in your superannuation.

WHAT IF YOU SIMPLY RELY ON EMPLOYER CONTRIBUTIONS?

Let's say you are age 23 and have landed your first 'real job', earning a salary of $50,000 p.a. Your employer contributes $4,750 p.a. as your 9.5% super guarantee. You make no other contributions. At age 67, your super balance may be around **$450,000**.

WHAT IF YOU ALSO CONTRIBUTE ($25 PER WEEK)?

If you contribute $25 per week from your salary into your super fund, what difference will that 'salary sacrifice' make to your account balance? In this scenario, at age 67 your super balance may be around **$540,000**. You can have an **extra $90,000** by retirement just by adding a small amount over a long time (plus some investment earnings). You also pay less income tax each year.

The contribution of $25 per week ($1,300 per year) is taxed at only 15%, instead of your personal tax rate (which is 34.5% including Medicare Levy for someone earning $50,000 p.a.). You save around $273 per year in overall tax. So, really, in net terms, you are only sacrificing $19.75 per week (not $25):

Salary sacrifice $1,300 ($25 per week)
Overall tax savings $273 ($5.25 per week)

Net salary sacrifice is therefore only $1,027 ($19.75 per week) So, you essentially give up $19.75 per week now to have $90,000 more at 67, even though you only personally contributed around $43,000 over that time. $19.75 per week should be affordable for most average salaries (and it's a good deal, tax-wise).

Over time, you want to be contributing around 15% of salary to super. Your employer will contribute 9.5%, so that means you need to salary sacrifice the other 5.5%. Not only will you have more for retirement, you will also pay less income tax along the way—after taking into account your tax refund, you end up sacrificing less than 5.5% (out of pocket).

That's not something that most 23-year-olds focus on in reality—hey, many 40-year-olds don't focus on super contributions. A lot of people prioritise other (short-term) savings goals over their retirement (very long-term) goals. This chapter is an introduction to superannuation because it's important.

As with other investing, adding a little money to your super fund, consistently over a long period of time can make a huge difference—because of compound interest. So, just be sure to add a little something extra to your super fund starting earlier rather than later.

Types of Super Contributions

SALARY SACRIFICE

Salary sacrifice is an arrangement with your employer to contribute part of your salary to superannuation. Contributions are deducted from your pre-tax salary and paid into your super fund by your employer (along with your 9.5% super guarantee). The amount you sacrifice is deducted from your salary before your tax is calculated, so you pay less tax.

This is an excellent way to contribute into your super as the deduction from your salary is done before you are paid your net income, so you don't have to do anything—just take home a little less each week in your pay packet. It's similar to the 10% Savings Rule—save first, spend second. Generally, you won't even notice the sacrificed amount, as you pay less income tax and therefore the overall net amount is less noticeable—just like your 10% Savings!

If you have many years to go until retirement then you won't generally contribute a lot to super because you won't be able to touch it until retirement, but a little bit added to your fund over those years can make a huge difference. So, you need a balance of investments held outside, as well as inside superannuation.

TABLE 2: Salary Sacrifice Example (assuming salary of $50,000 p.a.)

	No Salary Sacrifice	With Salary Sacrifice of $25 per week
Gross income	$50,000	$50,000
Super guarantee 9.5%	$4,750	$4,750
Salary sacrifice contributions	-$0	-$1,300
Taxable income	**$50,000**	**$48,700**
Income tax and Medicare levy	-$8,547	-$8,079
Net take-home salary (A)	**$41,453**	**$40,621**
Total contributions	$4,750	$6,050
Contributions tax (15%)	-$713	-$908
Net contribution to super (B)	**$4,038**	**$5,143**
Total tax paid	-$9,260	-$8,987
Total benefit after tax (A + B)	**$45,491**	**$45,764**
Income tax savings per year		$468
Total tax savings per year, net of extra contributions tax		$273

Salary sacrificing means more funds for retirement and paying less tax along the way.

If you have existing credit card debt, clear that first before worrying about making super contributions. Credit card debt costs you money and the interest rate payable will far outweigh the returns your super fund will make. Get rid of that first. Stop accruing new 'bad' debt. Then start a small amount of super contributions.

CONCESSIONAL (TAX-DEDUCTIBLE)

These are contributions made to super for which you claim a tax deduction. The tax deduction reduces the amount of income tax you pay. To have that benefit, concessional contributions are taxed at 15% when paid into your super fund (which is usually a lot less than your tax rate). Salary sacrifice contributions are classed as concessional contributions. There are limits on the amount you can contribute to super each financial year. You can make concessional contributions of $25,000 each financial year (this limit includes your employer super guarantee). You pay concessional contributions into your super fund directly, not via your employer.

NON-CONCESSIONAL (NON-DEDUCTIBLE)

These are contributions made with after-tax money. No tax deduction is claimed and therefore no tax is deducted from the contribution. You can make non-concessional contributions of up to $100,000 each financial year (or $300,000 over three financial years if you are under age 65). You pay non-concessional contributions into your super fund directly, not via your employer.

Government Co-Contribution

If you are a low or middle-income earner and make personal non-concessional (after-tax) super contributions to your fund, the government also makes a contribution (called a Co-contribution) up to a maximum amount of $500. To be eligible you need to earn an income of between $39,837 and $54,837per year and at least 10% of your income must come from eligible employment.

*Thresholds current for 2020/21 financial year.

Superannuation and Housing

On 13 December 2017, legislation was passed for the following two government schemes to reduce pressure on housing affordability in Australia.

FIRST HOME SUPER SAVER SCHEME (FHSS)

You can now make voluntary contributions to your super fund to save for your first home. The idea behind this is to help first home buyers save a deposit faster because of the tax savings made in super. When ready to buy your home, you apply to release your contributions, along with the associated investment earnings, to help you purchase your first home. This is a new way of accessing your super for reasons other than retirement.

To qualify you must:

◆ Have not previously owned property in Australia.
◆ Have not previously released any FHSS funds.
◆ Live in the premises you are buying for at least six months of the first 12 months.

You can apply for the release of voluntary contributions up to a maximum of $15,000 from any one financial year and $30,000 in total across all years. For more information visit: https://www.ato.gov.au/Individuals/Super/Super-housing-measures/First-Home-Super-Saver-Scheme/.

DOWNSIZER CONTRIBUTION

This allows people who are 65 years and over to make a contribution to their superannuation after selling their home. You may contribute up to $300,000 from the proceeds of downsizing your main residence (where you live). Your spouse may also be able to make a contribution. This contribution will not count towards the normal contributions limits.

Your Super Fund

Super funds invest in various asset classes such as fixed interest, shares and property, usually through managed funds (Chapter 12). You can choose how your super is invested. If you don't make a choice, your retirement savings will be invested in a diversified default investment option, which is selected according to your age. Each super fund will have their own investment approach. It is common for funds to have a balanced approach to investing by default, with 70% of assets in growth investments (e.g. shares and property) and 30% in defensive investments (e.g. cash and fixed interest).

When choosing an investment option, think about your investment timeframe (how many years you have until retirement) as well as the level of risk you want to take with your retirement savings. If you want high returns and retirement is many years away, you may be happy to accept a higher level of risk as you have time up your sleeve to ride out the ups and downs of market performance so you might select a higher growth fund. If you are more of a cautious investor or are close to retirement, you might choose a more conservative option (and accept lower returns) with less growth assets, so your returns aren't as volatile.

There are many different funds available in the marketplace today. The one that suits you best will depend on what features you want. To start with, keep it simple, fees will be one of your main concerns. Keep your account fees low as it makes a huge difference to your end retirement balance. If unsure, choose an Industry fund.

Most super funds also offer different types of insurance, such as Life, Total & Permanent Disability (TPD) and Income Protection. Often, a super fund will automatically give you a basic level of insurance. You can choose to change the amount or cancel the insurance to suit you. The insurance cover is generally basic but quite cost-effective. The premiums are deducted from your super fund balance.

If you have more than one fund, consider consolidating your money into a single fund. You will generally save on fees and charges and it will be easier to keep track of your retirement savings. Consolidating super funds is easy. Contact your preferred fund and they will process the transfer(s) for you. Note! Before you consolidate, make sure you check if you have insurances attached as that insurance will be lost when you close the fund. You need to replace insurances before you transfer. Be particularly careful if you have a pre-existing medical condition or are aged 60 or over, as you may not be able to buy new insurance without health checks.

As you change employers over your lifetime, be sure to give each new employer the details of your super fund to avoid having multiple funds open. Regularly opening and closing super funds is time consuming, costly and can eat into your investment returns.

Remember, this chapter is an introduction to superannuation. Knowing which fund is best for you depends on a few different things. If you are in doubt, seek professional advice. A Financial Planner can review your fund(s) and give recommendations.

Chapter 16 summary

- Super is one of the most tax effective investments because:
  - › Investment earnings in super are taxed at only 15%.
  - › Investment earnings in retirement are tax-free!
- Salary sacrificing to super increases the amount you have for retirement and reduces the amount of income tax you pay.
- You must personally contribute to super to have enough income in retirement (don't just rely on your employer contributions). Start sooner, rather than later.

CHAPTER 17

Insurance
(Do You Really Need It?)

What is insurance?
Insurance is an agreement with an insurer to pay you
a sum of money for a specified loss, damage, illness or death.
It's a form of protection, to protect yourself, your family
and the things you own if something goes wrong.

A lot of people have their car insured, however not their life. Think about that for a minute… Which is worth more? Not having the correct insurance in place can have devastating consequences, especially if you have debts and a family to take care of. However, in saying that, actually having the wrong insurances in place can also be a waste of money if you, for example:

◆ Have the wrong type and amount of insurance.
◆ Hold low-quality policies (not worth the paper written on).
◆ Pay too much in premiums.

Insurance is not the most exciting topic, it is however important.

Insurance is a gamble. It is a bet between you and an insurance company as to whether a particular devastating or debilitating event will occur in the future. Unfortunately, no one has a crystal ball, and you can't live in hindsight. All you can do is to pay to protect the most important areas of life—just in case something untoward happens.

I dislike paying insurance premiums because I have only ever claimed a policy once, so I get annoyed with paying premiums from my Bills Account. (It's a good thing not to have claimed insurance, I just wish I didn't have to pay the premiums.)

Yes, if you never claim a policy, then it was 'money down the drain' so to speak, but if you or your loved ones ever have to claim on a policy, especially a major claim... even just once in a lifetime then the benefit received from that insurance is priceless. In all my time,working in Financial Planning, I have never met a client who wasn't grateful for the money received from an insurance policy claim—regardless of the amount received or their financial position.

Protecting yourself adequately with insurance doesn't have to be expensive. The key is 'cost vs. value'—only insure what you need to and make sure your policies are suitable.

Only insure what will financially cripple you to lose. For everything else, wear the risk and rely on your emergency savings. You can't pay to protect everything.

You and your **income** are crucial to your ongoing survival. If you get hurt or die, everything changes. A car can be replaced. You can't be. The priority is to insure yourself. Everything else has a lesser priority. Unfortunately, a lot of people prioritise insuring *things* (home, contents, car, stuff, etc), rather than their *life*, or wait until later in life to buy personal insurance, only to have issues with their health which prevent them from being eligible for the cover they need.

Whether you are young or old, single or married, have children or not—you need certain insurances at certain times in life, for peace of mind and financial protection. You also need to be mindful of paying for 'rubbish policies' or paying for 'incorrect cover'. These can be overkill in balancing the payment of premiums for what could happen in the future vs. having money for what is happening now in your day-to-day life. There is a payoff between the cost of premiums vs. appropriate insurance. The type and amount of insurance you need depends on your own financial situation.

The main types of insurances are:

◆ **Personal Risk:** protects your life and income.
◆ **General:** protects things (home, contents, car, health and travel).

These are the most important areas which you need to pay to protect. Everything else is optional. If death, injury or damage to a person or thing in your life will financially cripple you, then insure it. If not, don't insure it. Here is a run-down of the most common insurance available, who needs it and who doesn't.

Protecting Your: Life & Income

LIFE INSURANCE

Pays a lump sum in the event of death to a beneficiary or your estate. Allows your family to meet their financial commitments (living expenses and debt repayment) if you are not around to support them. The amount needs to be sufficient to clear debts and costs, such as funeral expenses and child education, plus provide ongoing income for financial dependents (spouse and children under 18) for a number of years. A sum insured equal to 5–10 times your salary may sound like a lot. It is actually quite conservative and may only be enough to cover debts.

Who needs it? Anyone with debts or dependents (such as a non-working spouse/young children).

Who doesn't? People without debts or dependants, or enough assets to repay debts and funeral costs in the event of their death.

TOTAL & PERMANENT DISABILITY (TPD) INSURANCE

Pays a lump sum to you, if you are totally and permanently disabled and unable to work ever again (but don't die). The amount needed is similar to Life insurance, plus extra to pay for medical treatment or home renovations (wheelchair accessibility, etc).

Who needs it? Most people need some TPD insurance to cover debts, major medical expenses and home renovations. What would happen if you were hurt and bedridden for life? Where would you live? Who would look after you? You may receive some assistance from the government (i.e. a pension) however it will be a very small amount and not enough for long-term medical care, living expenses and rent/ mortgage payments. Do you have children, what about their full-time care and schooling costs?

Who doesn't? People with enough financial assets to repay debts and cover major medical expenses, in-home care and family expenses (child education, ongoing income).

TRAUMA INSURANCE

Pays a lump sum to you, if you are diagnosed with a major medical condition (cancer, heart attack etc). The amount needs to cover major medical costs or debt repayments (for 1–2 years), to allow you to take time off work (to recuperate without financial worry). It is more expensive than Life and TPD insurance, so the sum insured is usually a lot lower.

Who needs it? Most People—even if it is limited to providing just an amount for major medical expenses (not covered by Health Insurance).

Who doesn't? People with enough financial assets be able to repay debts and pay for major medical expenses.

INCOME PROTECTION INSURANCE

Pays a regular monthly amount to you to replace lost income if unable to work due to illness or injury for an extended period of time. Sum insured is usually 75% of salary.

Who needs it? Anyone working and earning an income they rely on for living expenses.

Who doesn't? Anyone not working or working less than 10 hours per week. Or those not relying on their income for expenses, i.e. they earn enough passive income from investments/business which will continue even if they are personally unable to work or have a spouse's income which will continue and be sufficient for household expenses.

Those ineligible for Income Protection, e.g. they are stay at home parents, part-time workers who can instead apply for Living Expenses Insurance, which also pays a regular monthly amount (where a claim is not occupation-based). For example, if a stay-at-home parent can't perform their normal household duties, there could be extra living expenses incurred to hire a cleaner for the upkeep of the house, a nanny to care for children or an in-home carer (assuming the other spouse continues to work full-time for income).

Did you know, according to The Lifewise/NATSEM Underinsurance Report—Understanding the social and economic cost of underinsurance (2010), cancer is one of the biggest reasons for Income Protection and Living Expenses Insurance claims. Sadly, one in two Australians will develop cancer before the age of 85 and 95% of Australian families don't have adequate levels of insurance. Mental Illness (Depression) and Back Pain are two other very common claims.

Life, TPD, Trauma and Income Protection all work in conjunction with each other. Rather than cutting out one or another due to cost, especially when budget restraints are an issue, look to reduce the sum insured a little, or remove policy extras or use superannuation (retirement savings) to pay some premiums.

Smoker Status significantly affects all premiums. Smokers usually pay double. You are only considered a non-smoker if you have not smoked for 12 months.

If you have any existing policies and stopped smoking over 12 months ago, be sure to contact your insurer to sign a Non-smoker Declaration and substantially reduce premiums.

STEPPED VS. LEVEL PREMIUMS

Stepped premiums are cheaper and increase each year with your age, whereas Level premiums generally remain the same, with possible small increases for inflation. Level premiums are more expensive initially but offer long term savings.

The crossover point when Level premiums become cheaper compared to Stepped premiums is around eight years. In my experience, most people tend to keep policies for a few years (much less than eight) before they change insurers (to save money or increase policy features, etc) and therefore don't hold Level policies long enough to achieve any cost savings.

Medical Underwriting vs. Moratorium

The process of underwriting takes place when you lodge an application for insurance. To assess a person's risk, an insurer relies on information from a range of sources. If you apply for a policy that's medically underwritten, as a minimum, you will be asked to complete an application form and a medical questionnaire. Any medical conditions from the past few years will be considered 'pre-existing' and may or may not be covered by an insurer (either excluded from cover or included, with a premium 'loading' of 25% - 100% + extra cost).

Medically underwritten policies can provide peace of mind as you are certain of what you are covered for. After the policy is accepted, if anything changes in your health in the future, you are not obliged to inform the insurer and will still be covered. Therefore, it makes sense to buy cover whilst you are young and healthy rather than later down the track, when you may have more health concerns noted on your medical history.

However, not all life insurance policies are fully medically underwritten. Some policies are accepted with 'moratorium underwriting', which means that you are not required to provide details of your medical history upfront (no health assessment is done). This type of policy can be established much faster but only covers future medical conditions, no past conditions. Only in the event of a claim is an assessment of your health history done to determine whether the claim is related to any past medical conditions—if yes, then your claim will be denied. It's essentially the opposite of a medically underwritten policy.

Each method of underwriting has advantages and disadvantages. It's very important to get that right. The method used can have a large impact on what's actually covered.

'Over-the-Phone' Insurances

Life insurances applied for over the phone or online (insurance hotline style policies) are generally 'moratorium' policies. That way insurers can offer cover quickly and without fuss to entice you to buy. Unless you read the fine print, you may not realise those policies generally don't cover pre-existing conditions. You might end up paying premiums for insurances that don't cover you in your time of need if something appears in your medical history which can be related to a future claim.

> *Personally, I am not a fan of over-the-phone life and disability insurance policies. I feel that they leave too much to chance. I would rather be medically underwritten now, whilst young and healthy, than in the future (at claim time). Sometimes the cost is even more expensive than a fully medically underwritten cover. I often see Financial Planning clients being recommended to replace moratorium policies with fully medically underwritten cover, to reduce premiums and increase certainty. It depends on your personal situation and your actual policy of course, so when paying good money for those insurances, it's best to seek advice.*

Superannuation Fund Insurances

Life, TPD and Income Protection insurances (not Trauma insurance) can be held inside a superannuation fund, so those premiums are paid with your retirement savings, from the account balance. There are extra considerations to consider when holding cover inside superannuation, including tax consequences, restrictions on receiving claim payments and prematurely using your retirement savings for purposes other than retirement. However, it can be a good way to compromise on cost and help afford the insurance cover that you need now, rather than being underinsured and at risk.

> *If you are concerned about cost or that your budget is too tight to pay for insurances out of pocket, then consider using your superannuation fund to hold your insurance. The quality of cover may differ to other policies that are available outside of superannuation, however at least you will have some of the most important insurances in place. Call your fund to apply.*

Protecting Your: Health
HEALTH INSURANCE (PRIVATE MEDICAL COVER)

Pays the cost of hospital and other medical treatments (known as 'extras'). Hospital Cover can be bought standalone or packaged with Extras Cover.

◆ **Hospital:** you choose your hospital, doctor, when you are treated and usually includes emergency ambulance services.
◆ **Extras:** benefits of dental, optical, physiotherapy, chiropractic, etc.

There are different levels of cover for different stages of life, so you are not at the whim of the public health system (Medicare) in a time of need. Medicare is not the same as health insurance. The Government provides a basic level of health care to every citizen under the Medicare system—your health insurance pays for everything else. Those who don't have health insurance must be prepared to rely on the Medicare system with longer waiting times (especially for elective surgery), no choice of doctor or hospital and the risk that some medical expenses are just not covered by Medicare—meaning you either go without treatment or foot the bill yourself, which can be very expensive. Without cover, you can still choose to be treated privately, but it's expensive.

The type of cover needed depends on what medical treatments may be likely in the future. If you have children, are planning to start a family or are older, then you need more coverage as the risk of needing costly medical treatment is greater. Younger people tend 'not to worry about it' because they are fit and healthy, however be aware that the cost of an ambulance is currently more than $1,100 in Victoria—you can usually buy cover for less, and it protects you for more than just an ambulance ride. Also, the Government will charge you a higher rate of tax if you don't hold Hospital Cover and earn over a certain income threshold. If you don't buy cover before age 31, an extra premium loading will also apply.

Who needs it? Everyone—at least Hospital cover (including Ambulance). Buy the best that you can afford. Basic cover for a young, single person starts from around $20 per week at the time of writing, so look to cut back other areas of spending to afford at least basic Hospital Cover. Extras Cover is just that... 'extras', add on depending on your stage in life and protection needs. If you know that you are prone to dental issues for example and feel that it will only get worse over time, then it may be wise to consider a policy that provides good dental cover. Likewise, if you are planning to start a family soon, then select a policy with good maternity cover. If you are young, fit and healthy then stick to the basics.

GOVERNMENT REBATES

A discount provided by the government to reduce premiums and encourage more people to take out private health insurance (to reduce the strain on Medicare).

MEDICARE LEVY SURCHARGE (TAX)

All taxpayers pay 2% of their taxable income as a Medicare Levy towards the system (except low-income earners). The Medicare Levy Surcharge is an additional tax for those who don't have Hospital Cover and earn above $90,000 for singles and $180,000 for couples/families (Australian Medicare Levy Surcharge income thresholds 2020/21 www.ato.gov.au). If the surcharge is payable, an additional 1%–1.5% of taxable income is payable on top of the usual 2% Medicare Levy.

For example, a single person with taxable income of $95,000 per year and no Hospital Cover will pay a surcharge of $950 per year. Ouch! For that cost, basic Hospital Cover can be purchased (and even some Extras Cover), which will provide greater protection and benefit, rather than paying extra government taxes for no additional benefits.

LIFETIME HEALTH COVER (LOADING)

People without Hospital Cover after age 31 who then decide to buy cover later in life will pay a 2% loading on top of their premium for each year they waited after age 31. For example, if you take out hospital cover at age 40, you will pay 20% more. Maximum loading is 70%. Ouch!

> *As a minimum, everyone needs to have at least Hospital Cover in place for protection and to avoid paying unnecessary additional taxes and loadings—which buys you nothing—no added protection. Then, add-on Extras Cover as afforded. Many insurers offer 'minimum packages' to meet the requirements stipulated by the Government. Hospital Cover is what counts for Medicare Levy Surcharge and Lifetime Loading purposes, not Extras Cover.*
>
> *If cost is an issue then check if the cost of your Extras Cover is worth maintaining. Is it better value for you to pay for Hospital Cover (only) and then pay for extras yourself when*

needed, e.g. trips to the Dentist or Physiotherapist (rather than paying premiums all year for services you rarely use)?

Protecting Your: Things

HOME & CONTENTS INSURANCE

Pays for loss or damage to your home (building), contents or other personal belongings. Allows you to repair or rebuild a home or replace damaged, lost or stolen contents.

- **Home:** consider the costs associated with rebuilding an entire home, such as demolition and builder fees plus the cost of driveways and fences etc. Include money to replace furnishings and fixtures—carpets, tiles, blinds, stove-tops etc.
- • **Contents:** important not only if you lose everything (fire/ flood etc.) and need to replace everything you own, but also for partial loss (burglary, etc).

Who needs it?

Home Building Insurance: All owners of standalone properties (non-strata title) especially with a home loan (mortgage) attached. If the property burns down, you still need to repay the loan. Repaying a loan for an asset that no longer exists can be financially devastating, especially one as expensive as a house!

Contents Insurance: Anyone with contents which they value and would want to be replaced in the event of loss, theft or damage. It's also possible to cover extra valuable jewellery and sporting equipment for an additional cost. Limit your premiums by simply selecting a lump sum amount such as $10,000, $15,000 or $20,000, for example, rather than covering too many individual items. Think about the potential loss which may happen in the future vs. the cost of insurance which is payable now. Imagine if an internal house pipe bursts and water damages your entire kitchen (floor, walls, built in appliances and the cupboards). The cost of those damages can run into the thousands of dollars. Without Home Insurance, will you be able to afford the repairs? What if the water reached the electronics in your lounge room? In that scenario, your Home Insurance policy won't replace your TV and Surround Sound System, you need to claim your Contents policy. The two go hand in hand.

Who doesn't? Owners of strata title properties don't need to buy separate Home Insurance because the body corporate will pay for a policy that covers all buildings in the strata complex. Those that rent where they live don't need Home Insurance, as it's the landlord's responsibility to protect the building, not the tenant's. However, renters still need Contents Insurance as their landlord's policy will not protect their personal belongings.

Those without many personal belongings of value to insure may not feel the need to have Contents Insurance, e.g. if you live in a furnished property and don't own the contents.

Some people may feel the cost of insurance doesn't warrant covering their low-value personal items, however, for peace of mind, having even $10,000 of cover can cost as little as $150 per year (a lot less than having to refurnish a whole apartment or house).

Home Contents Insurance will generally limit the payout for any one particular item such as a computer or a piece of jewellery to $1,000 per item. You can add on extra cover for the items worth more than $1,000 that you want to protect—this is an added cost. The more you add, the higher your premium will be. So, think carefully about which extra items to add to a policy (if any). Always check the policy Terms & Conditions, to know whether an item you want to cover is already included in the standard policy.

MOTOR VEHICLE INSURANCE (CAR, MOTORBIKE, ETC)

Pays a lump sum to you to repair or replace a motor vehicle. Apart from your home, your motor vehicle is often the most expensive item you own, therefore it makes sense to protect against theft, fire, and accidents—cover also protects you for damage caused to other people (personal liability cover—in case you hurt someone).

Who needs it? Vehicle owners who can't afford to lose their vehicle—especially if a car loan is attached. If it gets stolen or is 'written off' in a major accident you will still need to repay the loan.

Who doesn't? Those who feel the cost of cover is not warranted for their car (e.g. the car may be very old), instead they may choose a 'Third Party Indemnity' policy to reduce costs and protect only damage caused to other people (life/property), and not their own car.

TRAVEL INSURANCE

Pays a lump sum to you for loss of luggage, unexpected changes to your travel plans and trip cancellation, emergency medical treatment and personal liability. Adventure activities such as snow sports, water sports, bungee jumping, etc, can also be covered.

Who needs it? Anyone travelling internationally (overseas). Don't travel without it. If you can't afford travel insurance then you can't afford to travel. Whilst losing luggage is inconvenient and may warrant the cost of this type of cover, it is more so the major costs that will be payable if you are hurt whilst overseas (or worse), which need to be protected.

Who doesn't? Optional if travelling domestically—depends on what activities you will be doing. If travelling interstate to visit family or for business then perhaps it's not so important to insure you and your luggage compared to a ski/snowboarding holiday. Some Home Contents policies protect your valuables when travelling domestically, so check your policy document to avoid doubling up on costs.

PUBLIC LIABILITY INSURANCE

Provides protection if there is an accident in or around your home or business. For example, if a cleaner or builder injures themselves in your home, then public liability insurance helps to pay compensation.

Who needs it? Everyone—it's included in many Home & Contents policies.

Real-life story

I recently purchased a new Home Contents Insurance policy. I specifically wanted to cover a couple of pieces of jewellery which were worth more than $1,000 per piece and a brand new, state of the art, work computer which I had only just bought and which would have 'significantly annoyed me' to have to dip into my savings to replace in the event of loss. Those were most important to me (in addition to household furniture).

I went online to get a quote from two big-name insurers, with which I already held other policies (to benefit from an automatic 5%–10% 'existing customer' discount). Quoting online also meant a further discount of $25 per year from both insurers. One insurer quoted $300 per year including the extra cover for the jewellery and computer (I had to add all three extra items).

The second insurer automatically covered computers and personal electronics with no value limit, meaning I didn't have to add on extra cover for the computer (only for the jewellery), which resulted in a cheaper premium of $230 per year (for similar, like for like, cover).

A $70 difference may or may not be a big deal to you, remember though, that represents a 23% saving and is a big deal in percentage terms. Savings made here and there all add up and does make a difference in the long run.

It only takes a few minutes to check the Terms & Conditions for the items you want to insure—use the search function on your computer for keywords such as 'computer' in this case. Most insurers also offer a Fact Sheet—a shorter version highlighting the main policy features.

Waste of Money Insurances ... in my opinion.

FUNERAL INSURANCE

Pays an agreed amount (usually $7,500–$15,000) in the event of death for funeral expenses. Policies are quick and easy to buy online or over-the-phone without medical questionnaires. In the event of a claim, payment will be made to your family within 24 hours (of the paperwork being completed), which is quicker than a Life insurance policy.

Who needs it? No one. Instead, buy some Life insurance and make sure you have an emergency fund which covers the cost of an average funeral. Often, the premium payable for a Funeral Cover policy can buy a lot more Life insurance, for example:

TABLE 1: Life Insurance vs. Funeral Cover Cost: Female, non-smoker, 36 next birthday, Western Australia.

Insurer	Sum Insured	Premium
Sureplan Funeral Cover	$14,822 (max available)	$22.88 per month
NRMA Funeral Cover	$15,000 (max available)	$64.34 per month
Zurich Life Insurance	$100,000 (example)	$12.53 per month

Premiums current as at time of writing. The insurers shown are examples only and not a recommendation to hold cover with.

In this example, for a cost of $22.88 per month, the insured person could buy $14,822 of Funeral Cover, however for almost half that cost, she could buy $100,000 of Life insurance. The second Funeral Cover quote costs over five times more than the Life insurance (note though for only 15% of the sum insured).

MOBILE PHONE INSURANCE

Replaces your mobile phone (or tablet) in the event of loss, theft or irreparable damage. You know 'that' cover—sold to you when you sign up for a new phone contract? Premiums can be around $10–$15 per month on top of your monthly phone cost.

Who needs it? No one. Only people without savings think they need this type of insurance. It's expensive (for what you get). Instead, make sure you have an emergency fund which you can dip into to replace or fix your device on the off-chance something does happen. Theft of a phone from a home or car may already be covered by a Home Contents or Motor Vehicle policy—check to avoid doubling up.

Unfortunately, I've known people to pay their Phone Insurance premiums consistently, thinking they needed that type of cover because they have no savings and are worried that the replacement value of mobile phones can be around $1,500–$2,000+, only to be told when lodging a claim that their insurer will not fix or replace a phone because the damage was due to 'water damage' and not covered by the policy. One person was even told that the water damage was likely caused by sweat, from carrying the phone in his back pocket. Yes, you read that right.

The cost of a new phone will be a lot less than paying $15 per month in premiums each year over your lifetime. For example, say you first sign up for a mobile phone at age 18. For how long do you keep paying those premiums? A lot of people continue to pay phone insurance premiums year after year. That means that if a claim is made at:

Age 25 ($15 per month paid since age 18) = $1,260 paid so far.

Age 35 ($15 per month paid since age 18) = $3,060 paid so far.

Often, the likelihood of losing a phone doesn't warrant paying those premiums. Instead, save that $10–$15 per month towards an 'emergency fund' which can be used for any purpose. Draw the line somewhere when it comes to paying premiums and what you protect. If you pay $15 per month to protect a phone rather than $12.53 per month for Life insurance (from table 1), then reassess your priorities.

Don't walk around with inadequate Life insurance when you are paying for phone insurance because a salesperson scared you into it.

PET INSURANCE

Pays the cost of veterinary bills either once off or ongoing if a pet is sick or injured. Annual sum insured allows multiple claims and sometimes includes third-party liability.

Who needs it? People with pets and no savings think they need this type of insurance. It's expensive—instead, make sure you have emergency funds.

A furry friend is a member of the family, and their health is very important. Veterinary bills are expensive so having Pet Insurance can seem like a good idea, unfortunately, it's expensive (around $15–$55 per month+ for a cat and a whopping $65–$116 per month+ for a dog). Let's ignore the cost to insure a pet horse which is even higher!

I consider this type of insurance to be quite 'luxurious' in the scheme of things—especially if you hold this type of cover instead of protecting your own life. Instead, choose to save that money each month towards a general emergency fund. Having savings available to you means you don't need to pay for some insurances, or as much, compared to people without any savings. Having an emergency fund will negate the 'value' of Pet Insurance. Those without savings feel more 'at risk' and fear the 'cost of financial loss' and therefore are more willing to pay monthly amounts to insurers, rather than save that monthly amount, well before it's needed. Cost vs value. The likelihood of a claim vs actually paying premiums.

LOAN COVER

Offered by banks and other lenders to cover your loan repayments if you are unable to work due to illness or injury, or to repay the loan if you die. Usually offered when applying for a loan or later through a bank employed telemarketer.

Who needs it? No one. This insurance is irrelevant if you have enough life and disability insurances in place. For the cost of Loan Cover, you can buy other better value insurances.

> *Currently, the premium offered by CBA is $25 per month (added to your loan repayment) which equates to $300 per year. NAB charges a minimum of $150 per year (premium depends on your loan balance). Both are expensive.*
>
> *The protection offered by Loan Cover is not worth it compared to other types of available insurance.*
>
> *For example, Life insurance is used to protect debts (and other things) in the event of death and you can buy a lot more Life insurance for those prices, instead of paying to protect just one loan with expensive Loan Cover.*
>
> *Income Protection is used to protect the loss if income in the event of illness or injury and again covers more compared to Loan Cover, which protects just one loan (and none of your other living expenses).*

CREDIT CARD COVER

Offered by card issuers to protect an outstanding card balance (or repayments) if you become involuntarily unemployed or temporarily disabled (sometimes death). Usually offered over the phone from a telemarketer. The sum insured will clear the card balance or pay up to 10 times the amount due on the card.

Who needs it? No one. It is irrelevant if you have emergency savings available to you to cover repayments temporarily if you lose your job. Avoiding credit card debt in the first place definitely negates the risk.

> *Currently, the premium offered by CBA is 45c for every $100 (or part thereof) owing on a card at the time your monthly statement is generated. So, if you owe $3,000 then*

your monthly premium would be $13.50 (added to the card balance).

NAB is charging 79c for every $100 owed (or part thereof) so $23.70 would be charged to your card balance. The premium is payable even if you repay your card by the due date. That premium is expensive. What you are covered for (the 'value') for a recurring cost of $162–$284 per year is not worth it (assumes your card balance does not change throughout the year as a simplified example, otherwise the premium would change). Remember, banks are in the business of making money.

AIRLINE TRAVEL INSURANCE

Some airlines will offer Travel Insurance when you book a flight for an additional, sometimes fairly small, premium. Wait! Before you proceed with the cover thinking that it's cheap and will suffice, you must check what's actually covered and what's not. Many times, only flight cancellation is covered (cancellation only by the airline or because of personal injury/death). Medical expenses, loss of luggage and personal liability cover may not be included—especially if you opt-in for 'one-way basic cover' meaning cover ends when you reach your destination.

You don't have to accept the offer of insurance when booking a flight. Instead, purchase a separate comprehensive Travel Insurance policy elsewhere. Some airlines are cheeky and will automatically add the extra cost to your quote unless you intentionally untick the box. Read carefully. Pay attention when booking.

TABLE 2: Airline Insurance vs. Travel Insurance: 14 days in Thailand, 29-year-old traveller

Insurer	What it Covers	Premium
AirAsia Tune Protect One-Way	If the trip is cancelled, curtailed or unable to be completed because of the unforeseeable death, accidental injury, sickness or disease of your travelling companion. Includes some loss of luggage and travel delays. **Doesn't include** medical expenses or cover airline delays, cancellation or rescheduling except for strikes. Doesn't cover if you decide not to continue with the trip or change your plans. **Covers your one-way trip commencing in Australia and ending at your destination.**	$20.00 each direction in addition to the flight (i.e. $40 return)
World Care Travel Insurance	All the usual cover that Travel Insurance provides, i.e. unlimited trip cancellation and delays, unlimited medical expenses, repatriation, dental expenses, loss of luggage, rental vehicle excess and personal liability, etc. **Covers you before you leave, whilst you are away and until you return home to Australia.**	$74.14 for Comprehensive cover ($60.43 for Budget cover, i.e. medical expenses, repatriation cover and personal liability only)

Premiums current as at time of writing. The insurers shown are examples only and not a recommendation to hold cover with.

So in this example, if you had opted in for the AirAsia One-Way cover whilst booking your flight, you would have paid $40 ($20 for the flight there and $20 for the flight home) thinking it will provide 'standard travel insurance coverage'—it doesn't. If you also want to cover emergency medical expenses and loss of luggage (which most people typically do when travelling), then you need to buy another policy as well. So, the total cost to you becomes $114.14 for both policies shown, instead of just $74.14 which is all you really need.

Whilst the World Care Travel Insurance 'costs more' it also protects you more—the 'value' is greater. It covers you before you leave, whilst away and until you return home, plus so much more. You don't need to also buy the AirAsia One-Way cover.

The premiums shown above are examples only. As a comparison, Travel Insurance through other popular insurers for similar coverage to the World Care policy include $81.03 with 1Cover, $92.58 with Allianz and $107.00 with Cover-More.

You must read the Policy Terms & Conditions to know whether a Travel Insurance policy will cover you before you leave home, or if you are already travelling (and need to buy a new policy). Does it cover you if you're already outside of your home country? Price must not be your only deciding factor— the cheapest is not always best, nor is the most expensive.

How to Reduce Premiums

ASK FOR A DISCOUNT

Got existing policies in place? Have you asked for a discount? Why not? Everything in life is negotiable, well nearly everything. Insurance premiums can be. If you have existing policies in place and have not asked your insurer for a discount lately, or ever, I suggest you ring them today to do so. With so many competitors in the marketplace, your insurer will not want to lose your business and will often give you some sort of discount if you ask. Even if it's a small discount, that money is better off in your pocket than the insurers—it all adds up.

It's about 'stickability'—if an insurer thinks you won't change companies (because you can't be bothered), then they won't come to the party and give you what you want (a discount). If they see that you are prepared to change companies then they often meet your demands to keep your business.

REQUOTING AT RENEWAL

When you receive annual statements or renewal notices for a policy, it's a good prompt to spend a few minutes to requote with one or two other companies for comparison purposes, to make sure your renewal premium is still competitive or if savings can be made by moving the cover elsewhere—don't just simply pay the renewal out of habit and laziness. A lot can change in a year with regards to premium rates. It only takes a few minutes to get a quote online using the insurer websites—if you manage to save say $85 and it takes you 15 minutes to quote and change policies, then you essentially just earned yourself the equivalent of $340 per hour, tax-free. Even if it takes you 30 minutes, you essentially earned $170 per hour, tax-free.

I suggest you also requote your existing cover with your existing insurer's online quoting system. At times, your insurer may be offering the same cover to new customers at a cheaper rate than what you are currently paying. If so, ring your insurer and demand that they match the online quoted price. If not, change insurers.

PAY PREMIUMS ANNUALLY

Paying the premium on a yearly basis (rather than monthly or quarterly) will reduce your costs. Having savings available to you will make this possible for the first premium, then be sure to put a regular amount in a 'Bills Accounts' for when the premium is due again in 12 months.

INCREASE THE EXCESS

Some policies allow you to choose your excess. Generally, the higher your excess, the cheaper the premium. Sometimes, however, there may not actually be that much difference in cost for a policy with a $500 excess or a $1,000 excess.

When getting a quote on your policies, check the premium offered with the different excesses. If you can save a decent amount to warrant increasing your excess, then weigh up your 'risk vs. reward' and select the higher excess to save money from day one. Of course, this assumes that you have your emergency savings in place to be able to pay the excess in the event of a claim—those with savings can take advantage of the discounts in life. However, if you will save only a few dollars each month in the premium then why increase an excess from $500 to $1,000, for example?

CASE STUDY

Real-life story

I recently replaced an insurance policy for an investment property to reduce premiums—quite substantially. The premium for the existing policy, which I had for a few years, was increasing to $766.08 per year. Each year at renewal, I checked for a cheaper premium for similar coverage, to no avail—no savings were possible elsewhere, at least, having done my homework, I was sure that the policy was good value.

This year, however, I managed to find a premium through a large, well-known, reputable insurer for only $458.78 per year. A saving of $307.30 per year. Finally! Too good to be true—maybe—before I proceeded, I quickly checked the Terms & Conditions to make sure the new policy provided similar cover to what I already had and covered for Flood in particular (some policies don't) and Loss of Rent (for Landlords). Yes, the new policy covered both, however the Loss of Rent was for 14 weeks with the new insurer, compared to 15 weeks with the current insurer. The new insurer was also offering a $50 discount for online policies. So, to save $307.30 per year, I was happy to give up one week's worth of Loss of Rent cover, on the off chance I have to claim in the future. The property's rent was only around $375 per week—so it wasn't even a big difference overall.

The whole process to get a quote with the new company, buy the new policy and ring the old insurer to cancel the existing policy took me less than 30 minutes. Essentially, I saved (earned) myself $307.30 in that time, which is the equivalent of $614.60 per hour, tax-free. You tell me... was it worth it? Yes, it definitely was.

How Much Insurance is Needed

Here are two case study examples using fictitious but realistic figures. Swap the figures for your own, to calculate how much cover you need.

TABLE 3: Single Person, no dependants, earning $50,000 p.a. (example)

Commitments	Life	TPD	Trauma	Income Protection
Home loan to repay	$300,000	$300,000	$50,000 (partial)	-
Other loans/ debts to repay	$20,000	$20,000	-	-
Funeral/ Medical expenses	$10,000	$100,000	$100,000	-
Income to replace	N/A [1]	Income Protection [2]	Income Protection [2]	$3,125/ month
Time to go without income	-	-	-	30 days [3]
How long to replace income	-	-	-	Age 65
Total	**$330,000**	**$420,000**	**$150,000**	**$3,125/ month**
Less Assets To Sell				
Cash/ Shares etc	$10,000	$10,000	N/A	N/A
Superannuation	$25,000	$25,000	N/A	N/A
Insurance Needed	**$295,000**	**$385,000**	**$150,000**	**$3,125/ month**

1. No financial dependants and therefore no ongoing income needed.

2. Income Protection benefits could provide ongoing income.

3. Example waiting period assuming some annual/sick leave entitlements with employer and emergency cash savings to cover the first 60 days on claim (30 day waiting period plus 30 days payment in arrears).

Plus:

◆ Health Insurance (single package)
◆ Home & Contents Insurance (public liability included)
◆ Motor Vehicle Insurance
◆ Travel Insurance (when travelling)

TABLE 4: Married Person, 2 young children ages 2 & 3, earning $50,000 p.a.

Commitments	Life	TPD	Trauma	Income Protection
Home loan to repay	$300,000	$300,000	$100,000 (partial)	-
Other loans/ debts to repay	$20,000	$20,000	-	-
Funeral/ Medical expenses	$10,000	$100,000	$100,000	-
Child Education expenses	$100,000 [1]	$100,000 [1]	-	-
Income to replace	$550,000 [2]	Income Protection [2]	Income Protection [2]	$3,125/ month
Time to go without income	-	-	-	30 days [3]
How long to replace income	-	-	-	Age 65
Total	**$980,000**	**$520,000**	**$200,000**	**$3,125/ month**
Less Assets To Sell				
Cash/ Shares etc	$10,000	$10,000	N/A	N/A
Superannuation	$25,000	$25,000	N/A	N/A
Insurance Needed	**$945,000**	**$485,000**	**$200,000**	**$3,125/ month**

1. Funds for school fees of up to $10,000 per child per year (assume five years each).

2. Funds to generate income of $50,000 per year for the surviving spouse, until children are 18 (assume 15 years) using a 'Balanced' investment return, as an example.

3. Income Protection benefits could provide ongoing income.

4. Example waiting period assuming some annual/sick leave entitlements with employer and emergency cash savings to cover the first 60 days on claim (30 day waiting period plus 30 days payment in arrears).

Plus:

♦ Health Insurance (family package) including spouse and children

♦ Home & Contents Insurance (public liability included)

♦ Motor Vehicle Insurance

♦ Travel Insurance (when travelling)

In both examples, regular savings (emergency fund) are needed to cover the initial period off work before Income Protection payments start and any other 'possible losses' which may not warrant paying for extra insurance.

How To Buy The Right Cover (for you)

The amounts and type of cover you need will depend on your financial situation. Whilst most people can comfortably arrange home, contents, motor vehicle and travel insurance online or over the phone, it's best to seek advice from a Financial Planner to buy Personal Risk Insurances as that is a specialised area and with many variables.

Life, TPD and Income Protection insurances are available through most superannuation funds, with the quality of cover varying compared to policies held outside of superannuation.

Financial Planners don't provide General Insurance advice (home, contents, motor vehicle, travel)—a General Insurance Broker can help with that.

Who to Contact	For What
Financial Planner	Life, TPD, Trauma, Income Protection and Living Expenses Insurance and better insurance (more comprehensive) cover.
Alternative: Call your superannuation fund to buy some basic cover (at least) and pay some premiums from your account balance. The fund won't be able to provide you with any advice and can't offer Trauma cover, but you can instruct them as to the amount of Life, TPD and Income Protection (Salary Continuance) that you would like.	
Direct to Insurers (Online or Phone)	Health Insurance, Home, Contents, Motor Vehicle, Travel plus Landlords Insurance (for investment properties).
Alternative: Call a General Insurance Broker.	

Personal Risk Insurances

(LIFE, TPD, TRAUMA, INCOME PROTECTION)

Ideally, seek advice from a Financial Planner to put the correct insurances in place for your personal financial situation, especially if you want to use your superannuation. You can call your fund to implement low-cost basic insurances, and it's better than nothing, the fund though, can't help you with calculating how much or what type of cover you need.

Financial Planners are licensed to offer several insurance companies for you to choose from and will calculate what exact insurance you need, what policies are best for you (cost vs. features) and how to structure the cover. They will also review any existing policies you have to determine whether to keep or replace them (and why). As payment for their work, Financial Planners will receive a commission from the insurer just like any General Insurance Broker. The commission will often cover the cost of your consultation. Many of the policies will pay a similar percentage commission, and therefore that's not generally a driving factor when recommending a certain policy vs. another, compared to other factors such as premium, policy features, and wording and the insurer's claims history, which are much more important.

It's best to seek advice when considering holding cover inside superannuation as there can be some tax consequences and cover limitations to consider.

HEALTH INSURANCE (PRIVATE MEDICAL COVER)

There are large, well-known insurers in each state which provide good cover, with varying packages and premiums, arranged over the phone or online. Most offer easy to use online quotes with a few simple questions to determine which package may suit you best. A quick Google search will result in the most popular insurers. You must compare the packages available and check what they actually cover (and what they don't)—most insurers have an easy to read 'features at a glance' policy summary, and you will see that for the most part, a lot of policies are similar and only a few variables may change between companies e.g. if you are looking for specific cover such as Maternity, be sure to check for that in the policy summary. For example, basic Hospital Cover for a young, single person will not cover Maternity.

General Insurance
(HOME, CONTENTS, MOTOR VEHICLE & TRAVEL)

Again, there are many well-known insurers available in each state, with varying packages and premiums. Policies can be purchased over the phone or online. Online quotes available. With all quotes, you must compare like-for-like policies and check what they cover e.g. if looking for Flood Cover for a Home & Contents policy, be sure to specifically check for that in the policy summary as not all policies automatically cover floods (some insurers charge an additional fee to cover that and some don't cover it at all). There are new insurers coming onto the market each year, some offer cheaper premiums. If considering those insurers (for cost savings), be sure to read closely what the policy covers, the excess payable, the premium frequency and what waiting periods apply. Make sure you are comparing like-for-like products. Read online reviews about insurers, especially when it comes to claims. Does the insurer pay claims? Do other people constantly have issues with making a claim? Cheaper is not always better, especially if a company is known for not paying claims.

Chapter 17 summary

- You need insurances to protect your life, income, and assets.
- Not having the correct insurance in place can have devastating consequences in the event of major loss.
- There are a lot of insurances which are a waste of money.
- Insure wisely—if unsure, seek professional advice.

CHAPTER 18

Death and Your Money

Have you ever wondered what happens when you die?

This is not a chapter on the afterlife. Instead it focuses on what happens to your money, assets, liabilities, and family when you are no longer around, or if something happens and you can no longer make your own financial and health decisions. It seems counter-productive to have an organised money life and to have spent so much time making money for you and your family, only to then leave a mess for others to sort out when you pass away.

Estate Planning makes sure that the right assets are in the right hands at the right time. It's about putting in place some strategies now, so your final wishes are granted later on. Estate planning is important for everyone. If you own anything or have people who rely on you, then it's a good idea to have an estate plan. The more complicated your personal situation and financial affairs are, the more important estate planning is.

Your Assets

You have probably heard of a Will. It's a legal document that details what you want to happen to your assets etc in the event of your death. You need to make a Will, even if you think you don't have much to leave. If you have children, you definitely need a Will.

There are three parties to a Will:

◆ **Executor:** person appointed to administer your estate.

- **Beneficiaries:** person(s) named to receive your assets.
- **Guardian:** person(s) nominated to be legally responsible for caring and otherwise managing the affairs of underage children.

The legal requirements for preparing a valid legal Will vary from state to state. A Will is generally revoked in the event of marriage or formal divorce through a court.

What happens without it?

Dying without a valid Will is called 'dying intestate'. When this happens, your estate will be distributed using a fixed formula determined by the Government. The formula may not be in line with your intentions, and the outcome may not be in the best interests of your family and loved ones and can cause significant delays and heartache.

Making a Will can be easy and doesn't have to be expensive. A 'Will Kit' is available from your local post office for around $19.95 (at the time of writing) and can be a good way to put your instructions in writing, in the correct format, though only if your personal and financial situation is straightforward, e.g. single person, minimal assets, no children.

For everyone else, married couples, blended families, people with children, take the time to have a professional Will prepared by a lawyer or estate planning professional. Costs vary if completed online or in person but assume a starting price of around $200 for online. I paid around $300 which was worth every cent. To have the peace of mind in knowing it was done correctly (in person) is extremely important for me, considering the property assets I am building.

Keep your Will in a safe place and make sure you tell your family where it is. Review your Will every few years or as life circumstances change, e.g. marriage, the birth of children or grandchildren, etc.

Your Children

Ensure you have a Guardianship Clause included in your Will for children under 18, which details who you want to take care of your children in the event of your death, as well as how you want them to be cared for. Your Will must include instructions for the appointment of a guardian who can legally act on behalf of your children, as well as specific instructions for their upbringing. This is an area that you don't want to get wrong. It can be tricky to get right if you use a Will Kit instead of having a professional Will prepared. If you have children, it is imperative. Have a professional Will prepared.

What happens without it?

There may well be messy feuds later down the track, especially in blended families and if both parents pass away at the same time.

> *Make sure you have adequate Life insurance in place to leave funds to your children, for the nominated guardian to use. Children cost money. It's not fair to 'leave your children to someone' and not leave any insurance money for their upbringing and education costs.*

Your Financial Decisions & Health

A Power of Attorney is a legal document allowing you to appoint someone to act on your behalf. When in force, the signature of the person you appoint as your Power of Attorney has the same legal force as your own. There are different Powers of Attorney, each with a different purpose:

- ◆ General Power of Attorney: Allows someone to act on your behalf about your personal and financial affairs. You can set limitations around the powers if you wish. The powers granted are voided if you lose your mental capacity to make decisions.
- ◆ Enduring Power of Attorney: An Enduring Power of Attorney is similar to a General Power of Attorney, but it's

not automatically revoked if you become mentally incapable and allows someone to make important financial decisions on your behalf if you are unable to.

◆ Enduring Guardian/Medical Power of Attorney/Advanced Health Directive: An Enduring Power of Attorney allows someone to make financial decisions on your behalf, although not lifestyle and medical decisions.

◆ An Enduring Guardian allows you to nominate someone to make health care decisions on your behalf.

◆ A Medical Power of Attorney allows the person nominated to make medical decisions on your behalf if you are ill or incapacitated.

◆ An Advanced Health Directive allows you to nominate the types of medical treatment or care you do or don't want to receive if you are unable to make the decisions for yourself.

What happens without it?

Your family will have to apply to the State Authority to have an Administrator manage your affairs. That takes time and could cause costly or life-threatening delays.

> *A lawyer or estate planning professional can arrange a Power of Attorney for you, which is often done at the same time as a Will.*

Your Superannuation (Retirement Savings)

A 'beneficiary' is a person you nominate to receive your superannuation account balance (death benefit) when you die, and that includes any Life Insurance attached to the fund. For your superannuation fund to know your instructions, you need to nominate a 'beneficiary'. This is generally, a 'dependant' according to Superannuation Law such as a spouse and children under 18. You can nominate a non-dependant as your beneficiary, such as adult children over 18, but there can be some tax consequences. Beneficiary nominations can either be non-binding or binding:

- Non-binding: the fund trustee will make a decision about who to pay your death benefit to and is legally obliged to determine who your dependents are at the time of your death. So, your nomination is more of a 'suggestion' rather than an 'instruction' in this instance. The trustee can pay benefits to a person who is not the person you nominated.
- Binding: the fund trustee is required, by law, to pay your benefit to the person/s you nominated, as long as the nomination is valid at the time of your death. Binding nominations generally only remain valid for three years and then need to be renewed.
- Non-lapsing Binding: same as binding but doesn't lapse (no need to renew every three years).

Not all superannuation funds offer binding nominations, so you need to check with your fund. If you have no dependents, you can nominate your legal personal representative (your estate), which means your benefits will be distributed as per your Will instructions. It is therefore important to have a valid Will in place.

What happens without it?

The trustee of your fund will decide who receives your death benefit. The trustee has to pay your benefit either to one or more of your dependents or to your estate for distribution according to your will (or both). It can take some time to determine who your dependents are, which means delays until your loved ones receive funds.

> *Contact your fund to ensure you have a beneficiary nomination in place. If not, request a beneficiary nomination form to complete. If yes, then double check your nomination is still valid and appropriate for your current situation. Do you have the right person nominated? It's a good idea to review your beneficiary nomination each year in case things change.*

Your Life Insurance

A beneficiary can also be nominated to receive the proceeds of a Life Insurance policy. If you own a Life Insurance policy personally (in your name), then you nominate a beneficiary for that policy. If you own Life Insurance in your superannuation fund, then the beneficiary nominated on your superannuation fund, will also receive the insurance benefits in the event of your death.

Total & Permanent Disability, Trauma and Income Protection insurance claim payments are paid to the policy owner (you), and therefore no other beneficiary is nominated.

What happens without it?

If the policy is owned personally, then the claim payment will be left to your estate, to be distributed by your Will (or intestacy laws if no Will is in place). If the policy is owned by superannuation, then normal fund trustee discretion applies, as mentioned above.

> *If you have any existing Life insurance policies in place, contact your insurer(s) to review your beneficiary nomination (or request a Beneficiary Nomination form to complete). Make sure your nomination is still appropriate. Review each year in case things change.*

Making a 'List for Mum'

Many years ago, when I had a Will prepared, I wondered how on Earth (if anything did happen to me) would my executor and beneficiaries ever know what assets I owned—with bank accounts and insurance policies held with different institutions and investment properties at different addresses. Would the executor go searching? Would that cause delays? Would some assets be missed and sit in limbo? Would my beneficiaries miss out? Would that hard-earned money disappear into the ether or worse yet, end up owned by the government by default if left unclaimed for too long? This was too much uncertainty for me, which is not my style, so I simplified things and prepared a 'List for Mum'. Simplicity at its' best. A list of the who, what and where with the following details:

- Will Location: Lawyer's contact details and instructions to give them a copy of the List if anything happened to me.
- Important Contacts' Details: Accountant, Mortgage Broker and Insurance Broker and instructions to give them a copy of the List.
- Life Insurances: details of policies and who to contact to claim.
- Superannuation: details of funds and who to contact to withdraw.
- Assets (personal and financial) such as car, bank account details, plus all investment property addresses and real estate agent details.
- Loans such as investment property loan account details.
- Debit/Credit Card(s) to be cancelled, with bank details and account numbers.
- Services to Cancel such as mobile phone, home internet, car insurance, private health insurance with company details and policy numbers.

I gave the list to Mum for safe keeping. Truth be told, Mum got a little emotional when I gave her the list and with the thought of something ever happening to her daughter. We need to face our mortality when organising our money lives. It's better that Mum be a little upset now and to know that every single dollar will pass to my loved ones than leave a mess for them to clean up later on.

Who you use as your trusted person to hold onto a copy of your list is totally up to you. Whilst the list doesn't include account balances or asset values, it still incorporates a lot of personal information, so consider your chosen person wisely.

Chapter 18 summary

- Everyone needs a Will and Enduring Power of Attorney at least.
- Marriage or divorce will revoke an existing Will.
- Will-Kits are very basic. It's better to pay for professional advice—especially if you have children or significant assets/debts.
- Nominate a beneficiary for superannuation and life insurance.
- Someone needs to know where your Will, assets, and liabilities are. Make a list!

FINAL WORD

And Your Next Steps...

At the start of this book, I promised to share with you my financial secrets and to show you the strategies, which I personally use in my day-to-day finances to get the most out of money. You too can achieve more with your money.

I promised to teach you the forgotten fundamentals of money management and to fill the knowledge gap of what's not taught at home or school—to teach you the things you need to know about money. The aim was to reprogram your everyday spending habits, so you better control your own money, whilst also exposing some common, but unknown truths about money. You should have learnt some facts about money which perhaps before you didn't know.

The financial secrets and strategies shared in this book are simple to follow. They are tried, tested, proven to work and suitable for all ages, whether just starting out, or starting over. They are the essential foundation of successful money management, regardless of how much you earn or where you are at in life.

Now you can:

- Control your money to have the life you want.
- Stop living payday to payday to reduce financial stress.
- Pay yourself first and increase savings.
- Set up your bank accounts correctly (put bills on auto-pilot).
- Know the hidden truths behind personal debt.
- Get out of credit card debt in 3 easy steps.
- Stop wasting money and increase income.
- Understand the basics of investing and compound interest.
- Buy your first property (or multiple properties).
- Decide whether it's better to buy a home or an investment.
- Buy multiple properties over time (if you want).
- Understand superannuation and insurances.

- Be in control of your money, even after death.
- Master the fundamentals of successful money management!

Things to Remember

- An asset is something that pays you. A liability costs you.
- Poor People buy 'stuff' (liabilities). Rich People buy assets.
- Buying more stuff will not make you happy. It will make you poor.
- Save money regularly to have a healthy cash flow and choices.
- Pay yourself first. Always. That is the secret to saving.
- Use different accounts, to separate savings from spending money.
- Use automated transfers to move money out of sight.
- Save 20%, spend 80%.
- Never buy 'things' on credit. Personal debt will financially cripple you.
- You must repay 100% of a credit card balance to avoid interest.
- For a home loan, save a minimum 10% cash deposit. Use any first-home buyer government grants towards other fees and charges.
- Rentvesting can be a great way to have the lifestyle you want, whilst also being able to invest.
- The suburb you live in doesn't always make the best investment.
- You must personally contribute to superannuation to have enough by retirement.
- You need insurances to protect your income, life and your assets; there are a lot of insurances which are a waste of money.
- Everyone needs a Will and Enduring Power of Attorney.
- Will-Kits are too basic if you have children/significant assets/debts.
- Someone needs to know where your Will, assets, and liabilities are. Make a list!

**These lessons are REAL. They WORK.
They are TIMELESS.**

Your Next Steps

INCOME & EXPENSES (CASH FLOW)

- ◆ Be conscious of money decisions. Be observant of spending.
- ◆ Track your expenses for at least one month, preferably three.
- ◆ Categorise your expenses as 'essential' or 'non-essential'.
- ◆ Create a budget: income on one side and expenses on the other.
- ◆ Review and reduce each area of spending to create a surplus. In time, consider ways to increase your income.

START YOUR LONG-TERM SAVINGS (FOR GETTING AHEAD FINANCIALLY)

- ◆ Set up a 10% Savings Account (save 10% of your income)
  - › Use a high-interest account (make sure it's fee-free, has no ATM access and is with a different institution).
  - › If you have a home loan, use an offset account.
  - › If you have personal debts use these savings to make extra repayments.
- ◆ Before anything else, use an automated transfer to move your 10% Savings the day after payday.

START YOUR SHORT-TERM SAVINGS (FOR EMERGENCIES & LIFESTYLE)

- ◆ Check that your Everyday Bank Account is fee-free (if not, change it).
- ◆ Open extra accounts (fee-free) and set them up as follows:
  - › Account 1: Everyday Account
  - › Account 2: Bills Account
  - › Automate payment of bills/loans using Direct Debit/BPAY.
  - › Account 3: Emergency Account
  - › Build the balance to at least $1,000. Keep building up to 1 month worth of expenses (preferably 3 months).
  - › Account 4: Just In Case Account
  - › When your initial emergency fund of at least $1,000 is done, redirect some savings here for better lifestyle.
- ◆ Use automated transfers (lodge the day after payday).

Transfer a set amount to each account every payday.

DEBTS

- Credit Cards and Personal Loans:
  - › Stop spending on credit. Switch to a Debit Card.
  - › Contact all lenders to ask for an interest rate discount.
  - › Set up a repayment plan—always make minimum repayments. Make extra repayments on the card/loan with the highest interest rate. Once repaid, snowball the extra repayments to the next highest interest rate.
  - › Consolidate multiple credit card balances to a Balance Transfer Card, so long as you also cut up that card and repay 100% the balance by the end of the interest-free period.
- Home Loans:
  - › Contact your lender to ask for an interest rate discount.
  - › If making monthly repayments, switch to fortnightly or weekly.
  - › Use an offset account for your 10% Savings Account.
  - › Clear all credit cards and personal loans before making extra home loan repayments. (They usually have higher rates.)

SUPERANNUATION

- Review your existing super fund.
  - › If you have multiple funds, think about consolidating.

> Make sure you have invested correctly for your timeframe until retirement. The longer you have until retirement, the more growth assets you can hold, for the potential of higher long-term returns.
- Consider making extra contributions—talk to your employer about salary sacrificing an amount to your fund each payday.

INSURANCE
- Review all existing insurance policies that you have.
  > Requote with other insurers to reduce premiums.
- Establish/Increase Personal Insurance (Life, TPD, Trauma, Income Protection).
  > If worried about premiums, use your superannuation fund.
- Establish/Increase Private Health Insurance.
- Establish/Increase General Insurance (Home, Contents, and Car).

ESTATE PLANNING
- Establish a Will (with Guardianship Clause for underage children).
- Establish an Enduring Power of Attorney and Medical Directive.
- Review your superannuation beneficiary (or nominate one).
- Review your Life Insurance beneficiary nomination (or make one).
- Make a 'List for Mum'.

If in doubt, seek professional advice:
- Investments, Superannuation & Insurances: Financial Planner
- Home Loans: Mortgage Broker
- Wills etc: Estate Planner/Lawyer/Solicitor
- Tax: Accountant

Remember, this is a journey.
A Lifestyle. Take it slow. You can do it.
Control Your Money. Live the Life You Want.

ABOUT THE AUTHOR

Angela Santalia has over two decades of experience working in the Australian Financial Planning industry as a Financial Paraplanner (strategist) (Dip. FP). From her experience with clients and other financial planners she has learned a lot about money, people, and which spending habits do and don't work.

In her work as the Money Messenger, Angela's mission is to increase financial literacy in everyday Australians by educating and empowering people to take control of their finances, get out of debt and use their income in better ways to create the life they want.

Angela runs a thriving website, Money Messenger, which features a blog, resources, tools, videos and more where she shares her money management knowledge with the public.

Angela was 'Young Investor of the Year' Runner Up in 2017 for *Your Investment Property Magazine*.

Connect with Angela online to access more financial secrets and strategies to become wealthier

www.moneymessenger.com.au

@money_messenger

/themoneymessenger

/MoneyMessenger